THE BLUESMAN

THE BLUESMAN

The Musical Heritage of Black Men and Women in the Americas

Julio Finn

Illustrations by Willa Woolston

INTERLINK BOOKS
An imprint of Interlink Publishing Group, Inc.
NEW YORK

First American edition published 1992 by
INTERLINK BOOKS
An imprint of Interlink Publishing Group, Inc.
99 Seventh Avenue, Brooklyn, New York 11215

Copyright © Julio Finn 1986 and 1991
Illustrations copyright © Willa Woolston 1986 and 1991

Originally published in Great Britain by Quartet Books Ltd.

Library of Congress Cataloging-in-Publication Data
Finn, Julio.
The bluesman: the musical heritage of Black men and women in the Americas /
Julio Finn : illustrations by Willa Woolston. — 1st pbk. ed.
p.   cm.
Includes bibliographical references and index.
ISBN 0-940793-91-1 (pbk.) / ISBN 0-940793-93-8
1. Blues (Music)—History and criticism.   2. Blacks—Music-History and criticism.
I. Title.
ML3521.F56   1992
781.643'09—dc20
91-25984
CIP
Printed and bound in the United States of America.

To: Billy Boy Arnold, the teacher; Margo Crawford, the historian; Latonga Gadamu, the Ethiopian; and Jerome Arnold, the dreamer

Thanks are due to University of Chicago Press, Chicago, Ltd for permission to quote from *Lay My Burden Down* by Benjamin A. Botkin; to the School of Oriental and African Studies, London; to Giles Oakley, whose *The Devil's Music* inspired portions of this book; to Arc Music Corporation: 'Louisiana Blues' by McKinley Morganfield, copyright © 1959 by Arc Music Corporation, reprinted by permission, all rights reserved; 'Gypsy Woman' by McKinley Morganfield, copyright © 1966 by Arc Music Corporation, reprinted by permission, all rights reserved; 'She Moves Me' by McKinley Morganfield, copyright © 1959 by Arc Music Corporation, reprinted by permission, all rights reserved; 'Hoochie Coochie Man' by Willie Dixon, copyright © 1957 by Arc Music Corporation, reprinted by permission, all rights reserved; 'Spider in My Stew' by Willie Dixon, copyright © 1973 by Arc Music Corporation, reprinted by permission, all rights reserved; and to the copyright holders whom we have been unable, despite our efforts, to trace, and for whose indulgence we ask. Lastly, the author wishes to thank Memphis Slim, Bo Diddley and B.B. King for their friendship and guidance and Chicago Beau, Eric Feinblatt and Maurice Oliver for their comradeship.

Contents

THE BLUESMAN

Introduction

When I want to study some mystical aspect of black people, I go to the blues — then I feel I'm in touch with black people.

Leo Smith

There are many books about the blues currently available: books by musicologists, sociologists, journalists and other 'investigators'. Unfortunately, all but a few have wholly missed the mark when it comes to explaining the true nature of the blues and its roots. Even when these authors have 'gone to the source' — that is, interviewed the blues performers themselves — they have come back empty-handed. This is not because the musicians intentionally led them astray, but because they invariably asked the wrong questions. These have been historical and sociological; they should have been psychological and spiritual. Asking bluespeople questions such as 'What is the blues to you?' can hardly get to the heart of the matter. Such naïve questions provoke naïve answers. Worse still, countless erroneous opinions about the blues and the people who make it have been drawn from these well-intentioned but misleading accounts. Both black and white authors have failed in these attempts to discover the roots of the blues, their mistake being to seek this precious source in the *history* of black Americans instead of looking into their *souls*. Plantation songs, work songs, etc. are stages along the blues' development but they have nothing to do with its origins. By the same token trips to Africa to unravel these roots may provide interesting travelogues but not much more, serving to show only just how far off the mark their researchers are, how out of touch they are with the minds of the people they would explore. In order for these journeys to bear fruit their Columbuses would require a . . . *time machine* . . . for the roots of the blues *lie in the psyche of all peoples of African origin*.

1

The story of the blues is inseparable from the history of black people – not only in the United States, but throughout the Americas. And it is inseparable from black religion – African, as well as its American offspring: Hoodoo. The blues defies simplistic explanation and ready-made definitions; my method is to take the reader through a step-by-step analysis of its various components, so that a comprehensive understanding of the subject can be arrived at. To achieve this, I have utilized techniques used in performing a song: varying the rhythm, modulating the pitch and syncopating images and dynamics.

My thesis, unlike that of other books on the subject, is born of my experiences – thus, I speak of 'initiations' of which other writers have been ignorant. For me, the blues is neither an 'interest' nor a 'study', but a way of life.

This book is about a song which derives its name from the colour of a people; it is also about the things I have experienced and felt, the things which have sustained me in my career – I, Julio Finn, a bluesman from Chicago. My hope is that this book will situate the blueswomen and -men in their rightful place – as *artists* – in American culture.

Origins:

What is the Blues?

If you've ever been mistreated — then you know what I'm talkin' about . . .

Eddie Boyd

The seeds which were to come to fruition as the blues were in the African psyche thousands of years before blacks were enslaved in America. Africans, whose gods were never suppressed, didn't have the blues – they had no reason to have them. But a people deprived of religion, language, customs and human dignity *did*. The first slaves were the first bluespeople: America, literally, gave the slaves the blues.

Under slavery the black mind took refuge in the spiritual resources of its past and tapped (like a well under pressure which finds a new outlet) a hitherto unused part of its godhead. John the Conqueroo and Erzulie, Damballah and the other *loas* were forced to retreat underground but, far from being extinguished, new forces were born: new hardships call for new remedies.

Jealous – like all gods – they haunted blacks, visiting them with lovely, strange visions of life back home, of the Garden of Eden they had lost, of sweet liberty and of how good life *could* have been. It's a peculiar kind of haunting which I believe only black people in the New World can understand: the blues is the black people's shadow, their companion down the lonesome road.

Africana Americana

The Priest or Medicine Man was the chief surviving institution that African slaves brought with them. He early appeared on the plantation and found his function as the healer of the sick, the interpreter of the Unknown, the comforter of the sorrowing, the supernatural avenger of wrong, and the one who rudely but picturesquely expressed the longing, disappointment, and resentment of a stolen and oppressed people.

William E.B. Dubois

African religion travelled with blacks wherever the slavers took them. Invisible to the whites, it was the *visible* symbol of blacks' past, the tangible part of their dream to return home, a psychological shadow cast by the light of the past.

As we will see, blacks wed their gods with those of Christianity. In Brazil this fusion − along with Indian contributions − gave birth to Maumba and Candomblé; in Cuba to Santeria and Nyannego; in Jamaica to Bongoism and African Cumina (also known as the Maroon Dance); in Trinidad to Shango; and in the United States to Hoodoo: 'Initially the veneration of the saints must have provided the slaves with convenient disguise for the secret worship of African gods.'[1]

This mélange of African, Indian and European cultures produced many new and varied offspring, complex in nature but all clearly traceable to their respective origins. And, naturally, it was everywhere persecuted:

> The white Cubans charge the Negroes with still maintaining in their midst the dark Vudu or Hudu mysteries of West Africa. There seems to be no doubt that the black people of Cuba (not the mulattoes) do belong to a number of secret masonic societies, the most widely heard-of being the Nyannego; and it is possible that these confraternities or clubs are associated with immoral purposes. They originated in a league of defence against the tyranny of the masters in the old slavery days.[2]

Each of the new religions adapted itself to the particular circumstances of the country in which it had to survive. In the United States, Hoodoo, cousin of Voodoo, produced a stepchild called the blues.

For reasons to be elucidated in later chapters in this book, the blues was all but divested of its religious role: it donned the cloak of secularity. Still, its role was of the first importance to the black community. Unlike their fellow blacks in Haiti black Americans have never known the freedom of ruling a country of their own. Their lives were fragmented in a world which outlawed their 'Africanness'; in America there was none of the cohesion which characterized black life in the West Indies. Even so, Hoodoo has survived in the legacy of the blues.

Haiti:

The Invisible Religion

We wear the mask that grins and lies
It hides our cheeks and shades our eyes
This debt we pay to human guile
With torn and bleeding hearts we smile
And mouth with myriad subtleties

Paul Laurence Dunbar

Voodoo was, or rather *is*, the most successful of the many African religions to flourish in the slave garden of the New World and hence is the most worthy of examination here. The reason Voodoo survived and grew is that its destiny is inextricably bound up with that of Haiti, the oldest black republic in the world. Haiti wrenched its freedom from the French in 1804. It became an African state out of Africa and was able to go its own way with less harassment than the other black communities of the Americas, not one of which won its freedom by contest of arms. Despite Haiti's independence, however, Voodoo has remained a secret religion, preserved for the initiated.

The origins of Voodoo lie in the dark mists of Africa's past, in the quasi-universal belief in ophiolatry (serpent worship), which (to simplify a great deal) held that the founder of the race (mankind) originally sprang from a serpent. For this the serpent was revered as a symbol of fecundity and wisdom and as a life-giver. Other honours included those of god of war, great spirit of the waters, and goddess of fertility.

Serpent worship sprang up, independently, throughout the ancient world: in Egypt, India, Africa, Peru and China. The beliefs with which we are concerned have been traced to Uganda, *circa* 700 A.D. Canon Roscoe, who visited the temple of the python god Selwanga at Budu on the shore of Lake Victoria, reported that:

the appearance of the new moon was celebrated by a ceremony extending over seven days . . . A drum was sounded as soon as the moon was seen . . . [the priest] went into the temple to the medium and gave the latter a cup of beer and some milk from the python's bowl mixed with white clay. After the medium had drunk the beer and milk, the spirit of the python came upon him, and he went down on his face and wriggled about like a snake, uttering peculiar noises and uttering words which the people could not understand. The priest stood near the medium and interpreted what he said. During the time that the medium was possessed the people stood around, and the temple drum was beaten.[1]

Another explorer, Hambly, also investigated African ophiolatry:

The distribution of python worship is clear. The main foci are the south-west shore of Lake Victoria Nyanza; also several centres in the coastal regions of the west, from Ashanti to the south of the Niger. Python worship was probably indigenous to ancient, possibly aboriginal Negro populations, which were driven west by racial pressure in the east. . . West Africa undoubtedly yields evidence of python worship, especially in Dahomey and southern Nigeria [and in Uganda there is] a definitely organized python worship with a sacred temple, a priesthood, and definite ritual acts, including sacrifice.[2]

It should be stressed that the python was not itself the Great Spirit; rather it was revered as the messenger of the gods – snakes were affectionately called 'brethren' and woe unto the foolish person who harmed them! For they were also held to be the reincarnation of the dead, the living spirits of ancestors: 'According to the belief of a great many Bantus, especially in South Africa, the dead appear chiefly in the form of snakes.'[3]

Another traveller, Arthur Glyn Leonard, who spent ten years in Nigeria, came to this conclusion: 'Irrespective of the tribe or locality, one fact in connection with these natives impressed me very forcibly, and that was that in every case, with regard to snakes, the emblem revered is the python.'[4]

King Python was the messenger from the other world who came back to watch over his children, to advise, warn and instruct them in propitiating the gods:

The fact is that the serpent was only a symbol, or at most an embodiment of the spirit which it represented, as we see from the belief of several African and American tribes, which probably preserves the primitive form of this superstition. Serpents were looked upon by these peoples as embodiments of their departed ancestors.[5]

Père Labat recorded the story told him by Père Braquez of how he witnessed the rites of the python ceremony at Whydah:

The people on their knees and in silence were withdrawn some distance

apart; the King alone with the priest of the country entered the enclosure, where after prolonged prostrations, prayers and ceremonies, the priest drew near to a hole where supposedly he has a serpent. He spoke to him on behalf of the King and questioned him as regards the number of vessels that would arrive the following year, war, harvest and other topics. According as the serpent replied to a question, the priest carried the answer to the King who was kneeling a short distance away in an attitude of supplication. This by-playing having been repeated a number of times, it was finally announced that the following year would be prosperous, that it would have much trade, and that they would take many slaves. The multitude expressed their joy by loud shouts, dancing and feasting.[6]

Apart from these set ceremonies the sacred serpent was consulted during any crisis and his guidance was invariably followed. Moreover, he functioned as the symbol of the nation – no matter what hardship befell it there was still hope if the cult of the python were preserved. When the Kingdom of Whydah fell to Guadja, King of Dahomey, 'the remnant of the Whydahs who had escaped the edge of Guadja's sword were abundantly thankful to him for permitting them to continue in the enjoyment of their snake worship'.[7]

About the same time a Report of the Committee of Council noted: 'They have a great number of men they call Fetiche men, or padres. The word *fetiche* is derived from a Portuguese word meaning witchcraft.' And in 1893 Pierre Labarthe wrote in his *Voyage à la Côte de Guinée:*

they have a kind of high-priest whom the Negroes call the Great Fetisher or Great Voodnoo; he claims to have descended from heaven and poses as the interpreter of the gods on earth; under this guise he demands the same honours as are shown to the King – [the people] seek him to placate Him [God] through their fetishers.

This is significant: the priest has encroached upon the formerly exclusive preserve of the Python. We shall see how he came wholly to take on the serpent's duties.

At the time of which we are speaking the Vodun (or fetish) and the serpent were interchangeable. Indeed, the Supreme Being was everywhere – in the waters, in trees, thunder, the winds – and the road to him lay through the Voduns, who had the ear of the lesser gods and of the ancestors.

Pierre Bouche, who resided at Whydah in 1868, told how he was walking with a native boy when a snake appeared: 'Father,' cried the boy, 'a fetiche! You are my father, you are my mother,' he said, prostrating himself.

Thus we see that the Africans of the so-called Slave Coast worshipped the python as the intermediary of the Supreme God and that the Vodun or Fetish-keeper (python priest) took on the attributes of his charge. Included in this was a very real respect for, even fear of their ancestors, to whom they never neglected to address themselves when they invoked the spirits. It would take more than a boat ride to make Africans abandon these age-old beliefs.

Voodoo Defined as a Religion

So . . . these serpent worshippers are abducted, stolen from their native land and transported across the sea to swell the coffers of English milords, Spanish grandees, Portuguese doms and French nobles – maintaining one's position in the gilded salons of the Faubourg Saint-Germain and making the grand tour were essential for any cultured gentleman or lady – after all, it *was* the Age of Enlightenment. The serpent worshippers also footed the bill for the development of the Industrial Revolution which, among other 'improvements', spewed forth the cotton gin which held the Afro-American in thrall for decades. King Cotton, Milord Tobacco, Emperor Sugar, and Prince Coffee held sway over a dominion of 'soulless' sufferers. For, after all, they were only heathens, peoples without cultures – no languages, no arts, no sciences, no society worth speaking of. One wonders *just how did they live?* They had to have the benefits of civilization forced down their throats – could a life be worthwhile if one did not know the story of Hamlet and the divine melodies of Bach and Haydn? In return for their freedom and labour they would receive the benefits of grace in the Hereafter. Be that as it may, slavery was certainly calculated to result in misery.

The first step was to rid them of what passed for their languages, customs and beliefs. National and family ties must be rent asunder in order to initiate them into the New Order of things in a New World. And above all their superstitions – never honoured with the title of 'religion' – must be rooted out. To accomplish that would have been tantamount to depriving them of their past, of their collective unconscious, of memory itself. And is that not synonymous with possession of the soul? In short, the goal was to take Africa out of the Africans, to dehumanize them. Africa was declared *persona non grata* in the very dwelling (souls) in which it held sway. Like a mother protecting her children, Africa went underground, shielding its religions with a cover as dark as night.

> The evil thing that the slave brought with him was his religion. You do not need to go to Africa to find the fetich. During the hundred years that slavery in our America held the Negro crushed, degraded and apart, his master could deprive him of his manhood, his wife, his child, the fruits of his toil, of his life; but there was one thing of which he could not deprive him — his faith in fetich charms. Not only did this religion of the fetich endure under slavery — it grew. None but Christian masters offered the Negro any other religion; and by law, even they were debarred from giving them any education. So fetichism flourished. The master's children were infected by the contagion of superstition; they imbibed some of it at the Negro foster-mother's breast. It was a secret religion that lurked thinly covered in slavery days, and what lurks today beneath the Negro's Christian profession as a white art, and among 'non-professors' as a black art; a memory of the revenges of his African ancestors; a secret fraternity among the slaves of far distant plantations, with words and signs — the lifting of a finger, the twitch of an eyelid — that telegraphed from house to house with amazing rapidity (as today in Africa) current news in old slave days and during the late civil war; suspected but never understood by the white master; which as a superstition has spread itself among our ignorant white masses as the 'Hoodoo', 'Vudu' or 'Odoism', is simply African fetichism transported to American soil.[8]

So . . . they lost everything except their religion. Ewe, Fulani, Ashanti Mandingo, Wolof and dozens of other tongues were replaced by Spanish, French, English, Dutch and Portuguese. Seh, Damballah, Ogoun and the King of Engole (Angola) were forced out of the African heavens and replaced by Christ, the Virgin and the saints.

The African worked, watched the systematic destruction of his mores, saw his family broken up and his women raped, and prayed to the white man's god. No doubt about it, the slavers could be well proud of themselves. What they didn't know — and it was a seminal aspect of African worship — was that the *loas*, the gods, *demand service*. No peril in the world could stop Africans from paying them their dues. The *loas* were also the only thing which gave them the strength to endure: they were their protection, their guide and their hope. They were their *bond* to Africa, the *connection* with their ancestors, their *unity* with their fellow slaves. Stolen out of Africa, *loas* became Africans' home, a sanctuary the whites could not enter for the simple reason that they did not know where it was. Whites' futile attempts to destroy this worship only drove it underground. It progressed from secrecy to obscurity, its very name becoming a magical byword of faith to its initiates. In their ego-besotted blindness the whites failed to realize, to accept the fact that Voodoo was a religion, and that far from being a mere sect, it was the faith of a quarter of a continent. Alas, even today, this fact is rarely understood . . . and hardly ever accepted. I hope that my readers will bear this in mind as they read these pages.

Voodoo is a religion because all the adepts believe in the existence of spiritual beings who live in part of the universe in close touch with human beings whose activity they control. These invisible beings constitute a numerous Olympus of gods, of whom the highest among them bear the title of Papa or Great Master and have the right to special homage.

Voodoo is a religion because the cult developed to its god demands a hierarchical sacerdotal body, a congregation of faithful, temples, altars, ceremonies, and in fine, altogether an oral tradition which certainly has not come down to us unchanged, but thanks to it, has transmitted the essential part of the cult.

Voodoo is a religion because through the medley of legends and the corruption of fables one can disentangle a theology, a system of representations, thanks to which, primitively, our African ancestors had an explanation for the natural phenomena and which in a hidden way lays the foundation of the anarchistic beliefs on which rests the hybrid Catholicism of the masses of the people.[9]

To end with I shall quote two further sources which give insight into Voodoo's transmigration and the origin of its name: 'In the south-eastern portions of the Ewe territory, the python deity is worshipped, and this vodu cult, with its adoration of the snake god, was carried to Haiti by the slaves from Ardra and Whydah, where the faith still remains today.'[10] And: 'I may observe that from the Slave-Coast "Vodun" or Fetish we may derive the "Vaudoux" or small green snake of the Haitian Negroes, so well known by the abominable orgies enacted before the [Vaudoux King and Queen]; and the "King Snake" is still revered at S'a Leone.'[11]

God's Basement

When the early Christians refused to render unto Caesar what was God's Rome unleashed a campaign of persecution and drove the believers from the towns. The believers retaliated with a network of secret passwords, signs and rites, the sum of which the curious may witness on any Sunday wherever there is a Christian church. Caesar's wrath spurred them to heights of zeal and sacrifice they might otherwise never have reached had they been left to their own devices. What those stalwart martyrs would have had to say about the Christian institution of slavery can safely be left to the reader's honest and fruitful imagination.

The enslaved Africans found themselves in a terrifying religious circus — shades of the catacombs! They too formed clandestine associations but, sadly, the lives and activities of the Ben Hurs of these holy rebellions were not documented.

The slavers believed that the Africans were frightened, ignorant men and women and undoubtedly some of them were: people usually experience a queasiness of the stomach when faced with the barrel of a cannon. But we must dispute the opinion that the majority of them were spiritless weaklings. Countless observers contradict this. They speak of Africans throwing themselves overboard into the sea, of rebellions on both land and ship, and of many acts of great courage.

> The man who emerged from this African chrysalis was a courageous, warlike individual. He was not soft; he was hard. He had fought the tsetse fly, the mosquitos and hundreds of nameless insects and he survived. He had wrested from the hungry jungle gaps of land and had found time to think beautiful thoughts and to make beautiful things. He was used to hard work and he was accustomed to an elaborate social code . . . In fine, as Stanley M. Elkins said, 'he was the product of . . . cultural traditions essentially heroic in nature'.[12]

Africans arrived in the New World with some of the material manifestations of their worship: seeds, plants, talismans, stones, idols, prayers, proverbs, legends and forbidden formulae. With these they laid the foundations of their new Church: 'After studying the history of Haiti, one is not astonished that the fetish worship continues to flourish. The Negroes imported from the west coast of Africa naturally brought their religion with them, and the worship of the serpent was one of its most distinguishing features.'[13]

The gods of Africa were being worshipped in the caverns of Jamaica, in the forests of Trinidad, and in the back streets of Port-au-Prince, Havana, and New Orleans. Even when they knelt and imbibed Latin in the 'official' Church they had Legba and Erzulie on their minds: the Africans of Brazil painted the faces of the icons of Jesus, Mary and Joseph black. Neither Church nor State was willing to countenance this and stringent laws were passed in an attempt to extinguish it.

At Jamaica, in 1696:

Be it enacted by the aforesaid authority, that no master, or mistress, or overseer, shall suffer any drumming or meeting of any slaves, not belonging to their own plantation, to rendezvous, feast, revel, beat drum, or cause any disturbance . . . [and in 1717] And whereas the permitting or allowing of any number of strange Negroes to assemble on any plantation, or settlement, or any other place, may prove fatal to this Your Majesty's Island, if not timely prevented: and forasmuch as Negroes can, by beating on drums, and blowing horns, or other such like instruments of noise, give signals to each other at a considerable distance of their evil and wicked intentions . . . no proprietor, attorney, or overseer, [shall] presume to suffer any number of strange Negroes, exceeding five, to assemble on his plantation or settlement . . .

An edict, dated 21 December 1781, carried this dire pronouncement:

As regards amusements which are permissible among their own slaves, the use of 'drums, horns and such other unlawful instruments of noise' are of course prohibited . . . That from the first day of January, aforesaid, any Negro or other slave who shall pretend to any supernatural power, and be detected in making use of any blood, feathers, parrots'-beaks, dogs'-teeth, alligators'-teeth, broken bottles, grave-dirt, rum, eggshells, or any other materials relative to the practice of Obeah or witchcraft, in order to delude and impose upon the minds of others, shall upon conviction before two magistrates and three freeholders, suffer death or transportation . . .[14]

Africans must have smiled at these weighty proclamations: they could outwit the whites because they knew the enemy's mind without the enemy knowing theirs. Their altars were hidden in the thickest of uninhabited forests, their incantations were as indecipherable to the whites as Latin was to them, and they knew that none of their fellow slaves would betray them. How, then, could the whites lay hold on them?

> Voodoo is not a written creed over which a house of bishops presides publicly, a fact which should account for the many and extremely varied versions of its practices which are in circulation through the world. It is certainly not a mere veneer or an old garment from the Congo days of the black race which has not yet been cast away. But it is a substantial edifice of West African superstition, serpent worship, and child sacrifice which exists in Haiti today, and which would undoubtedly become rampant throughout the island were it not for the check and control upon native practices which foreign residents exercise.
>
> Several Roman Catholic priests, who have long resided in the heart of Haiti, told me that one of the hardships and difficulties of the combat against African darkness upon which they are engaged, is the extreme reticence not only of the active Voodooists themselves, but of all blacks in regard to fetish-worshipping rites.[15]

As the creole proverb says: '*Z'affe mouton pas z'affe cabrite*': the sheep's affairs don't concern the goat.

Perhaps Voodoo's greatest foil was Christianity itself. It provided a mould into which Africans could pour their own beliefs. After all, the Africans believed in a Supreme Being and a pantheon of lesser gods and saints. And wasn't the Virgin just another name for Erzulie?

> 'Take Erzulie, for instance. This creature is the Dahomeyan Aphrodite, the goddess of love. She is supposed, in the superstitions of the natives, to be the wife of several of the greater African deities, and also unites herself in mystic marriages to mortals. *Elle est, en somme, une fameuse trainée* . . .Well, that is Haitian tradition. But,' he continued gravely, 'who do you think this wretch is identified with in the minds of the adepts of Voodoo? With the Blessed Virgin herself. One shudders to think of it.' (Father Cosmo in conversation with Patrick Leigh Fermor, 1949)

And Francis Huxley, who studied Voodoo in Haiti in the mid-sixties, tells of how '. . . Agenci began the prayers . . . His wife fumbled her way through Catholic prayers and through the great prayer of Voodoo itself, in which all of the *loas* are named.'[16]

The blacks' thinking probably ran something like this: the whites are so certain of our ignorance that they can't imagine that we could trick them so let's make them believe that we believe in their religion while we practise our own.

Africans saw no incongruity in adding the Christian saints to their own pantheon. The Church had unwittingly played into their hands.

We overtook a troop of Negroes. We recognized them as our companions from the first *tonnelle* (Voodoo temple) and exchanged *bonjours*.

'Where are they going to, Rodolfe?'

He looked slightly surprised at the question.

'Où? Mais à la messe.' (Where? To mass, of course)[17]

Praised be the Lord

The war between Voodoo and Christianity has never abated. It is a battle for souls complicated by racial and social factors. To the Christian Church Voodoo is an unholy superstition, a pernicious weed growing in its American Eden, an embarrassment which refuses to go away. The problem is all the more thorny because the blacks have accepted Christianity, but on their own terms, blending it with their own beliefs, so that it is no longer a 'white' religion, but a *mulatto*. This half-breed wasn't in the European Church's plans, and it fervently desires that Christianity be a white religion. Hence, this bastard, this amalgamation of Christianity and African religion, this Voodoo, must be destroyed, dug out at the root and consigned to the inquisitorial flames. But that devout task is easier wished for than accomplished, for Voodoo is one of the most profoundly *lived* systems of belief in the world. Lip-service is rarely met with in its convenants; its ceremony is no mere social rite, but an act of personal communication with and possession by the gods.

Voodoo in Haiti is a profound and vitally alive religion . . . Voodoo is primarily and basically a form of worship, and . . . its magic, its sorcery, its witchcraft (I am speaking technically now), is only a secondary, collateral, sometimes sinisterly twisted by-product of Voodoo as a faith. Voodoo is not a secret cult or society in the sense that Freemasonry or the Rosicrucian cult is secret; it is a religion, and secret only as Christianity was secret in the catacombs, through fear of persecution. Like every religion it has its inner mysteries, but that is secretness in a different sense. It is a religion towards which whites generally have been either scoffers, spyers, or active enemies, and whose adherents, therefore, have been forced to practise in secrecy above all where whites were concerned. [18]

From the very outset the representatives of the European Church acted hand in glove with the secular authorities to enslave the blacks. Sharing in their material benefits reaped by the regime, the so-called holy men did their utmost to instil in the slaves the belief that their position was justified by the decree of heaven and the whites' innate superiority.

Priests and congregations owned slaves, possessed personal and landed property, managed plantations, were large-scale planters and sugar manufacturers, and owned oxcarts or coffee mills. In spite of their pastoral commitments, the Capuchins, Jacobins, Dominicans and Jesuits were all colonizers and were trapped in the colonial mentality and the dissolution of the cities, in the cupidity and debauchery. Abbot Enos offered for sale 'some skilled slaves, one of whom is seven months pregnant'. Abbot Castellane was tried in Cap on 19 November 1765 'for having killed a slave on the grounds of his presbytery'. A Cayes-Jacmel priest suffered 'shameful illnesses resulting from debauches'. Numerous priests 'bring up little bastards born of their concubines'. [19]

In his book, *Ruling on the Disciplining of Negroes Addressed to the Priests in the French Islands of America* (1776), Father Coutance gives vent to his heartfelt humanity:

Unfaithful and wicked servant, since you have strayed from the service of your master and the obedience you owed to God and the Holy Church in order to give way to the sinfulness of your heart and to expose yourself to the certain loss of your salvation and your life, we, by the authority of our holy ministry, condemn you to serve penance for the period of [. . .] warning you that should you fail in this and show no clear proof of repentance and making amends you will be rejected among Christians, forbidden entry to the church and abandoned to a death without sacrament, without mourners and without a burial place.[20]

Another holy sermonizer, worthy of being crowned the High Priest of Hypocrisy and Cant, was Coutance's contemporary and comrade-in-arms, Father Fauque, who delivered the following sugar-coated poison to a band of captured runaways:

Remember my dear children that though you be slaves you are nevertheless Christians like your masters; that from the day of your baptism you profess the same religion as they which teaches you that those who do not live the Christian life shall be cast into hell after death. How unfortunate for you if, after having been slaves to men of this world and time you should become slaves of the devil for all eternity. This misfortune will certainly fall upon you if you do not return to your duty since you are in a condition of habitual damnation for in addition to the wrong you do your masters by depriving them of your labour, you do not come to Mass on holy days; you do not approach the sacraments . . . Come to me then, my dear friends.[21]

I make so bold as to ask readers to read the above again, and again; for in this sermon is contained the whole of the black experience in the Americas, the whole of the whites' attitude towards blacks, the whole of hypocrisy as exercised by the Christian Church towards black people: if readers fail to grasp this they may as well close this book now, for its remaining pages will profit them but little.

After Haiti's proclamation of independence Voodoo was the State religion in all but name. However, this continued 'invisibility' left it open to attack from those blacks who sought to Europeanize the country. Both Dessalines and Christophe, having used it to gain power, instituted anti-Voodoo policies, and both paid the price for them. They opted for Catholicism and thus lost the support of the people, who never forgot that they owed their freedom to the *loas*. 'The double failure of L'Ouverture and Christophe signified the triumph of Vodoun . . . A chief who was not credited with supernatural power was lacking "something" . . . The crux of the matter is that in order to play the game of realpolitik they could not ignore the usefulness of Vodoun as a means of control and prestige.'[22]

Until the beginning of the present century Voodoo and Catholicism lived side by side in an atmosphere of peaceable if somewhat jealous toleration. As long as the people performed the external rites of the Church, the white priests were content, even countenancing the work of the *pères savanes* (bush doctors) who, in a mixture of Voodoo and Christian rites, performed baptisms, marriages and funeral services. All this was to change in 1896, when the Catholic synod began its crusade to drive the African religion out of the land. To begin with, it created what it called the League Against Voodoo, which body was directed by Monseigneur Kersuzan, Bishop of Cap Haitien. By his orders persecution bureaux were set up throughout the country, their task being to get people to follow the 'true' Church. The people turned out in great numbers, cheered and applauded the speakers, and then marched off in the direction of the sound of the drums. The bishop grew desperate and passed a series of edicts: Voodooists were forbidden to receive communion, *houngans* and *mambos* (priests and priestesses) were deprived of the right to serve as godparents, and only a high Church official had the power – on the off-chance that they should apply for it – to administer absolution to them. Gangs of the faithful were sent trooping around the countryside, praising the joys of belief in Christ and calling upon those who were not thus blessed to get in on the good thing before it was too late. The total effect of all this drum-tapping was . . . nil! Bewildered, the crusading minister told a convention of the synod that the authorities – yes, the president included – were actively doing everything they could to ensure the crusade's failure.

In the face of this resounding defeat the white Church backed off, that it might live to fight another day. In 1913 it issued the pious lament that 'the monstrous mixture continued unabated'. Then, in 1939, this wide-awake clergy was astonished to find that 'the mixture . . . this abomination was not only the way of isolated persons but the current practice of the whole body of converts!'[23] A new campaign was launched, spearheaded by a new convert and lay preacher by the name of Ti-Jules (Uncle Jules). He was a peasant who had experienced a vision to spread the gospel and wean the people from Voodoo superstitions. Crowds flocked to hear the 'no-mixture' preacher who commanded them to get rid of their charms and destroy the Voodoo altars. Henceforth, they must live as 'pure' Catholics, and have no truck with the *houngans*.

Many were converted; many others weren't; but all took an interest in what must evolve as a contest between the two creeds. The inspired hierophant was reported to the Catholic authorities, who ordered him to appear before his local curé. After a long and serious discussion, the churchman pronounced that Ti-Jules' work was in keeping with the duties of a good Christian. When this result reached the ears of the Voodooists they were enraged and denounced him as a charlatan who 'organized meetings dangerous to the State'. With the swiftness of a message transmitted by drum-telegraph the no-mixture proselyte's doings moved from the farmyards to the salons in the capital, with the result that he was arrested – for being a good Christian? for being seditious? – tried, acquitted but fined; such an outcome being clear proof that the authorities were aware of the tightrope they were attempting to walk. In any event, the publicity of the trial made him famous and new converts flocked in. As a result, the synod decided that it was now or never that the power of Voodoo could be broken. With typical effrontery it commanded that he send his followers to the curés to receive 'official' recognition that they were *rejétés* (rejectors of the Voodoo cult), and good Christian that he was, the worthy believer submitted. At the same time the most zealous of his disciples were sent out on pilgrimages, the aim of which was to bring in new converts. Among other ploys, they threatened the Africanists with eternal damnation if they didn't embrace 'unmixed' Catholicism. Bloated with a confidence as chimerical as it was unwarranted, the synod then issued an 'Anti-Voodoo Oath', to be sworn unconditionally by all the faithful.

I, before God, stand in the Tabernacle, before the priest who represents Him and renew the promises of my baptism. With hand on the Gospels I swear never to give a food-offering of whatever kind – never to attend a Voodoo ceremony of whatever kind, never to take part in a service to *loa* in any way whatsoever.

I promise to destroy or have destroyed as soon as possible all fetishes and objects of superstition, if any – on me, in my house, and in my compound.

In short, I swear never to sink to any superstitious practice whatever.

[For married persons]: I promise moreover to bring up my children without exception in the Catholic and Roman religion, outside all superstition, submitting myself fully to the teaching of the Holy Church.

And I promise that with God's help I shall abide by my oath until death.

This was too much: a bolt of indignation hit Haiti! Did it not owe its very existence to the strength Voodoo had given the national heroes? This Anti-Voodoo oath wielded by a white clergy was an insult to black people,

an attack against national pride and a slur on the memory of the martyrs of
the revolution. 'Haiti,' the people cried, 'is a BLACK country!'

Caught up in this trick-bag of their own invention, the Catholic clergy
sought frantically to make amends, but the outraged people would have none
of it: a series of conferences, at which the whites offered garbled
explanations, were held, but nothing could temper the justified ire of the
blacks. That diabolical oath was but another of the whites' attempts to
'divide and rule'. As in the past, Voodoo became an instrument of black
solidarity. Driven to the wall, the Christians now played their trump card
and had pressure brought to bear from throughout the powerful economic
enclaves of Christendom: Rome, Madrid, Washington and other right-
minded places, with the effect that President Lescot 'ordered the army to
co-operate with the curés in their hunting down of all objects to do with the
Voodoo cult'.[24]

It was the old witch-hunt, the foul cleansing by the bloodthirsty
inquisition, the holy enslavement of men's souls all over again. Like rogues
out to redeem their sins, the sanctimonious bigots fell upon the Voodoo
relics with wanton fanaticism.

> Strengthened by the more or less open support of the government, the
> curés had the *humfo* shut up or destroyed and thousands of the sacred
> objects were burnt in a veritable *auto-da-fé*. I was in Haiti in 1941 and I
> remember seeing in the backyards of the presbyteries vast pyramids of
> drums, painted bowls, necklaces, talismans – all waiting for the day fixed
> for the joyous blaze which was to symbolize the victory of the Church over
> Satan.[25]

But it would take more than fire, more than government troops, more
than the brandishing of the Bible to defeat the heirs of Macandal. Once
again, talismans carved in his image made their appearance; drums played
the tattoo of his dance, voices swept through the night invoking him to
return yet again and renew his people. And faithful to his promise, he did.
People from every condition and walk of life: peasants, intellectuals,
businessmen, all formed together and declared a series of religious strikes,
condemning this brutal affront to the national conscience. Soon, the press
added its voice to the complaints and the President, seeing the consequence
of weak action, recalled the army and left the clergy to get on as best they
could. Embittered by what they termed the army's desertion, the press
accused the government of sending *agents provocateurs* to fire shots in the

church of Delmas while a black priest was preaching against Voodoo. The enraged government reacted by banning the Anti-Voodoo campaign. Since then, Voodoo has basked in the warmth of the Haitian sun.

In his novel, *Les Arbres Musiciens*, Jacques Stephen Alexis puts these words into the mouth of the *houngan*:

> The *loas* are immortal, priest. The *loàs* have not allowed you to raise your sacrilegious hands against the ancient shrine of Remembrance. It is no longer anything but flames and ashes, but the *loas* live! Watch the light glowing on the ashes; La Remembrance lives! Bois-d'Orme can go to his death now, for the ancient shrine will rise one day, at the same place, greater, higher, more beautiful, eternal like the *loas* of eternal Africa. You, to your misfortune, you will survive, but no one will be more dead than you. When you look at the trees you will see in their symmetry the mystic and invisible body of the *loas*. When you hear the wind sighing over the land, it is their voice that will be cursing you. For you did not respect the right of men to believe according to their hearts. Go, son of no one! Man of no race! Man of no land! Man of no nation! The hands of the gods are upon you.[26]

This statement of faith by one of the Caribbean's leading writers, put into the mouth of a Vodun to a Christian, of a black man to a white, tellingly illustrates both the strength of the Haitians' belief and their position *vis-à-vis* the white Church. It is more than just a proclamation of faith: it is evidence that the Invisible Religion had come out of hiding.

Black Power in the Black House

The importance of Voodoo in the lives of its believers can hardly be over-emphasized. It was omnipresent and affected every facet of Haitians' lives: it was their way of thinking. The *loas* were ever-present to guide and admonish; and not only that, they *possessed*. Voodooists were forever ready to receive the god in their persons and co-religionists to welcome the divinity with its particular drum, rhythm, song and dance.

Vaudou is so inextricably woven in with every side of the Haitian's life, his politics, his religion, his outlook upon the world, his social and family relations, his prejudices and peculiarities, that he cannot be judged apart from it. In Haiti the nominal religion is Roman Catholicism, but it is no more than a thin veneer; beneath it you find, not traces merely, but a solid groundwork of West African superstition, serpent worship and child sacrifice.[27]

Every class and level of society, from the peasant to the ruling family, was permeated with adherents. Naturally, they all professed to be Catholics. After all, one had to survive, had to be diplomatic: Europe was too powerful a trading partner to upset seriously. Still, Haiti gave itself over to Voodoo very publicly, as this account by Stephen Bonsal amply shows:

Last February there was assembled in the national palace what might justly be called a congress of serpent worshippers. During the life of Mme Nord, which came to an end in October 1908, not a week passed but what a meeting of Voodoo practitioners was held in the executive mansion, and her death bed was surrounded by at least a score of these witch doctors.

General Antoine Simon, who recently achieved the presidency, may be the intelligent man he is represented to be by not a few white residents who have come in close contact with him during the years of his government of the southern *arrondissements* of the island. But one thing is quite sure: if he wishes to remain in the Black House and rule, he must share his sovereignty with the Voodoo priests. If he should exclude them from power and banish them from his presence, his term of office will be of short duration . . . upon this point there is practical unanimity. No government can stand in Haiti unless it is upheld by the Voodoo priests or by foreign bayonets.[28]

And might not the same be said throughout the world? To deny religion its political clout is to deny it its social function. Bonsal understood this well enough but the rub derived from the fact that it was an African religion triumphing over its European equivalent.

Métraux goes so far as to deny Voodoo's importance in Haitian politics, insisting that 'we must remember that the people of little Haiti are always tempted to establish a chain of cause and effect between sorcery and success'.[29] He then goes on to state that none of the black presidents who held office under the American occupation of 1915–33 was charged with being a Voodooist. They were, he says, 'educated bourgeoisie'. Begging his erudite pardon, it must be pointed out that as a white foreigner he would hardly have been in a position to gain the confidence of the Voodooists; and he himself speaks of the violent anti-Voodoo campaign instituted with refined barbarity by the American army:

> During the American occupation Voodoo was looked upon as a sign of barbarism and served as a butt for the spite of military authorities. One of the Marine officers, John Craig, treats it in his book *Black Bagdad* with as much naïveté as horror. In reading some of his accounts, allegedly authentic, you cannot help wondering which is the more gullible and has the greater weakness for marvels – the unsophisticated peasant or the white chief of police. All the same, the persecution of Voodoo, which went on throughout this period, was limited to the arrest of a few *houngan* (Voodoo priests), the laying waste of a few sanctuaries and the confiscation of drums.[30]

Again, it must be noted that I take strong exception to M Métraux: religious persecution is never to be taken lightly, and nor is eighteen years of occupation by a government with a deeply ingrained philosophy of white superiority. May I suggest that the black presidents of the period had reverted to the time-honoured ruse of concealing African religion in the face of another Christian onslaught? Indeed, it would be a very strange thing if Voodoo did not play a leading role in the life – political or otherwise – of a self-determining black nation. Besides, Voodoo has always been a rallying point for Haitian liberation. All of its 'liberators' were adherents: Toussaint, Dessalines, Henri-Christophe, Mulatto, Pètion, Boyer. Voodoo's strength as a natural rallying point was obvious.

Macandal, the great visionary who led the first revolt in 1757, relied heavily upon it to charge his people with the ardour of sacrifice. A Guinean by birth, he escaped from the plantation he worked on and led a small band of followers into the hills, where he plotted the overthrow of the whites. Métraux calls them 'fanatics'; I see them as freedom-fighters. This may appear merely as a semantic quibble, but in history semantics can be as important as fact. Macandal, the One-Armed (he had lost the other in an accident on the plantation) was revered by his followers to the point of idolatry (it was the age of Napoleon) for though he walked among them as a mere slave they knew his true identity, that he was a messenger of the Great Vodun, and had only adopted his present guise the better to confound their enemy. His knowledge was without bounds and his powers bordered upon the supernatural. The gods had marked him out, had selected him as the intermediary between themselves and their stolen children. The memoirs of the period leave no doubt as to the respect and fear he inspired.

> Of all the Maroon chiefs, none had a greater, more deserved reputation than François Macandal, executed in 1758. This Macandal was a black from Guinea and long-time slave on Plantation Le Normand, in Limbe . . . He ran away and hid in the mountains, where he soon exercised the most extraordinary dominance over his companions. In addition to very great leadership skills he possessed all the qualities necessary for reducing and fanaticizing the credulous and primitive creatures around him. 'He predicted the future,' wrote a contemporary. He experienced revelations and possessed an eloquence far different from the imitative eloquence of our orators, and much stronger and more vigorous. In addition he was possessed of rare courage and the staunchest spirit which he was able to maintain in the face of the most cruel torments and punishments. He had persuaded the Negroes he was immortal, and he had indeed imbued them with such terror and such respect that they considered it an honour to sit at his knees and to pay him reverence due only to the Divinity whose envoy he claimed to be. The most beautiful women vied for the honour of being admitted to his bed. (*A.M.C. Correspondance générale de Saint-Domingue, Tome II*, 1779)

One certain fact is that Macandal was more than a simple Maroon leader. Not because he disdained the pillaging of plantations, the sacking of mansions, the stealing of herds and other common slave exploits; but he appears to have envisioned the possibility of making *marronage* the centre of an organized resistance against the whites. He had a notion of the races on Saint-Domingue. One day, amid a crowd, he had brought to him a vase full of water into which he placed three kerchiefs, yellow, white and black. First he pulled out the yellow. 'Here,' he said, 'this stands for the first inhabitants of Saint-Domingue; they were yellow. Here are the present inhabitants.' He showed a white kerchief. 'And here are the ones who will remain masters of the island.' It was the black kerchief. (*Notes Historiques, A.M.C.*)

Macandal's career as a Maroon revolutionist lasted for eighteen years, during which period he was responsible for the deaths of hundreds of whites. His knowledge of herbs gave him power over life while his ascendancy over his own people guaranteed that his commands would be unquestioningly executed.

His orders on this point were carried out with a passive and blind obedience by which the Old Man of the Mountain had been able to lead all his disciples. He caused the death of all the masters and mistresses against whom they harboured some slight resentment. The slave most attached to his master would have felt he was committing a crime against the Divinity had he delayed the slightest in carrying out his orders or if he had not most religiously guarded the secret. For more than six years the colonists were ignorant of the fact that within the bosom of the colony there existed so dangerous a Maroon, with the possible exception of the master who had bought him and long ago thought of him as being dead in the woods. At last this Negro set about to execute his plan of destruction which he had followed with a constancy and skill one is almost tempted to admire. The day and hour were set when every vase holding water in every house in the City of Cap was to be empoisoned. The hour at which he and his troop were to surprise the whites in the anguish of their death throes was indicated. He had an accurate list of all the blacks who from that point were to follow him and then fan out across the plain massacring all the whites. He knew the names of all his followers in every work gang . . . (Ibid)

Macandal was captured before his victory could be accomplished. Condemned to death by fire, he told his brethren that he would not die but would transform himself into an insect and escape his enemies.

In any case, when finally he was apprehended in 1757, the colony was terrorized and the news of his capture was greeted with universal thanksgiving . . . For the terror he had caused he was cruelly repaid. By order of the Cap court, 20 January 1758, he was condemned to be burned alive. He had succeeded in persuading the blacks that it would be impossible for the whites to have him killed in case they caught him, and that the Creator would change him on the point of death into a mosquito to reappear more terrible than ever. As chance would have it his neck ring was poorly secured to the stake so that with the first torments the fire brought him he pulled it out. No more was needed to persuade those of his colour that the prophecy had been fulfilled; so much so that three-quarters of the blacks are still steeped in this belief, and are daily expecting to see him return to keep his promises, and that the first black who dares to call himself Macandal can a second time imperil the dependency of Cap.[31]

The blacks were forced to watch his execution. And, very coolly, they did. Much to the consternation of the whites they appeared unduly unaffected by what was taking place – Macandal had given his word, so what was there to fear? When he broke his stake his followers were jubilant. 'Macandal saved!' they yelled. 'Immediately there was an every-man-for-himself scramble . . . House doors were banged shut; soon the whole town was in a state of alarm.' The white soldiers restored order and Macandal was again consigned to the flames. But the show backfired, its impresarios forced to admit that they had miscalculated on the efficacy of their *tour de force*: none of the blacks believed that the Messenger was dead; he had escaped to fight another day; he, the powerful nightshade come to brighten their day.

> . . . the slaves of the Lenormand de Mezy plantation continued unshaken in their reverence for Macandal. Ti Noel passed on the tales of the Mandingue to his children, teaching them simple little songs he had made up in Macandal's honour while currying and brushing the horses. Besides, it was a good thing to keep green the memory of the One-Armed, for though far away on important duties, he would return to this land when he was least expected.[32]

Macandal had boasted that he was immortal, that his spirit would remain to protect and guide his people, to lead them out of bondage and into freedom. Subsequent events proved that he kept his word.

> The sudden deaths attributed to poison did not stop. The Conseil du Cap took preventive measures against the unknown malefactors: on 11 March 1758, prohibiting the making of 'Macandals' or witchcraft items, because of their profaning of holy matters, the prohibition against any slave making and distributing *garde-corps* (gris-gris) and Macandals is extended to freemen . . . None of these measures proved effective. Poison took its toll as before, that is if all the mysterious deaths of the time are to be attributed to poisoning.[33]

Ostensibly, Macandal had failed. In the train of his death hundreds of his followers were put to death. As far as the slavers were concerned no black could be trusted, and if the whole race was not dispatched to the next world it was only because such a solution was not economically viable. Many blacks, both men and women, took to the hills, where they lived as Maroons, awaiting the day when they would gain their liberty. Macandal's memory was kept alive in songs and legends. Chary lest these 'superstitions' might miraculously come true, in 1760 the whites passed a series of edicts:

> Whereas the dance known as Vaudou is antagonistic to good morals, to Republican institutions, to decency, to the very health of the participants in these scandalous scenes; that frightful oaths, which if carried out can compromise public safety, are taken upon the direction of the presiders at these ridiculous yet frightful orgies, always followed by prostitution; that these infamies are carried on under the eyes of the young, even of children who, for shame, are admitted to a spectacle as disgusting as it is pernicious to their education; the commission has decreed and does hereby decree the following:
> Article 1: Vaudou Dance gatherings are strictly forbidden.
> Article 2: Any citizen apprehended in such dances shall be arrested and suffer a month's imprisonment.
> Article 3: Individuals who permit their homes to be used for such gatherings, and those in charge shall be arrested and suffer three months' imprisonment and a fine of one hundred pounds.[34]

The next major revolt came thirty years after Macandal's demise. Led by Boukman, a Voodoo *houngan* of prodigious physical and mental strength, it put the writing on the wall as far as slavery in Haiti was concerned. Like his predecessor, he knew that it was through their religion that his people could be united to throw off the shackles of oppression. In a sacred ceremony held in the Caiman Woods he proclaimed the opening of the Great Revolt, a scene dramatically described by Pauléus Sannon:

> He exercised over all the slaves who came near him an inexplicable influence. In order to wash away all hesitation and to secure absolute devotion he brought together on the night of 14 August 1791 a great number of slaves in a glade in Bois Caiman near Morne-Rouge . . . suddenly Boukman stands up and in an inspired voice cries out: 'God, who has made the sun that shines on us from above, who makes the sea to rage and the thunder roll, this same great God from his hiding place on a cloud, hear me, all of you, is looking down upon us. He sees what the whites are doing. The God of the whites asks for crime; ours desires only blessings. But this God who is so good directs you to vengeance! He will direct our arms, he will help us. Cast aside the image of the God of the

whites who thirsts for our tears and pay heed to the voice of liberty speaking to our hearts . . .[35]

On 16 August, the revolutionaries took to the field, their first blow being aimed at the Plantation Chaband, which was razed to the ground. Next, the regions of Petite Asne, Limonade, La Plaine du Nord, Plaisance, and Port Margot were ravaged; in these incidents, over a thousand whites met their end by strangulation. The strategy of the blacks was that of guerrilla warfare, turning up where least expected, striking a telling blow and then returning to their camps in the hills, which strongholds the white army dared not attempt to penetrate. Shocked by this fresh outbreak, many of the whites escaped abroad, to Cuba or France, for the might of the blacks seemed irresistible. Then, two months after the revolt had begun, Boukman fell in action, his death dealing a severe blow to his forces. Still, the Maroons held out, and though their raids became less frequent, they yet harassed the slavers enough so that they attempted to sue for peace. From their headquarters at Gallifet the Maroon generals and chiefs sent the whites a historic rebuke, ending with the words: 'We shall never have any other motto than: Liberty or death!' Among these leaders were Jeannot Bullet, Toussaint Breda, Michaut and Romaine the Prophet. All were staunch Voodooists.

The role black women played in the liberation wars must be emphasized. They were an integral part of the action, and sacrificed their lives on the battlefield alongside the men.

In February 1792 we marched to attack a camp of blacks at Fonds Parisien in Plaine du Cul-de-Sac. On approaching the camp we were astonished to see stuck in the ground along the route large perches on which a variety of dead birds had been affixed. After a quarter of an hour's march I saw the camp which was dotted with *ajoupas* ranged like army tents. What was our surprise to see black males leaping about and more than two hundred women dancing and singing in all security . . . The Voodoo high priestess had not fled . . . She was a very beautiful black woman, well dressed. Had I not been hunting down the blacks, I would not have allowed her to be killed, at least not without extracting from her a great deal of information about her activities. I questioned several women in detail; some of them, from the little Gouraud plantation in Fonds Parisien knew me; they could not understand how we were able to pass through the obstacles the grand mistress of Voodoo had strewn in our way. It was due to this assurance this woman had given them that they so confidently had taken to dancing . . . The priestess was a beautiful creole black from the des Boynes plantation . . . In the Sainte-Suzanne Mountains we captured an Arada woman. She was of the Voodoo cult. She was taken to Cap; she was questioned, but she spoke no Creole . . . Both the men and women frankly said that there could be no human power over her . . . At Gouraud there was a Voodoo high priestess and a black high priest. I learned this from a woman initiate. There was a password but she would never give it to me: she claimed the women did not know it. She gave me the hand recognition sign: it was somewhat similar to that of the Masons. Very few creoles are initiated, only the children of Voodoo chiefs. She told me this as a secret, assuring me . . . I would be killed or poisoned if I tried to penetrate the great mystery of the sect.[36]

A white nun at the convent of the Daughters of Our Lady of Cap Français, reporting that the black penitents remained loyal to African religion and the fight for freedom, also testifies to the part played by women.

A former pupil later known to history as Princess Amethyste, the leader of a company of Amazons, was initiated into the Gioux or Voodoo sect, a sort of religious and dancing Masonry brought to Saint-Domingue by the Aradas, and brought into the sect a large number of her companions. The class regents used to note a certain agitation which would increase particularly after this round which they had adopted to the exclusion of all others:

> Eh! eh! Bomba eh! eh!
> Canga bafio te
> Canga mousse dele
> Canga do ki la
> Canga li

We don't know if this is Senegalese or Yolof, Arada or Congo; we do know . . . these words are a sacramental Voodoo hymn. One evening the Negresses left the building accompanied by a large number of female companions and went out of town into the night, singing these words incomprehensible to the whites. Now, however, the attention of the nuns had been piqued; for some time the Negresses had adopted an almost uniform dress, around their bodies wearing kerchiefs in which the colour red dominated; they wore sandals. At night these words foreign to the whites could be heard in chant, now in single voice, now in chorus. The Voodoo king had just declared war on the colonials, and, diadem circling his forehead, and accompanied by the queen dressed in a red scarf, and agitating the little bells decorating a box containing a snake, they were marching to the assault of the colony's cities . . . They came to lay siege to Cap-Français. By the light of large braziers which notched the silhouettes of the magnificent rounds the nuns from the windows of their monastery which overlooked the countryside and city were able to see the nude black women of the sect dancing to the sad sound of tambourines and *lambis* alternating with the shrieks of the sacrificial victims.[37]

Twelve long years of war followed Boukman's revolt, a dozen years which were to see men such as Toussaint, Dessalines, Pètion, and Henri-Christophe lead their people to freedom – not, however, until they had dealt the 'Little Corporal' what can rightly be called his 'Caribbean' Waterloo. In this noble struggle, surrounded by white racist governments on all sides, Voodoo played a central and decisive role.

And when the war years were over the African cult and African gods gave the fighters the courage, toughness and faith which were necessary to inflict upon the First Consul Napoleon Bonaparte his first defeat. The animal sacrificed in the ritual was not only a gift to the *loas*; its blood bound together those who made the sacrifice, it demanded of each individual who voluntarily entered this ritual group absolute confidence and complete reliability – otherwise the blood of the sacrificial animal would come over him and destroy him. That is the traditional blood pact of Dahomey, which was assimilated to the Voodoo cult and which swore the former slaves to a community that was able, despite being badly armed, to oppose a drilled European army, and which, despite many defeats, repeatedly stirred the rebellion up anew. Thus the Haitians broke down the army which Napoleon had sent under his brother-in-law Leclerc, 35,000 men, picked troops of the army of the Rhine . . .[38]

Politically speaking, Voodoo is the triumph of the African way of life over the European; the triumph of freedom over slavery, the triumph of dignity over inhumanity. It remains the axis of the Haitians' world, and is the seed of their language, music, art, dance, medicine and spirituality. It restored to them their pride in being black. When, in 1804, the country declared itself independent, one leader, Boisrond-Tonnerre, called for a 'parchment from the skin of a white man, his skull for an inkwell, his blood for ink, and a bayonet for a pen' to write the proclamation.

Jamaica:

My Name is Obeah

The obi men provided the blacks in the Caribbean with a foundation upon which they could build a new culture.

Dennis Bovell

He was staring hard, straining his eyes to their utmost, somehow trying to make them do the impossible that they might forever retain what he was seeing. The impossible was happening . . .

It was growing smaller, getting dimmer by the moment. Which reason made his eyes drink all the more greedily: they were like travellers embarking for a perpetual stay in the desert. The impossible was happening . . .

And yet, no nightmare could be more real. Death itself dwindled into insignificance besides this. The ship and all its miseries – the stench, the heat, the air-tight crowdedness – all ceased to exist. Only the awed silence was real. It filled the hole to suffocation . . .

It was sinking, down low, like the last breaths of a candle. And his eyes, mothlike, danced around it with despair-laden wings . . .

He saw the savannah, the endless river, the great mountain rising to the clouds; they initiated him into manhood; he hunted; war stirred his blood; he caught a butterfly; he sang a song; he picked a flower – her name was Djouma; the drums were riding the wind; the drums were dancing in his soul; the drums were guiding his life . . .

Rain? Yes, it was raining. If only it had been simply rain – but, ah!, these were rains from the heart, rains which fell from the spirit. He felt like a young girl embarrassed by her first menstruation: this rain had come so unexpectedly . . .

Young warrior of Senegabia! He peered into the fetid darkness. Warriors of Senegabia: they were all crying. Softly. Tenderly. Unabashedly . . .

Such rains are accompanied by thunders. He trembled; he was going to fall apart, be bashed to pieces, lose reality . . .

A momentary calm steadied him. A hand. Its owner's eyes were portals of hope. His gaze was the dawn of wisdom. His expression like a sun which never sets . . .

Then it happened: the Theft of Hope. The Rape of Freedom. The Ruin of the Future.

'What have we to fear as long as the Gods are with us?' the old man whispered.

'What do you mean?'

'I am an Obeah,' he said.

The Obeah Man was a wizard. He was priest, herb doctor, diviner, guide and judge. His knowledge was the sum of a long and trying apprenticeship at the hands of formidable masters. He was the product of an ancient and respected line. Nature was his goddess and he knew and understood her to a fearful degree. His devotion to her combined the labour of a scientist with the passion of a lover: he lived a life of austerities and trials. Addicted to solitude, he sought out uninhabited places in the jungle where he could pursue his studies and meditations undisturbed. In these lonely haunts he found God – happiness without attachments and evil without the aid of men. He could see into the future, bring about good or bad luck, and give or take life. His was the alchemy of herbs and the jungle was his storehouse and laboratory.

Obeahism had its origins in the Ashanti belief in animism: the belief that inert 'things' are also the abodes of the gods. (The word itself is derived from the Ashanti *obayifo* which means wizard or witch and is in turn derived from the Egyptian *ob*: a snake. *Ob* is also the Hebrew word for python.) The Ashanti believed in a Supreme Being, Onyame, who was invisible and never represented in material form. Access to him was by way of subordinate deities, of whom they made idols and housed them in shrines. They were assiduously worshipped, as were the ancestors. Every shrine was equipped with stools in case any of the latter should decide to visit. The other side of this worship of the gods was the worship of the Devil.

There was a clear distinction between the two. The good priest was called *okomfo* and the bad *bonsam komfo*. As in all religions the Ashanti worshipped the former and appeased the latter. Hence charms, beads and talismans were employed to attract blessings and to ward off evil.

Such men would not have cowered before slavery: the elite of any nation are known by their dignified indifference to adversity. Their immediate preoccupation would have been to put their heads together with the other leaders of their people to arrive at a plan for survival and by this is meant, foremost, survival in a psychological sense. Apart from loss of bodily freedom, slavery meant the threat of the loss of cultural values, the forfeit of which spelt disintegration of the race. As a result, the first thing to do was to see that the memory of the ancestors and the rituals proper to their worship were preserved.

> . . . the professors of Obi are, and always were, natives of Africa, and none other, and they have brought the science with them to Jamaica, where it is so universally practised . . . The oldest and most crafty are those who 'usually attract the greatest devotion and confidence . . . The Negroes in general, whether African or Creoles, revere, consult and abhor them; to these oracles they resort and with the most implicit faith, upon all occasions, whether for the cure of disorders, the obtaining of revenge for injuries or insults, the conciliating of favour, the discovery and punishment of the thief or the adulterer, and the predicting of future events.[1]

Another report says: 'Negroes formerly called Obeah men, but now more commonly called Doctors, do exist in Barbados, but I understand that they are not so many at present as formerly.' However, the Council of the Island reports at the same period:

> There is hardly any estate in the island in which there is not some old man or woman who affects to possess some supernatural power. These are called Obeah Negroes, and by the superstitious Negroes much feared . . . It has been so long known here, that the origin is difficult to trace, but professors are as often natives as Africans.

The Obeah doctor derived his power from knowing how to propitiate the gods. He knew the hour of the night and the place to make the offering; he knew the correct roots, herbs and stones and their combinations and proportions. To this he added the sacred words handed down to him from his teachers. The gods entered into his charms and poisons and gave him extraordinary powers and thus he could wield power over men.

He hated the slavers and promised his brethren protection from them:

> Amalkir, the Obeah practitioner, dwelt in a loathsome cave, far removed from the inquiring eye of the suspicious whites, in the Blue Mountains; he

was old and shrivelled; a disorder had contracted all his nerves, and he could hardly crawl. His cave was the dwelling-place, or refuge of robbers; he encouraged them in their depredations; and gave them Obi, that they might fearlessly rush where danger stood. This Obi was supposed to make them invulnerable to the attacks of the white men, and they placed implicit belief in its virtues.[2]

And the whites did everything within their power to destroy him. The following sentences are from the record book of the parish of St Andrew's in Jamaica:

1773: Sarah, tried for having in her possession cats' teeth, cats' claws, hair, beads, knotted cords, and other materials relative to the practice of Obeah, to delude and impose on the mind of the Negroes – sentenced to be transported.

1776: Solomon, for having materials in his possession for the practice of Obeah – to be transported.

1777: Tony, for practising Obeah, or witchcraft, on a slave named Fortune, by which means the said slave became dangerously ill – not guilty.

1782: Neptune, for making use of rum, hair, chalk, stones, and other materials, relative to the practice of Obeah, or witchcraft – to be transported.

The Obeah man posed a threat to white rule and his preaching of African glories gave the institution of slavery short shrift. This clause from the Acts of the Jamaican Assembly (1827) eloquently delineates white fear: 'Neither health nor life can be secure, if the slaves are allowed to unsettle the understanding of each other, by mutually inculcating their crude notions of religion, and have free licence to meet under the pretence of preaching at unseasonable hours and in improper places.' Obeah became punishable with death. In 1840 the Rev James Phillippo was able to boast that 'the spell of Obeism and its kindred abominations is broken'.

Be that as it may, at the trial of George William Gordon (who was later executed) in 1866 the following testimony was given:

Q: Are these Obeah men still much consulted?

A: (*By Beckford Davis, a white man*) Very much indeed; and their influence is so great that nothing that can be said to the black population can induce the more ignorant of them to question the power of the Obeah man.

And they still survive today, as this song of the Maroons of Accompong, heard and copied down by Fermor in 1950, testifies:

> When you want to get money to send to the war
> They gather up thousands of pound.
> The Obeahman visits the parishes then
> And drives in a buggy-go-round.

Obeah concerns itself with protection by means of homeopathics. The Obeah man is no magician, but a skilled herbalist who has spent his life attaining knowledge of those plants useful in removing bodily and spiritual ills. It is impossible to believe that the whites couldn't see that his practice was pretty much the same as that of the Western physician. Hence, the source of their irritation was their realization that he was a black person looked up to by his people. And a man thus revered might become a man who commanded, and it didn't take a genius to guess what that command would be. Obeah men and women were stringently persecuted, and even when white rule ended they were still attacked with every available resource. Apart from laws prohibiting the practice of Obeah, the whites spread racist calumnies about it. Obeah practitioners were 'self-hypnotized', 'dirty, ignorant, and deformed in some way', and 'conscious of their own fraud'. These were the observations published by white travellers. One such was Martha Warren Beckwith, who in 1929 published an insidious little tome, *Black Roadways*, which contains her horrifyingly ignorant ideas about Obeah. From her visit to Jamaica she gleaned the information that 'the Negro has a credulous mind', and 'many of these people are heathens – still, and Obeah is the religion of the shadow world, the religion of fear, suspicion, and revenge'. However, this cultural philosopher does concede that 'it is true that as the Negroes become better educated and more intelligent the spiritist beliefs (upon which Obeah practices depend today) lose their hold upon the mind . . .'[3]

Edward Kamau Braithwaite, a black man who lived in Jamaica and has first-hand black experience of Obeah, expresses a radically black and different opinion about it:

Obeah (the word is used in Africa and the Caribbean) is an aspect of the last two subdivisions (healing and protection), though it has come to be regarded in the New World and in colonial Africa as sorcery and 'black magic'. One probable tributary to this view was the notion that a great deal of 'pre-scientific' African medicine was (and is) at best pyschological, at norm mumbo-jumbo/magical in nature. It was not recognized, in other words, that this 'magic' was (is) based on a scientific knowledge and use of herbs, drugs, foods and symbolic/associational procedures (pejoratively termed *fetishistic*), as well as on a homeopathic understanding of the material and divine nature of Man (*nam*) and the ways in which this could be affected. The principle of Obeah is, therefore, like medical principles everywhere, the process of healing/protection through seeking out the source or explanation of the cause (*obi*/evil) of the disease or fear. This was debased by the slavemaster/missionary/Prospero into an assumption, inherited by most of us, that Obeah deals *in* evil. In this way, not only has African science been discredited, but Afro-Caribbean religion has been negatively fragmented and almost (with the exceptions of Haiti and Brazil) publicly destroyed.[4]

In the light of this clear-sighted explanation it is abundantly obvious that the men and women who practise Obeah are nothing more or less than members of that profession which practises medicine around the world, each according to its own customs and with the materials available. Obeah can be used for evil, but that is a characteristic inherent in all power. The men who made the atomic bomb are still referred to as 'scientists'. As long as black culture remains rooted in Nature, the Obeah man will have his place in it, an exceptional position for one who fulfilled an exceptional task.

Rastafarian Sunrise

While the Jamaica of old is something of a social historian's treasure-trove – the Maroons, pocomania and the inspiring deeds of Cujoe and Mary Secoulie – contemporary Jamaica has managed to live up to that proud past by producing the most socially significant black music in the world today and, in doing so, has usurped the palm formerly held by the blues. This music – reggae – can justly be called the 'music of Négritude', for, like the poems of those who waged their struggle against colonialism under that banner –

Césaire, David Diop, Derek Walcott, Gotran-Damas, Nicolas Guillen, Senghor – reggae is an affirmation of black cultural and spiritual values. Reggae has its roots in the Ethiopian Church movement, begun by George Liele in 1784, and brought to fruition in 1920 by Marcus Garvey, one of the most outstanding and important (to black people) figures of this century.

Garvey was born at St Ann's Bay, Jamaica, on 17 August 1887, the son of a descendant of the Maroons. His early years may be described as one long, unremitting course of studying the effects on blacks of colonialism. As a young man he took part in political rallies, and at twenty began to travel widely throughout the Caribbean and Central America. No matter where he went, the plight of blacks was the same: racial discrimination and economic exploitation comprised the sum of their lives. In 1912 he went to London to further his studies and came into contact with many Africans who were able to acquaint him with conditions in their countries. These dire revelations, coupled with his reading of Booker T. Washington's autobiography, fired him to the mission which was to become his life's work.

> I read *Up from Slavery* by Booker T. Washington, and then my doom – if I may so call it – of being a race leader dawned upon me . . . I asked: 'Where is the black man's Government? Where is his King and his kingdom? Where is his President, his country, and his ambassador, his army, his navy, his men of big affairs?' I could not find them, and then I declared, 'I will help to make them.'[5]

Like a man possessed, he set to work. Returning to Jamaica in 1914, he founded the Universal Negro Improvement and Conservation Association (UNIA), the aim of which was to unite black peoples everywhere in the struggle against their oppressors. Within the short span of two years he had turned his attention to the blacks in the United States and, in March 1916, without any 'official' backing, 'an obscure young man named Marcus Garvey arrived in Harlem . . .'[6] Almost overnight he cast off the cloak of obscurity, for it at once became apparent that he was a charismatic orator fired by the righteousness of his cause. In his speeches he never failed to stress the fact that blacks were not a people without a past; that they, too, had 'made history'; and that the white race had done their best to hide the truth of the black past from them. Black people were the heirs of a civilization which had existed long before the whites had become 'civilized'.

When Europe was inhabited by a race of cannibals, a race of savages, naked men, heathens and pagans, Africa was peopled with a race of cultured black men, who were masters in art, science and literature; men who were cultured and refined; men, who, it was said, were like the gods. Even the great poets of old sang in beautiful sonnets of the delight it afforded the gods to be in companionship with the Ethiopians. Why, then, should we lose hope? Black men, you were once great; you shall be great again. Lose not courage, lose not faith, go forward. The thing to do is to get organized.[7]

Garvey understood that the use of history as a weapon wasn't a white monopoly. 'Negroes,' he said,

teach your children they are the direct descendants of the greatest and proudest race who ever peopled the earth . . . Sojourner Truth is worthy of the place of sainthood alongside Joan of Arc; Cripus Attucks and George William Gordon are entitled to the halo of martyrdom with no less glory than that of any other race. Toussaint L'Ouverture's brilliancy as a soldier and statesman outshone that of a Cromwell, Napoleon and Washington; hence he is entitled to the highest place as a hero among men.[8]

Garvey was indefatigable in championing the black cause. Publicist, organizer, fund-raiser, publisher and orator, he took daring steps to provide blacks with visible manifestations of the power they wielded when united. In 1918 he founded the *Negro World*, a weekly publication which became the foremost black journal of the day. The next year, 1919, saw the advent of the Black Star Line, the black-owned and -operated shipping line subscribed to by thousands of poor Afro-Americans. Then, in 1920, he convened the first international congress of the UNIA. Held in Harlem, it drew raving throngs who filled the streets of the black metropolis to overflowing to hear the First Black President of the Negro World.

These successes naturally brought him into conflict with the US government, and in 1922 he and three associates were indicted for supposedly defrauding the mail. Due to bad management, the Black Star Line had folded and Garvey, who died in poverty, was accused of fattening his bank account. In this case of the White People of the United States *v* the Black People (with Garvey in the role of scapegoat), the Great Guide pleaded his own case, using the courtroom as a platform to plead the plight of his brethren. The white press had a field day with the proceedings, shamelessly rolling out reams of racist propaganda and cant. The outcome was as was to be expected: the all-white jury found him guilty and the judge, a white member of the NAACP, sentenced him to five years' imprisonment. Oddly enough, his co-defendants were ajudged not guilty and released – they were not dangerous to the racist status quo but Garvey, a man made of the stuff of a Boukman, was: a fact clearly illustrated while he was free on bail pending his appeal. He started another shipping company, the Black Cross Navigation and Trading Company, and sent a delegation to Liberia to put forth his plan for the creation of a new colony of Afro-Americans. When, in 1925, his appeal was overruled, he was imprisoned in the penitentiary at Atlanta, Georgia, where he remained until 1927 when President Coolidge commuted his sentence, after which he was deported to Jamaica as an undesirable alien.

Though he was never again to attain the heady heights he had achieved in Harlem, he never gave up the struggle. In 1928 he lectured in Europe, and petitioned the League of Nations (which did nothing whatever) to turn its attention to the sufferings of black peoples. In 1929 he returned to Jamaica where he founded the Jamaican People's Political Party, and chaired the sixth internationale of the UNIA. Elected to the Kingston City Council in 1930, he failed in his bid for a siege in the national assembly. After that, ill-health and the frustrating sense of the movement's growing weakness took their toll. Garvey died in London at the age of fifty-two.

Garvey was a Pan-Africanist visionary who laid the foundations for black liberation movements everywhere. Phoenix-like, his aspirations have been reborn in the likes of Nkrumah, Elijah Muhammed, Martin Luther King, Jr, Malcolm X (the son of Garveyite parents), the Blank Panthers, Jesse Jackson, Andrew Young and many others. Their achievements have redeemed the labours of this founding father, this West Indian freedom-fighter who opened the road to black liberation and spiritual awareness. It was he who, in his Declaration of the Rights of the Negro Peoples of the World, demanded 'that instruction given Negro children in schools include the subject of "Negro History" '. It was he who rekindled the black people's faith in their race, and who told them that no matter where they were presently living – in Africa, the Caribbean, the United States or Europe – they were one people and one nation.

In the Black World, Garvey is thought of as a member of that elite pantheon of liberators which includes Macandal, Toussaint, Nat Turner, Jomo Kenyatta, Malcolm X and Martin Luther King, Jr. (Thus, in his prospectus for an independent black nation in the US, Manning Marable projects the creation of an African Cultural Institute under whose auspices, 'The complete works of influential black intellectuals, from Dubois and Garvey to Julius Nyerere and Imamu Amiri Baraka, would be published and distributed at a nominal cost to the public.'[9]

Garvey's greatest contribution proved to be his concept of a black Church which worshipped a black God. Given the high spiritual inclination of peoples of African descent, he early realized that the myth of white superiority could never be destroyed while blacks paid homage to a white God – a God who had no problem accommodating himself with slavery and its attendant evils. Therefore he admonished them to turn away from the blue-eyed Son of God and to seek their salvation in a divinity made in their image: 'We have only now started out (late though it may be) to see our God through our own spectacles . . . We Negroes believe in the God of Ethiopia.'[10]

This injunction set off one of the greatest religious revivals of this century, culminating in the founding of a new Church: Rastafarianism. Garvey chose Rev George Alexander McGuire, an Episcopalian minister from Boston, as General Chaplain of the UNIA. Ordained a bishop in 1921 by the Greek Orthodox Church, McGuire took up his duties as head of the newly founded African Orthodox Church with a zeal which rivalled Garvey's. 'Erase the white gods from your hearts. We must go back to the native Church, to our true God.'

By the time the Fourth International Convention of the Negro Peoples of the World met in 1924, moreover, the leaders of the black religion were openly demanding that Negroes worship a Negro Christ. During the opening parade through the streets of Harlem, UNIA members marched under a portrait of a black Madonna and Child. The convention session of August 5, 1924, drew the attention of the white press when Bishop McGuire advised Negroes to name the day when all members of the race would tear down and burn any pictures of the white Madonna and the white Christ found in their homes. 'Then,' he said, 'let us start our Negro painters getting busy and supply a black Madonna and a black Christ for the training of our children.' Bishop McGuire gave added weight to his words by speaking under a large oil painting that clearly portrayed the type of Madonna and Child he had in mind.[11]

Garvey told his people to turn their eyes to the black continent, for it was from there that their salvation would come. 'Look to Africa, where a black king shall be crowned, for the day of deliverance is near.' And he adopted Burrel and Ford's 'Ethiopia, Thou Land of Our Fathers' as the Pan-African anthem.

> Ethiopia, thou land of our fathers . . .
> [. . .]
> We must in the fight be victorious
> When swords are thrust outward to gleam
> For us will the victory be glorious
> When led by the red, black and green.

The black 'saviour' he spoke of was Ras (Prince) Tafari, the Regent of Ethiopia who, upon ascending the throne in 1930, was crowned Haile Selassie (Power of the Trinity), Negus Neghest (King of Kings). Sebastian Clarke's summary of the movement is masterful:

> Ethiopianism was essentially a church movement, and . . . Marcus Garvey combined political objectives with religious expressions to create an impact, not only on the Jamaican masses, but on black peoples all over the world. In the face of their general lack of literacy and of education – a deliberate British colonial policy – these people did not have a coherent understanding of history. But they could understand a religious prophecy. So the masses awakened to the birth of the Black Redeemer, the same black king that Marcus Garvey spoke of.[12]

Selassie's arrival on the throne marked the real beginning of Rastafarianism, and while Garvey had no direct role in the movement, he is rightly held to be its founder. The early thirties saw the rise and proliferation of the cult, led by the Rasta preachers Leonard P. Howell, H. Archibald Dunkley and Joseph Hibbert. Harassed by the colonial authorities, Howell was sentenced to two years' imprisonment for selling photographs of the Negus. In 1940 he founded the Ethiopia Salvation Society, a part of which was the first dreadlocks commune. By 1953 there were a dozen of these, highly organized groups, varying in size from twenty to upwards of two hundred members. The Rasta code is at once a religious and a social bulwark, by which the devotee both gains salvation and lays down the burden of colonialism.

Six doctrines stand out in the Ras Tafari belief system. The first is that black men, reincarnations of the ancient Israelites, were exiled to the

West Indies because of their transgressions. Second, the wicked white man is inferior to the black man. Third, the Jamaican situation is a hopeless Hell; Ethiopia is Heaven. Fourth, Haile Selassie is the Living God. Fifth, the invincible Emperor of Abyssinia will soon arrange for expatriated persons of African descent to return to the Homeland. Sixth, in the near future black men will get revenge by compelling white men to serve them.

. . . [During their meetings] a speaker may follow the first song with remarks of this type: 'How did we get here?' Chorus: 'Slavery.' 'Who brought us from Ethiopia?' Chorus: 'The white man.' 'The white man tells us we are inferior, but we are not inferior. We are superior, and he is inferior. The time has come for us to go back home. In the near future, we will go back to Ethiopia and the white man will be our servant. The white man says we are no good, but David, Solomon and the Queen of Sheba were black. The English are criminals and the black traitors [middle-class Jamaicans] are just as bad. Ministers are thieves and vagabonds. The black man who doesn't want to go back to Ethiopia doesn't want freedom. There is no freedom in Jamaica. Ras Tafari is the living God.'[13]

In 1954 the authorities launched an offensive against the Rastas, culminating in police assaults and imprisonments. Among foreigners (mostly English and Americans) and brainwashed Jamaicans, the Rastas were held in contempt. 'It is widely believed that the members of this cult are hooligans, psychopaths and dangerous criminals. Ras Tafarians are often referred to as "those dreadful people".'[14]

In the light of the history of black and white relationships, it is not difficult to understand why the colonials found the Caribbo-Ethiopians distasteful – these 'dreaded' dreadlocked women and men wanted the whites off their backs. 'The Rastas were always loyal to their religion and philosophy, and were never cowed by the system. Rather, they were quite vociferous and dramatic in demonstrating the extreme neglect to which the British colonial system had subjected poor blacks.'[15]

Reggae arose out of the logical need for the Rastas to praise the black God in music and verse untarnished by connotations and values handed down by the white oppressor. These called for a radical break with Christian church music and a return to African roots. 'At the inception of Rastafari in the late 1920s, there was already a doctrinal credo, but no music . . . if Afrika were being projected, it would be contradictory to project the music of the (white) Christian Church . . . The words of church songs were altered to project

Rastafari and they were accompanied by handclaps.'[16]

African music was alive in Jamaica in the music of the Burru and Kumina religious sects, whose modes of worship were based on the dances and drumming of Ghana. The Rastas would attend the Burru ceremonies in the slums of Kingston, and it was here that, in the late 1950s, reggae evolved. Among the pioneers, men like Count Ossie, Rico Rodriguez, Cedric Brooks and the preacher Brother Love hold pride of place. Theirs was the glory of providing the Rastafarian creed with a music whose content fulfilled the need of a revolutionary religion. Just as the Voodoo of Haiti liberated its slaves, the aim of reggae — in its rhythms and lyrics — is to deliver the West Indian from the Babylonian nightmare left over from colonialism. Thus, the Jamaican-born, British-resident poet Linton Kwesi Johnson (see p. 54) says in his poem, 'Reggae Sounds':

[. . .]
foot-drop find drum, blood story,
bass history is a moving
   is a hurting black story.
Rhythm of a tropical electric storm
cooled down to the pace of the struggle,
flame-rhythm of historically yearning
flame-rhythm of the time of turning,
measuring the time for bombs and for burning.

[. . .]
shape it into violence for the people,
they will know what to do, they will do it.[17]

Johnson is one of the many poet-musicians of reggae who is not a religious devotee of the sect. His is the poetry of black socialism concerned, Garvey-like, with the destiny of his people wherever they might be. Others, like Peter Tosh, Robbie Shakespeare, Burning Spear, Ras Michael and the Sons of Negus, are firmly committed to the concept of Rastafari, as was the much-missed guiding light of the music, Bob Marley. London's West Indian community has added to this list of socially aware artists Matumbi, Third World, Barry Ford, Steel Pulse, Candy and Bunny Mackenzie, Aswad and the awesomely gifted Dennis Bovell.

Reggae has carried the West Indian's cry of righteous indignation around the world, and if there are those who refuse to heed its message, everyone is aware of the implications of its black beat. It is a revolutionary pounding, calling black people to take their rightful place in the world. As Jan Carew puts it:

> Echoes of singing drums speak
> of Garvey and Fidel
> Malcolm and Fidel
> Lumumba and Fidel

Rastafari is the West Indians' passionate No! to white domination, and their ecstatic Yes! to their self-won liberty. With its inception, a black sun rose over the isles, bathing them in glorious waves of red, black and green. Garvey's prophecy (here given) has come true.

> When I am dead wrap the mantle of the Red, Black and Green around me, for in the new life I shall rise with God's grace and blessing to lead the millions up the heights of triumph with the colours that you well know. Look for me in the whirlwind or the storm, look for me all around you, for, with God's grace, I shall come and bring with me countless millions of black slaves who have died in America and the West Indies and the millions in Africa to aid you in the fight for Liberty, Freedom and Life.[18]

Cuba:

The House of Images

I am Yoruba, I am Lucumi, Mandingo, Congo, Carabali . . .
Nicolas Guillén

The Rolling Stones

Whereas the bulk of the Africans taken to Haiti were Aradas, Dahomeans and Ibos, the majority of those enslaved in Cuba were Yorubans and Bantus, peoples of the Niger River in southern Nigeria. The heirs to a rich civilization, they managed to keep intact their religion, music and much of their language in spite of stringent prohibitions decreed by their enslavers. One can very well imagine their amazement upon being told by the priests that there was only one God, that Christ was the saviour, and that Catholicism was the true religion for, by comparison with their own religion and its splendid pantheon Christianity was extremely pale. Jesus and his gang of saints were no doubt powerful spirits but hardly to be compared with Obatalá and Oddudúa, the father and mother of the gods; Oggún, the god of iron; Elegguá, the keeper of the crossroads; Ifá, the lord of the impossible; Olasa, the goddess of fishermen; Oyá, goddess of the River Niger; Oshún, the Vigin Venus; and Shangó, the god of thunder and lightning. It would take more than the likes of a carpenter and his disciples to remove this formidable line-up of supernaturals from the Africans' minds. The whites told them that the Bible was the word of God – but the Bible didn't sing, and it didn't dance! More importantly, Africans were in the habit of calling on their gods for help, and the whites' religion denied Africans that recourse. Besides, they knew that the white God was bound to help his own, just as the black one would his. So be it: all's fair in religion and war.

There was no way the zealous soul-savers sent out from Spain were about to tolerate the blacks' religion. Schooled in the bloodthirsty arts of the Holy Inquisition, their methods of instruction resembled those of the Conquistadores rather than those of a Church. They were devils preaching religion, a religion whose God had proclaimed white supremacy and black enslavement.

Dedicated to the 'golden calf', they were rosary-carrying bankers and merchants whose cross was a dollar sign. Apart from the profits from its own holdings and plantations (worked by African and Indian slaves), for over two hundred years the Church received a tithe (ten per cent) of everything produced by anyone in Cuba. For all practical purposes, to the Church the island was but a counting-house. An idea of some of the pernicious aspects of their devoted existence may be seen in the pages of Esteban Montejo's *Autobiography of a Runaway Slave*:

> The priests came in the morning and started praying and kept it up for hours. I hardly understood a word and didn't pay much attention to it. Some of them were the next thing to criminals. They flirted with the pretty white women and slept with them, they were lecherous and pious both at once. If they had a child they would pass it off as a godson or nephew; they hid them under their cassocks and never said, 'This is my son.'
>
> They kept tabs on the Negroes, though, and if a black woman gave birth she had to send for the priest within three days or she would be in hot water with the plantation owner. That was how all the children came to be Christians.
>
> If a priest went by, you were supposed to say, 'A blessing, Father.' Sometimes they didn't so much as look at you.
>
> Priests and lawyers were sacred in those days, because their titles won them great respect. But Negroes were never any of these things, least of all priests. I never saw a black priest. The priesthood was for whites of Spanish descent.[1]

Having lost their freedom the Africans now risked losing their souls. The brainwashing to imbue them with Catholicism never let up. It was like a miraculous sun which shone during the day but didn't set at night. With pitiless importunity the whites droned into African ears the fact that their lives on earth were of no consequence; what mattered was the fate of their souls. And the bigots were successful, to a degree: in order to continue practising their own religion with a minimum of persecution, the Africans incorporated the fetish symbols of the Catholic Church into the pantheon of their own. Had the whites had any idea of the sophistication of Yoruban beliefs they would certainly have employed other tactics than the hymn and the whip. So dynamic is Yoruban religion that many authorities consider it the richest and most complex to have survived since antiquity. Adapting itself to circumstances, gathering unto itself bits and pieces from the Catholic stockpile, it became known as Santeria – 'saint worship'. The gods, though, kept their original name, *orisha*; while their devotees are known as *lucumi* or Santeros.

Like the Vodun, Santeros see reality as the constant interreaction of supernatural forces, these powers being under the control of the *orishas*. Thus they implore them to intervene in their affairs. No matter how trivial or serious the case, they can call upon their gods to aid them in their endeavours and to help them on their journey through life. They invoke them in their love affairs, for their business, to bring about good luck, to ward off malevolent influence, and to bring about the downfall of their enemies. For to the Santero the gods are not either good or evil, they have the power to be both. Shangó can get angry and hurl thunderbolts or he can smile and wreathe the sky in rainbows. 'The secret of the Santero's life, then,' says Jahn, 'and the purpose of *orisha* worship is to establish a constructive relationship with these powers.'[2] The influence of Santeria, then, can cut both ways. And yet, if a Santero does call upon the gods to work harm, the cause must be just and the Santero the offended party.

> The Santeros do make use of chaotic forces in their magical work. Their allies, the Yoruba gods, are direct manifestations of the Creative Principle and thus are spirits of light. When he does magical work of an apparently destructive quality, the Santero is using the negative aspect of a positive force. For example, when he seeks revenge upon an enemy, he may be using the devastating forces of Oggún, god of war, or Shangó, god of fire, to correct an injustice or to 'right a wrong'. In order to avoid becoming the eventual recipient of cosmic reprisal for a work of destruction, the Santero is careful to state that he has been the victim of the evil machinations of his enemy, and therefore he is entitled to 'divine justice'. Thus he is able to carry on all the negative aspects of his magical works under the protective aegis of the cosmic laws.[3]

To start with, then, in order to undertake 'bad' magic, the Santero must be sure that his cause is righteous, for there can be no lying to the *orishas*. If a Santero is foolhardy enough to attempt to trick them they will make his life hell. For they have all the attributes, good and bad, of humankind. They can be merciful, loving, tender, understanding or spiteful, wilful, headstrong, or downright nasty. Elegguá, the master of the crossroads, is a malicious mischief-maker, held to be the cause of all bad luck. Oba, the wife of

Shangó, is so jealous that she never lets him out of her sight. Chiyidi, the god of nightmares, delights in tormenting. So whoever would beg their aid had best have scrupulously honest intentions.

Africans' belief in their native faith was never really threatened by the whites, for there was no question in Africans' minds that their gods were the more powerful. And even when a few Christian elements were mixed in, the faith was still wholly African in character. Writing of the belief in magic during the 1890s Montejo says,

> The plantation was full of witchcraft. The Filipinos were always meddling in this sort of thing, stirring up the Negroes and even sleeping with Negresses. They were a bunch of crooks. If one of them died they would bury him near a Negro, and soon afterwards he would appear dressed in red and scare the wits out of everybody. The old men tended to see these apparitions more than the young ones, who hardly ever did. A young man does not have the gift of seeing much, and he rarely hears voices either . . . All this is to do with the spirit world, and we should face it without fear. The living are more dangerous . . . That's the way to look at it, fairly and squarely. If a dead person comes up to you, don't run away, ask him, 'What do you want, brother?' He will either answer or take you away with him somewhere . . . The Congolese were different, they weren't afraid of the dead. They would put on serious faces, but they weren't frightened. There was no weeping when a Congolese died, only a great deal of praying and singing in a low voice, without the drums . . . Some people said that when a Negro died he went back to Africa, but this is a lie. How could a dead man go to Africa? It was living men who flew there, from a tribe the Spanish stopped importing as slaves because so many of them flew away that it was bad for business.[4]

Santero worship presupposes a belief in magic – that is, in the *orishas* actively participating in human life, without which the very idea of life is impossible. The slavers might control Africans' bodies but their spirits belonged to their gods – the Catholic priests might preach until doomsday and still not make any headway with them. Besides, a priest soon found that he was preaching to the converted, for the *orishas* had adopted their Christian fellow divinities and made them part of the Yoruban family of deities. Every African believed in Christ – believed that he was a friend of Shangó's, and that Mary and St Peter consorted with Ibeyi and Ochumare. And indeed, the two creeds did have many points in common, like, for instance, the holy rosary beads and the sacred stones, those blessed rocks the Africans had brought with them from their homeland. No, not in their suitcases. Nor did the captain of the vessel allow them the use of his coffers. Those sancrosanct stones, around which their religion revolved, were brought to the New World in the stomachs of men, heroes who sacrificed their lives that their people might keep, if not their freedom, at least their gods with them. Some of them died choking while attempting to swallow them; others died in agony during the voyage — itself a deadly risk — as their stomachs swelled and burst. When that happened, a dozen volunteers came forward, eager for the opportunity of sacrificing their lives. For to be a carrier of one of the stones meant certain fatality. Death awaited these heroes once they landed in the New World: their stomachs were cut open and the stones removed and hidden out of reach of the whites.

The noble and tragic destiny of those martyrs is the source of the term 'rolling stones'.

Black Religion — White Faces

The Yoruban religion did not long remain the exclusive preserve of Africans. The whites, intrigued by its mystique, cautiously began to take an interest in it. Unknown to their own clergy, behind the backs of friends and lovers, they stealthily made their way to the secret meetings where, once the Africans were convinced of their sincerity, they were initiated into the cult. As with the black Christians, these whites found out that god practises no colour bar. These men and women, brought up in a culture which found its highest value in reason, broke through its psychic straitjacket and delivered themselves up to Yemayá, Bacoso and Ibeyi. The spirit of rhythm took hold of them and they danced, wildly, freely, 'lasciviously'. The formerly 'savage' sound of the drums became the open-sesame to an enchanted world — as if with new ears they became aware of its sweet sonority. The African hierophants' invocations, their balletic gestures, held the essence of a hitherto unperceived meaning to life; hungry for knowledge, they hung on to the *vriddhis* as a drowning man clutches at a piece of bark. The Yoruban religion dealt with things Catholicism at best only hinted at, revealing the existence of those who worked behind the scenes of ordinary phenomena. 'Chance' was a fool's explanation of the world; the initiated knew that the auguries foretelling events of today had been manifested yesterday, and that today itself was but a presage of tomorrow. Besides, how could they be reproached with heresy when the saints of Catholicism had been syncretized with the African cult? Was not Jesus represented as Olorún, Joseph as Aganyú, St Peter as Oggún, and St Barbara as Shangó? True, the latter is represented in the African Church as a gigantic black man, but who said that the gods had to be white? By the time the 'straight' Catholics became aware that many whites were practising Santeria it was much too late for anything practical to be done about it. Threats of excommunication were useless against people who had already voluntarily removed themselves from the orthodox viewpoint. Why be content with the prettiness of the dish when they could have their cake and eat it too? The dogma they now adhered to, born of the cultural symbiosis of the three races which fused in Cuba, formed a more satisfying and complete credenda: a national religion.

The Syncretic Mixture in Santeria

Yoruba God	Catholic Saint
Olorún-Olofi – God, the creator	Crucified Christ
Obatalá – father of the gods	Our Lady of Mercy (Las Mercedes)
Oddudúa – mother of the gods	Saint Claire
Aganyú – son of Obatalá and Oddudúa	Saint Joseph
Yemayá – sister and wife of Aganyú	Our Lady of Regla
Orungán – son of Yemayá and Aganyú	Infant Jesus
Shangó – son of Yemayá and Orungán	Saint Barbara
Oyá – daughter of Yemayá and Orungán	Our Lady of La Candelaria
Oshún – daughter of Yemayá and Orungán	Our Lady of La Caridad del Cobre
Ochosi – son of Yemayá and Orungán	Saint Isidro
Dada – son of Yemayá and Orungán	Our Lady of Mount Carmel
Ochumare – goddess of the rainbow	Our Lady of Hope
Oggún – god of iron and war	Saint Peter
Babalú-Ayé – god of the sick	Saint Lazarus
Ibeyi – patron of infants	Saints Cosme and Damian
Elegguá – keeper of the doors	Holy Guardian Angel
Orúnla – owner of the Table of Ifá	Saint Francis of Assisi
Ifá – god of impossible things	Saint Anthony of Padua
Bacoso – founder of the dynasty	Saint Christopher

As the magical rites of the Yorubas became more popular, the white man, slowly overcoming the natural reticence of the African priests, managed to learn most of the intricate legends and rites of the cult, until he was finally allowed to participate in the initiation ceremonies. As soon as he reached adeptship, he rebaptized the cult and named it Santeria, that is, worship of the saints. He himself became known as a Santero, or practitioner of Santeria.

The modern Santero practises nearly the same type of primitive magic as the old Yoruba priests. He is a jealous guardian of the African traditions and is usually notoriously uncommunicative about his belief and practices. Since some of his magic would be hard to explain to an *aleyo* (non-believer), this reticence is not difficult to understand.[5]

To the Catholic clergy this was the worst possible slap in the face. It was the Cubano's way of rebuking them for all their sanctimonious hypocrisy. It was telling them that they had failed in their mission. A natural reaction against a religious oligarchy made up exclusively of Spanish-born priests! Of course, the 'official' Church was still very powerful (and vengeful) and lip-service was paid to it, but everyone knew that the most pious of little old ladies, who went to Mass three or four times a day, was also a devout Santera.

In this country Catholicism always seems to get mixed up with magic somewhere along the way. This is a fact. There is no such thing as a Catholic pure and simple. The rich people were Catholics, but they also paid heed to witchcraft from time to time. And the overseers were really impressed by it, they didn't dare take their eyes off the Negro magic-men for a second, because they knew that if the Negroes wanted they could split their skulls open. Lots of people here tell you they are Catholic and Apostolic. I don't believe a word of it! Here almost everyone has their missal and their stick. No person is one thing pure and simple in this country, because all the religions got mixed together. The African brought his, which is the stronger one, and the Spaniard brought his, which isn't so strong, but you should respect them all. That is my way of thinking.[6]

The basis of Santeria is faith — faith in the *orishas*, faith in oneself, and faith in one's cause. The Santero feels that firm faith is sufficient to bring about his desires. What others call miracles he calls 'sympathetic causality', or natural magic. As Montejo points out: 'A man who doesn't believe in miracles today may come to believe in them tomorrow. Proofs occur every day, some more convincing than others, but all quite reasonable.'[7] The Santero's magic cannot be carried out without the artifacts of Nature: plants, stones, flowers, herbs, trees, water, etc. Jesus, he believes, was a master herbalist. 'He was always around herbs; he was a Santero.'

The Santero always asks permission before taking anything from Nature, and he always pays for it. He leaves money, or some object of personal value, or pours liquor on the ground, as payment for what he requires. Trees are especially revered, and none more than the ceiba, which to the Santero is 'the house of god'.

A tree is very important to a Congolese, because everything comes from it and is to be found in it. It is like a god; they feed it and talk to it and ask things of it and look after it. Everything they do is with the help of Nature, especially the tree, which is the soul of Nature. Witchcraft makes use of trees and herbs. There were thickets and good-sized trees on all the plantations during slavery, which were ideal places for the Congolese magic-men.[8]

The Secret Society of Naniguismo

What is known as Naniguismo is often either confounded with Santeria or held to be a separate religion. Both views are erroneous; Naniguismo is a secular sect based upon African ritual and the mutual protection of its members. Born in the time of slavery, its aim is the preservation of a wholly African style of brotherhood; no women are allowed. This called for the courage to circumvent the vigilance of the whites, the risks involved being too severe to be undertaken lightly. The Nanigos were brave men dedicated to the rules of their fellowship and, by implication, to the customs of their people. Dauntless once they had set themselves to achieving some objective, they were feared by white and black alike.

The rites of the sect are based upon Nigerian tradition and centre around Baron Samedi and the *gedés*, the spirits who rule the cemetery. Thus, the rituals act as a means of communication between the living and the dead.

The initiation of new members is held in the strictest secrecy and lasts from midnight to sunset the following day. 'It is a kind of sacred drama, played out to a secret script in which Death (through the human-made imitation of the roar of a leopard) accepts the initiate as his own.'[9] The drama makes use of all the props of theatre: speech, song, costumes, masks and music. The initiate is purified with a magic potion and painted with sacred symbols, while the 'drums of command' beat and the participants chant invocations to Death. After drinking of the blood of a sacrificial cock with the other 'brothers', the initiate is bound to them 'unto death' – he belongs to them and they to him.

The secrecy surrounding the society could not help but make it an object of speculation, but it was its dances which gained it mass popularity. Costumed as *dialitos* (little devils) men dance in the Dia de Reyes (King's Day) and other carnivals, strange, frightening dances imitative of ghouls and other wicked spirits. Forbidden any number of times since the 1870s, they go on being performed clandestinely until, sooner or later, they make their appearance in public again. It is to them that the rumba owes its origin.

For all its popularity, the sect's inner ceremonies are still jealously guarded secrets, as Jahn's report illustrates:

> The attempt was even made to put Naniguismo on the stage. In 1928 in the civic theatre of Guanaboacoa a piece with the title *Apapa Efi* was to have been performed, a one-act play which was to be given as an interlude. The public were newly enthusiastic for folklore and a group of Nanigos who wanted money were going to show them some sacred objects and some of their picturesque rites. Nothing secret was to be made public and no sacrifice was to be undertaken. Nevertheless the actors were 'suspended'.[10]

It was not, however, the Church that interfered; the Nanigos were punished by their own adherents, for such a performance would have been sacrilege. 'As if priests were to sing the "Te Deum Laudamus" in a cabaret,' remarks Ortiz.[11]

Black magic, or *brujeria*, as it is known in Cuba, is outside the domain of Santeria. Sometimes called *palo monte* or *palo mayombe* (*palo*=tree), it is a form of Obeah. Its practitioners, called Congos though actually of Bantu descent, are greatly feared: their witchcraft *works*. Instead of the *orishas* the *brujo* invokes the lords of the dark domain, the demons of evil. Their only fear is of the *orishas* – only one bent on destruction would oppose *them*.

The Devil is a Smart Fellow

Esteban Montejo's *Autobiography of a Runaway Slave* was published in 1963 when he was 105 years of age. It is a fascinating document about life in Cuba during and after slavery, and a cornucopia of black beliefs and culture. Finally, it is the testament of a proud and courageous man – proud to be black and jealous of his freedom, which he took. His statements about black magic are worth quoting at some length.

> When you hear people talk of black magic you should keep calm and respectful, because respect opens every door . . .
>
> This Congolese from Timbirito told me a lot about his meetings with the Devil. He saw him as often as he wanted. I think the Devil is a smart fellow; he obeys when people summon him so as to work evil and give himself pleasure. But don't try calling him for some good purpose because p-h-h-t! he won't come! If a person wants to make a pact with him, the old Congolese told me, he should take a hammer and a big nail, look for the young ceiba tree in the countryside and hammer on the trunk hard three times. As soon as the bugger hears this call, he comes, quite cool and cocky, as if he didn't care a damn. He sometimes appears dressed very smartly like a man but never as a devil, for he doesn't want to frighten people. In his natural shape he is all red like a flame, with fire coming from his mouth and a pitchfork in one hand. When he appears you can speak to him quite normally, but you have to make your meaning very clear because to him years are just days, and if you promise to do something in three years he will think you said three days. If you don't know this, you are in trouble – I've known it ever since I was a slave. The Devil reckons things up in quite a different way from men. He loves doing wickedness. I don't know what he's like now, but he used to give all the help he could, so that spells would work.
>
> Anyone could summon up. A lot of aristocrats, counts and marquises, had dealings with him. Also Masons, and even Christians.[12]

'Here,' wrote the Cuban author Juan Marinello, 'the Negro is marrow and root, the breath of the people; a music heard, an irrepressible impulse.'[13] The dynamism of the Yoruban religion gave it the wherewithal to resist Christianity, to incorporate it unto itself, and to make whites themselves its adherents. Today, there are more than a hundred million Santeros throughout Latin America, and the influx in recent years of Puerto Ricans and Cubans into the United States has seen it gain a foothold in Anglo-America as well.

The black peoples' contribution to Cuban culture is so great and omnipresent that it can be said that they made it what it is. Through the maintenance of their religion they were able to hold on to their culture; their native tongues have enriched the Cuban brand of Spanish; their music and dances have spread their countries' names around the world; the Afro-Cuban school of poetry is one of the most vital and influential of this century. But their greatest success was to spread an African religion in lands where the white man ruled, to have transformed the Americas into a 'house of images'.*

* *Ilé-ere* in Yoruban. Every Santero's home contains an altar on which sit images of the *orishas*, pictures of the saints, charms, etc., and food and drink for the deities.

Brazil:
Obatala in the Backlands

Bahia – town of All Saints – is also the town of all West African gods.

Alfred Métraux

'We Had Palmares!'

The Portuguese in Brazil personified the inveterate inhumanity practised by whites which may stand for their chief characteristic in the New World: they decimated the red peoples and enslaved the black. The Portuguese failed miserably in living up to the name of this 'new' part of the globe, bringing with them all the 'old' evils which had made their history the ignominious story it is. Long schooled in racism at shamelessly anti-Semitic institutes, they now applied their learning to the garden which was America, where it could be put to deadly use. As elsewhere, the Church claimed its share of the spoils. In Brazil, this meant vast tracts of land, plantations covering tens of thousands of acres, presided over by missionaries grown fat in sloth, with slaves to do their bidding. The few men in holy orders who raised their voices against this outrageous way of life were speedily dispatched back to the motherland or to some semi-inhabited outpost where the heat of the swamps soon curtailed their complaints. As usual, the titled, the rich and the officially pious set down and carved up the pie – a golden confection for which others would do the kneading and baking. As for the missionaries, when not gourmandizing they dedicated themselves to the task of converting their helots to Christianity – that is, to moulding them into compliant puppets. Infernal cabal! The wretches professed to be men of God and to hold sacrosanct the dogma prescribed by the Bible. Not content with Caesar's share they demanded that the soul also should be rendered to them. In Lope de Vega's words:

> Oh, blessed court,
> Eternal Providence!
> Where are you sending Columbus
> To renew my evil deeds?

The success of their scheme depended upon the annihilation of the Africans' culture: above all, their religion must go. Only then could they be 'enlightened'. With one stone, composed entirely of cant, they would kill two birds: they would control the blacks' minds and increase their own wealth. The guinea pigs were mostly Dahomeans and Yorubans, children of traditions as vibrant as they were ancient. They knew what the whites didn't: that so long as they did not abandon their gods, the gods would not abandon them. Invisible to the whites, the whole of the Yoruban theogony had crossed the sea with them, booking passage on those same ships of misery and death which had carried their flock. Oshún had placed himself in a stone, Obatalá had taken refuge in some person's memory, Babalu-Aye had concealed himself in the words of a song. And now they found themselves transplanted in a new field, virgin territory.

The far-flung valleys and uncharted savannahs which constituted the Brazil of yesteryear were ripe terrain for the Africans' pantheistic religion, having been cultivated for innumerable ages by the creeds of the Indians, a mysticism akin to that of the blacks. Their mutual adoration of Nature was the cause of this similarity: both felt that God was everywhere manifest in everything, and that the Ancestors were the guardians of the race. It was inevitable, then, that when the two groups of deities met they should form a bond. So alike were their religious beliefs that the two peoples hardly had to explain them to one another; the names of their respective gods and their modes of worship were different in detail, but the form and content were alike in their essentials. Both peoples worshipped the deities with music and dance, and in both creeds the gods manifested themselves through possession of the devotee.

The threat of the whites, naturally, strengthened these bonds. Brought together in their struggle for freedom, Indians and blacks combined forces to resist the common enemy. Living together, intermarrying, exchanging and blending customs, in time they produced new cultural and human hybrids. It is to this social juxtaposition that Brazil owes so many of its unique characteristics. The whole of its civilization is spiced by this Afro-Indian union; Brazilian history echoes with the sound of their heroic struggle. In the soft glow of Brazilians' ebony-rose skin and mysterious, quiet smiles there lingers the shadow of past injustices and unvanquished pride.

The struggle of blacks against whites has ever been a battle between their two Churches. The Christian Church identified itself wholeheartedly with slavery; the African religions with freedom. In spite of the usual restrictions the drums continued to call the faithful. Black religion provided its followers with a base from which they could defend their way of life against the impending psychological holocaust instituted by the Europeans. Counselled by their elders, over the years thousands of blacks took to the bush, the wild jungles of the *sertao* (backlands). Men, women and children, singly or in groups, took their all but hopeless chances. Spurred by the dual emotions of fear and hope, they braved all the obstacles of a savage and intractable landscape in their pursuit of liberty. Starvation, thirst, even almost certain death could not deter them, for death, too, has its gradations. The black Maroons believed that it was better to die savouring freedom than to live in the poisonous bosom of captivity. The yoke of slavery robbed life of its fruits while death, if met in a fair struggle, could be dignified and noble. This courageous dedication to the pursuit of liberty contrasts vividly with the pathological aim of oppressors in their ignoble ambition to subject slaves to a life of bondage. Those who sacrificed their lives perished from the earth, but not from humanity's memory.

It is a tribute to black people's intelligence and bravery that they not only survived in that hostile land but also flourished. They founded communities, established plantations, carried on trade and conducted their lives *à la Africaine*. Some of these settlements were no more than villages, while others grew to become towns. The greatest of these Maroon communities was that of the Republic of Palmares. Founded in 1631, it was, in every sense of the word, an independent country, with a standing army, a constitution and an elected council. Palmares exchanged ambassadors with foreign powers and made treaties. The Yoruban religion was practised with all the solemnity and purity it had known in the land of its origin. During the seventy-five years of its existence – during which period it had been attacked many times by the whites – Palmares inspired every black in the land with the hope of freedom. During the following two hundred years in which blacks were enslaved, they would always remember that their people had founded and defended a country of their own in the very heart of the land in which they were held in bondage. And even today, this republic of free black people, hewn from the midst of a wilderness once believed to be untamable, still stirs in the black Brazilian's memory nostalgic images of glory. 'We had Palmares!' they say with undisguised pride.

Candomblé

Those Africans who remained in bondage on the whites' plantations had no choice but to pretend to accept Catholicism as their faith, thereby providing themselves with a way of worshipping the *orishas*. Then, gradually, the saints of Rome became integrated into the black credenda.

The Black Religion of Brazil is known as Candomblé, or *macumba*, and is basically the same as Santeria. It is a mixture of Yoruban, Catholic and Tupi Indian beliefs, the latter's contribution being particularly strong in the domain of magic. The ritual is, however, preponderantly African. The Catholic saints are interchangeable with the African divinities. Shangó is St Peter; Yemanja=Our Lady of Good Parturition; Shapana=St Sebastian; Ogun=St John; Osain=St Francis; Eowa=Our Lady of the Conception; Nana Buroko=St Rita; Lisa=St Paul. This fusion is still evolving: a number of Gege-Nego and Congo-Angola *orishas* have yet to find their definitive Catholic doubles, and some believers hold that Shangó is distinctly African and has no Christian equivalent. Less powerful than the saints are the *encantados*, angels created by Jesus. They have the power to succour the needy, to bring about good luck, to aid in love affairs – in short, all the talismanic powers of the Haitian *wanga* or New Orleans *mojo*. Indeed, they are sometimes referred to as *budu* – an obvious variation of 'voodoo', the Dahomean word for god. The chief *encantado* is Kakamado. Legba, known as Legua Bogi, is also considered as one of these angels. But he is no longer keeper of the gate, that function being given to St Barbara.

> He goes when he wishes
> with *vunso* in his feet.
> He is John-Barbara,
> Titinikati,
> Keeper of the keys-to-heaven,
> Budu

The State of Bahia is the centre of the Candomblé, the rites of which are divided into three types: the Gege-Nego (Yoruban-Ewe), the Congo-Angola, and the Caboclo* in which Indian spirits are worshipped. Whereas the latter ritual is transacted in Portuguese and a smattering of African words, the others are carried out in their respective original tongues. Their *seitas* (cult temples) are located exclusively in the black sections of the communities. The services of the worship are performed with an air of sanctity and seriousness, and strictly along prescribed lines. The males sit to the left, and the females to the right, of the drums. The ceremony — composed of sacred dances and invocations — is carried out to the playing of drums, handclapping, and singing.

> Powerful One, I know thee as the first man.
> Even in the dark I can see thou art powerful.
> In the whole world, nothing is hidden from thee.

When the *orisha* deigns to descend, it takes possession of one of the worshippers by 'entering his head'. This person then dances the dance sacred to the deity, after which, more than likely aided, he withdraws, respectfully facing the drums. Then, having been dressed in the ceremonial costume of the *orisha*, he returns again to perform its dance.

Even after slavery was abolished (1889) and blacks were supposedly free, they still had difficulty worshipping as they saw fit. Whereas slavery could be declared null by a stroke of the pen, racism could not be so easily eradicated. To many, African religion smacked of blasphemy against the Catholic Church and of savage barbarity. In 1935 a pernicious campaign was launched in the press. Under the headline THE CITY THAT GOD FORGOT, the newspaper *A Tarde*, on 9 December, had the following report:

Your reporter . . . has set down in his notebook curious scenes which reflect discredit upon our civilization; things which . . . continue on for the eyes not only of those who live here but also of those who visit us from foreign places.

Bahia already has the reputation of being the city of *candomblés*, the paradise of the *macumbas*. However, these used to be localized in fixed zones where the devotees of Oxalá and Yemanjá beat their drums and 'fell into the *santo*'. Now they begin to encroach upon the most frequented streets, and the African cult is to be seen even in the best residential areas.

Your reporter verified this fact last Sunday night in the *bairro* of Barra,

* Caboclo: The mixture of Tupi Indian and African rites

an elegant and aristocratic suburb. Here is to be found Grenfeld Street, very close to the Avenida Oceanica. And on this very street is a *candomblé*.

Happily there is no noise of drums. But palms are used instead, which beat without ceasing until day dawns. And whenever anyone makes an inquiry, the *pae de santo* insists that he has a licence, and continues . . .

One morning not long ago, your reporter was passing in front of the State Treasury building, a spot very much frequented. A *bozó* had been left there and still remained exposed to the curiosity of all who passed.

A black hen, three copper coins, yellow *farofia*, a cloth doll stuck full of pins, a piece of a man's shirt, and other *bugigangas* [trinkets].

The thing was there until midday. This is no uncommon occurrence, but one which is frankly deplorable. That in the heart of our city, so close to the Rua Chile, *despachos* are made to Exú is, to say the least, disgusting.

Eighteen months later, the same newspaper reported:

A short time ago the *macumbeiro* known as Manoelzinho took up his residence in a *roça* at No.256 Cruz do Cosme, and since that time his *bozós* have led to continuous complaints from dwellers along that road and from those who chance to pass that way.

At the side of the road just below the *roça* is a *loco* tree, that species so much preferred for fetishistic practices. Here *bozós* accumulate from day to day until they constitute a veritable mountain of refuse in which may be found an increasing number of dead fowls.

We are informed that this Manoelzinho, who is a *pae de santo* with considerable prestige, is a specialist in sport *bozós*. For it is said that among those who consult him are certain members of the different soccer clubs. Recently a policeman, on the eve of a great game at Graça, noted in one of these *bozós* the initials 'T.V.' which are the same as those of a well-known athlete.

Since the street cleaners never pass along Cruz do Cosme, the *bozós* keep polluting the atmosphere and obliging those who pass by to cover their noses with handkerchiefs.

To whom shall we appeal? Who will do something about this?

To combat this racist threat an Afro-Brazilian Congress was convened in Bahia in 1937, the outcome of which was a demand for official recognition of Candomblé as a religion with rights equal to those of the other 'recognized' religions, all of which were Christian. Of course, it was not granted: that would have been giving the blacks too much equality. In his book, *Negroes in Brazil*, Donald Pierson reports an argument between a Catholic priest and a Candomblé *mae de santo* (priestess).

> Intelligent, quick-witted, agile in debate, she is one of the most widely respected and revered leaders of the Afro-Brazilian world. When a priest argued with her that, since she had not been ordained by the Pope, she had no 'spiritual authority' to carry on religious rites, she quickly inquired if Moses, 'that great prophet and leader of his people was ordained by the Pope'? The first man, she maintains, must not have been a white man but instead a coloured man: 'if not black, at least red. For do the scholars not say that man originated in Asia, and do white men ever come out of that continent?' Jesus also must have been an African, or at least a person quite dark. 'For did not his parents once hide him in Egypt? And is not Egypt in Africa? If Jesus was not dark, how could they have hidden him among the people of Africa?'

Her explanation of her religion is worth repeating:

> The *Africano* doesn't worship things made with human hands. He worships nature. What is the *pedra* [fetish stone]? Is is not a mineral? No human hands have made it.
>
> We are just as Christian as the Catholics. Only we follow the law of Moses. He commanded that sacrifices be made of sheep, goats, oxen, chickens, pigeons, and so forth. Is it not so? We merely obey his commandments.
>
> There are two parts to the Bible, are there not? The Old Testament and the New. We follow the Old as well as the New. In the days before Christ, the people worshipped God with singing and dancing. Is it not so? David played his harp and sang psalms and danced before the Lord. We have our songs, too, and each has a special meaning. Just as the Catholics have something to remind them of their saints, so we have something to remind us of our *orixás*. But we do not worship images made with human hands like they do. We worship nature.[1]

The Drum

Drums . . . epitomize the real definition of African music — a music that speaks in rhythms that dance.

Francis Bebey

Drums are held to be the African instruments *par excellence* – and they are – but not because of the generally held notion that they are the only type of instrument Africans have produced. On the contrary, every type of instrument known to man – strings, woodwinds, brass – exists in an African version. Likewise drums exist everywhere in the world. However, the special role they play in African music and life place them in a privileged category. Each drum has a specific function, and in the case of the 'sacred' drum, is the dwelling-place of a deity. All 'speak' the language of the community to which they belong; secular drums are treated with respect, and sacred ones with reverence. As such, the drum is an integral member of the community. It is housed and cared for like the person it is. The African drum can weep, laugh, rejoice, mourn and die. It is inseparable from its community and shares its fate.

Sacred drums are kept in special huts located in sacred groves known as *senufos*. These places have an aura of mystique about them, the like of which leaves no African indifferent. Francis Bebey, the Camerounais guitarist-poet, describes them in terms worthy of their importance:

> There is an atmosphere of magic in these places and the drums are revered as supernatural creatures. Some instruments are only removed from their hiding-places very briefly on rare occasions.
>
> Most *senufo* villages are built near a 'sacred wood' where the *poro*, a male secret society, carries out its initiation rites. Masks and certain musical instruments are also kept in the sacred wood and are only brought out when they are needed for a particular rite.[1]

The drum plays a role in every facet of Africans' lives: in birth, initiation, puberty, marriage, hunting, pregnancy, war, death and in the religious life of the community. Some countries possess 'royal' drums, instruments used

only for the recounting of the history of the monarchs. As played by the court
musicians, they relate the genealogy and auspicious events of the royal
family's past. Bebey speaks of a song of the Mossi people of Upper Volta
entitled 'A Drum Reciting the Genealogy of the Nana (King)', and says of a
recording by the *griot* Tala Kere, 'This is an amazing document which has
been faithfully transmitted from generation to generation without the aid of
writing!'

Sacred drums are made from special 'blessed' woods. The god, in whose
honour it has been made, is then invoked to take up his abode in it. This
ceremony is conducted by the religious head of the community, and is
attended by all leading notables. Once the god has descended into it, the
drum is treated with all the reverence due to the deity.

These ideas concerning drums were kept alive by the black slaves in the
New World. The continuance of their worship demanded that they retain
the fundamental tenets of their religion. In Haiti, for example, the most
highly revered of the many sacred drums used in the worship of the *loas* was
the *assotor*:

> The *assotor* drum is the largest and most sacred of all Haitian drums.
> Around it is built an impressive and elaborate service known as the *mangé
> assotor*, which, according to local traditions and circumstances, may be
> held as often as every three years or as infrequently as every twenty-one
> years . . . This is what a man from Jeremie tells about it: 'The *assotor* is
> the greatest of all things in the *hounfor* (voodoo temple). The Rada drums
> are only for the Dahomey nation. The Congo drums are for the Congo
> nation. The *assotor* is a man of Dahomey, but he is for all nations. It is for
> all *loa* — Petro, Congo, Bumba, Dahomey. The *assotor* belongs to
> Dahomey, but when there is a great service the *assotor* is the host to the *loa*
> (gods) of every rite, the *loa* of Haiti and of Africa. Some ancient spirits
> from far away come only to the *assotor* service, and when it is over they
> aren't heard of again. The *assotor* drum is not for small things, it is for
> great occasions . . . all other drums are its servants. You can make an
> *assotor*, but it is not necessarily an *assotor*. It may look like an *assotor* and
> not be an *assotor*. To be an *assotor* it must not only have the shape of an
> *assotor* but it must be accepted by the *loa* . . . To make an *assotor*, there is
> first a service. The *houngan* (voodoo minister) goes into the woods to find a
> great tree that is suitable. The trunk must be big enough so that the drum
> is at least as tall as a man. Most *assotors* are six feet high or more. The
> *houngan* must buy the tree from Mait Grand Bois (the *loa* of the woods).

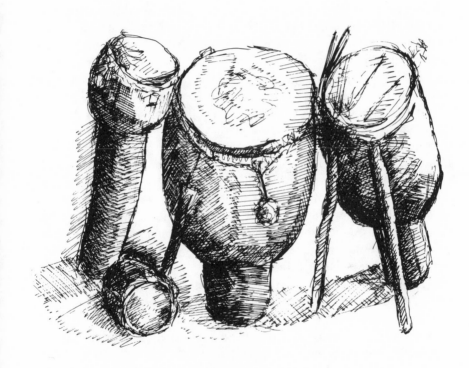

There is a service under the tree, a goat or a bull is killed, and the *houngan* places money on the ground for Mait Grand Bois. The *assotor* drum is not dedicated to Ogoun or Erzulie or any other single *loa*. If it is baptized, it is given its own name, *assotor*. During the ceremony, *mangé assotor* . . . the *assotor* drum is dressed in the finest of clothing and kerchiefs during the *mangé*. It is king of everything. When the *mangé assotor* is ended, when the drum has been fed, there is an immediate Mass held in church for the souls in purgatory. When there is no *mangé* going on, the *assotor* is kept in a special place in the *hounfor*. Every seven or nine months the *houngan* has a special *rappel* beaten for it on the Rada drums, and rum is spilled on the ground for it. It is a great responsibility to own an *assotor*. But it does great things for the *houngan* who owns it.'[2]

The above statements make clear the importance of the sacred drum in black religions, and though not all drums are held to be holy, all African drums 'talk' – that is, they speak: the rhythms played upon them have their source in the language and the sounds they make are reproductions of the human voice. 'It is scarcely an exaggeration,' says Bebey, 'to say that without African languages, African music would not exist. Authentic African music presupposes a practical knowledge of any one African language.' In Africa, the Man, the Drum and the Music are One: did the Man derive the intonations of his speech from the sounds around him or vice versa? Dennis Bovell, the Barbadian reggae artist, holds that, 'In the beginning there was the Sound,' a concept which breaks with the whole tradition of Western culture, which places its faith in the genesis of the world beginning with the Word, a factor which only Man possesses. Black music is based on premises closer to the nature of Bovell's idea: it is a compendium of everything which comprises life, it *is* sound. And the sound a musician makes on his or her instrument is the sound he or she lives.

In the more particular sense, there are drums which speak 'everyday' human languages. These 'talking drums' are the hour-glass drum and the slit drum. By holding the drums under the armpit and exerting pressure different tensions are obtained, and thus sounds imitative of the human voice. These drums literally 'speak' the language of the drummer, and can be as readily understood by members of the same language group as the drummer's own voice. Such is their precision that they are used on radio broadcasts.

In spite of the anti-drumming laws promulgated throughout the United States, black people managed to keep the institution of the drum alive, and when they found themselves deprived of those wondrous drums which sounded throughout the land of their origin they turned to adapting other instruments to serve as percussive substitutes. What, then, are we to make of this statement by Ortiz M. Walton?

> It is ironic that these laws against the use of drums during the slave era . . . account for the single most important development of Afro-American music . . . The enforcement of the anti-drum laws in the United States made it necessary to transfer the function of the drum to the hands, feet and body by way of spirituals during the slave era and by way of instrumental music after the Civil War in the new form of black music called Jazz.[3]

Sheer nonsense! Black people have always used their entire body as a rhythm instrument. Walton would have us believe that before they were deprived of their drums blacks made music and danced in the same way as Europeans. The truth is that blacks neglected no part of their persons in illustrating rhythm: 'This dance,' St Méry wrote in 1768, while in Haiti, 'in which the play of the eyes is nothing short of extraordinary, is lively and gay and the precision with which the step is kept gives it true charm.'[4] And as for the balderdash about purely instrumental music giving rise to Jazz, black peoples have been playing it since the dawn of creation. No matter what the instrument with which blacks make music – be it the piano, saxophone, guitar, harmonica, violin or the voice – to them it is always a matter of playing on a drum. No matter what the style – blues, holler, field songs, honky-tonk, ragtime, bebop, cool, modern or free – the basis is always the drum: 'Is not Rhythm my mother . . .? Furious music of the little drum whose body was still in Africa, but whose soul sang around a fire in Alabama . . . Congo gods talking in Alabama.'[5]

The tonic in the blues is but the stress of the tap on the drumhead. In singing, the stomach and chest, the lungs and larynx, are employed as a calabash or, if you will, in the same way as the talking drum: by the regulation of pressure and the rhythmic flow of the inflected tones. Black music is but a drumbeat.

The Dance

The African dance . . . has the nature of a visual prayer.

A.G. Keller

Perhaps black culture attains its most complete expression in dance. Within its limitless manifestations are embodied black music, poetry, body language and modes of worship. It is at once the internalization of everyday events and the externalization of the drama which takes place within. For black people, dance is a music performed upon the instrument of the human body. It expresses their ethos, their concept of theatre, and defines their place in the world. Always functional, it is used in the same way as speech: to convey emotions, to tell a story, to extol the wonders of Nature and the spirits which control it. In Africa and those parts of the New World where blacks managed to practise their own religions, dance was used to express the community's relations with the gods: to pay homage, to plead for rain or a good harvest, to offer thanks, etc. It was a religious act performed to sacred music played on sanctified instruments. The purpose of the dance was to invoke the gods to bless the offering by manifesting their presence, to 'enter into the heads' of the supplicants and to make use of their bodies. If the gods deigned to 'possess' them, then the invocation was deemed successful.

Black dancing is a pantomime and reflection of the events of human life: birth, death, eros, ambition, spiritual awareness and physical and mental prowess are only a few of the incidents with which its infinite catalogue deals. As such, it is liberated from all social inhibitions – and yet it is always moral. Its one goal is to be true to its subject; otherwise it would belie its purpose, which is to present a true-to-life picture of the event it has undertaken to pronounce upon. It has no other aim than this, and does not concern itself with Western ideas of morality. Its 'morality' is inextricably bound up with its purpose. Its ends are achieved if the spirit it invokes descends upon performers and spectators.

The whites' notion of the art was diametrically opposed to this. Raised on an unhealthy diet of religious bigotry – the main course of which was Original Sin – whites fell victim to the malady of moral hypochondria. In their infected eyes African dancing was sinful and debauched, its every gesture an offence to God. Such erotic displays were best left in the privacy of the bedroom – a scheme which, had it been adopted, would have robbed black dance of its meaning.

The whites were as little ready to countenance the Africans' style of dancing as the terrible noise of their drums and the infernal drone of their singing, all of which were proofs of innate savagery:

> The Negroes of the Gold Coast, warlike, bloody, accustomed to human sacrifice, know only dances as ferocious as themselves, while those of the Congo, Senegalese and other African shepherds or agricultural tribes, love dancing as a relaxation, as a source of sensual pleasure. Brought from all parts of Africa to our Colonies . . . the Negroes brought here preserved their taste for the dance, a taste so strong that, however tired out from work the Negro may be, he always finds strength to dance and even to travel a long distance to satisfy this desire.[1]

It would be an injustice not to draw attention to the fact that this author attributes to the African those qualities possessed in abundance by the whites of his day. 'Warlike' is a perfect description of the endless struggles which characterize the history of Europe; 'bloody' – take as an example the genocide of the American Indians who once populated two whole continents; 'accustomed to human sacrifice' – for this we have the edifying story of slavery, wherein whole peoples were sacrificed for whites' love of lucre.

Father Labat, a missionary who came to Haiti to do the Lord's work, described – with Christian goodwill – the dancing of the *calenda*, which he witnessed in 1698.

> Since the postures and movements of this dance are highly obscene, decent masters forbid their slaves to practise it and watch out to see that they give it up. Yet the slaves love it so that even children who can hardly toddle try to imitate their parents when they see them dancing and spend whole days practising . . . Some especially talented person among them sings a song he composes on the spur of the moment on some theme that he considers appropriate, and the refrain, sung by all the spectators, is accompanied by handclapping. [After describing the dance, which he calls 'lascivious', he goes on to add]: It is easy to see from this brief description how extremely this dance offends against the proprieties.[2]

Ortiz, the Cuban folklorist, called the *calenda* 'that dance which the moralists of the colonies so abominated'.[3]

Another dance which originated in Africa and was extremely popular among the slaves was the *chica*, which derived its name from the swaying of the female participant's hips. Her partner, while never actually coming into contact with her, comes tantalizingly close to doing so, but each time draws back, the object being to kindle desire and to seduce her into following him. As the rhythm quickens, the dance builds into a powerful caricature of love. Even such a staunch foe of black dance as St Méry could not conceal his admiration for the way it lived up to its intention: 'It would be impossible to describe the *chica* in its true character, and I shall confine myself to saying that the impression evoked by it is so powerful that an African or Creole of any colour who comes and dances it without excitement is looked on as a man who has lost the last spark of vitality.'[4]

The *chica* paved the way for black dancing to sweep the world. From it sprang the *fandango*, which became the national dance of Spain, no easy feat when moralists were up in arms against anything of African provenance, and especially 'lewd' dances. The Spaniards got around the problem by adding a good deal of 'national modesty' — otherwise, 'the symbolism of the dance would far exceed all the limits of moral censure'.[5] Spaniards think that they are performing a mild version of the *chica* when dancing the *fandango*; in fact, they are performing one of the oldest Voodoo dances of Haiti, the *loaloachi*, of which the *chica* is the secular version. Nearly all of the national dances of Spain have their origins in black dance: the *randena*, the *madaquena*, the *grenadina*, the *muriciana*, the *bolero* and the *sequidilla*. Another Europeanized dance with Voodoo origins is the *sarabanda* (the French *sarabande*). Its antecedents go back to 1500, when it was first danced in Cuba. When it reached Spain in 1660 it was declared obscene and proscribed by law. By the time it reached Versailles, it had been completely 'frenchified'.

The roots of all these popular dances were in the sacred ones, the themes of which the world knows little or nothing about. Many a boogie aficionado would be surprised to know that letting it all hang out is but an imitation of the ritual dancing which has been going on for centuries. Contemporary popular dance has its origin in the holy dance of the Afro-Cuban goddess Oshún, the 'compassionate virgin' of Santeria religion. This dance is divided into three parts. First, Oshún lies alone on the bank of the river; then she performs her ablutions, during which she becomes aware of her divine beauty; finally, having dressed herself, she raises her arms to heaven, invoking the love of her consort, Shangó.

Sometimes, Oshún meets the sensual Shangó, they recognize one another, and surrender themselves to a fervent dance of love in an unconcealed and incomparable imitation of carnal lust. Oshún used to dance naked, her body shining with honey . . . Today the dance is no longer performed in the orthodox fashion, but perhaps we shall soon see it again, not in temples, but in the cabarets and theatres as a great success of 'white' civilization . . . These pantomimic dances, their gestures, steps, costumes and symbols are as carefully planned as ballets. They were created by the Yoruba, an artistic people, said to be the best choreographers in Africa and possessing a highly dramatic mythology, as rich in narrative and as developed as the Graeco-Roman. Their allegorical movements are so highly stylized that the uninitiated are unable to understand them without interpretation.[6]

Out of this dance came the secular *yuka* (though the drum it is played on is not sacred, the drummer wears a set of maracas on his wrists to protect the instrument from evil powers). Its rhythm is fast, and the action consists of the female resisting her partner's advances. In this is the seed of modern dance as we know it. In making her *botao* (resistance) she opened the gateway for dancing based upon the 'couple'. This *botao* is the core of the frenzied gestures we see on today's dance floors, in which it appears that the partners are fighting one another.

The secular dances of the blacks were the only ones the whites could adopt. And, of course, their content had to be strictly controlled. For the whites dancing suggesting flirtation and sex was anathema – hence the innumerable complaints about obscene postures and gestures. The authors of these complaints were expressing their own cravings and frustrations. In castigating the blacks they were demonstrating their own pent-up erotic desires; the lewd tales they spread were but the mirrors of their own minds, reflecting a pathological condition which manifested itself in the wholesale rape of black women and the fable of the superior sexual endowment of the black man. It is not a coincidence that Europe produced Freud.

From the *yuka* came the *rumba*, which went from being the *rumba bara* to the *rumba picaresca* and finally to the empty and degenerate *salon-rumba*. Each of these developments took it further away from its original meaning. 'The *salon-rumba*,' says Ortiz, 'can be danced in society.' It is 'altogether modest yet it still retains a minimum of its inexhaustible grace and therefore also something of its original character'.[7] Now, as everyone knows, it has degenerated into a ballroom hop. The season for this 'success' is that of all

Afro-Cuban dances it is the one which has lost the most of its ritual character, and is thus easily assimilated by whites.

Black dancing in the United States has had a fate different from that of the Caribbean. As long as the blacks north of Mexico kept their religion alive, the African roots of their dancing thrived, being, as it were, an integral part of their worship. It was when they tried to become Americans that their art of dancing underwent an unseemly bastardization. During the antebellum period African dances such as the *juba*, the *congo*, the *babouille*, the *chacta*, the *counjaille*, the *calenda* and the *voodoo* flourished. In his book *The French Quarter*, Herbert Ashbury tells how the blacks used to gather in Congo Square, New Orleans, to dance:

> Before the Civil War the Congo Dances were one of the unusual sights of New Orleans to which tourists were always taken. At times almost as many white spectators as dancers gathered for the festive occasions. That the Negroes had not forgotten their dances, even after years of repression and exile from their native Africa, is attested by descriptive accounts of the times . . . Though discontinued during the war, the Congo Dances were again performed after the emancipation and were not entirely abandoned even two decades later, when a correspondent of the *New York World* reported: 'A dry-goods box and an old pork barrel formed the orchestra. These were beaten with sticks or bones, used like drumsticks so as to keep up a continuous rattle, while some old men and women chanted a song that appeared to me to be purely African in its many-vowelled syllabification . . . In the dance the women did not move their feet from the ground. They only writhed their bodies and swayed in undulatory motions from ankles to waist . . . The men leaped and performed feats of gymnastic dancing . . . Small bells were attached to their ankles . . . I asked several old women to recite them (the words of the song) to me, but they only laughed and shook their heads. In their patois they told me – "No use, you would never understand it. *C'est le Congo!*" '8

Cable, who witnessed these sessions, left this predictable account:

> The ecstasy rises to madness; one-two-three of the dancers fall – balloucoutoum! boum! – with the foam on their lips and are dragged out by the arms and legs from under the tumultuous feet of crowding newcomers. The musicians know no fatigue; still the dance rages on . . .

It was a frightful triumph of body over mind, even in those early days when the slave was still a genuine pagan; but as his moral education gave him some hint of its enormity, and it became forbidden fruit monopolized by those of reprobate will, it grew everywhere more and more gross . . .[9]

Not long after they were proclaimed emancipated, blacks began shying away from their traditional dances, distancing themselves from the Black Annie, the Pas Mala, the Strut, the Walkin' the Dog, the Ballin' the Jack. In their place they opted for the dances of the whites. The Black Christian Church, ever ashamed of black culture, laid down strictures about dancing, and the 'faithful' followed them — waltzin', polkain', and mazurkain' with a panache which did full credit to the spiritual advisers. 'As one approaches the US through the West Indies,' Herskovits wrote, 'the introduction of European dance patterns becomes more and more evident, until in the US, as well as among the more acculturated upper socio-economic groups in the islands generally, pure African dancing is almost entirely lacking, except in certain subtleties of motor behaviour.'[10]

Not only that, but the blacks actually named a dance in honour of a white American, who, it is safe to assume, could have never looked upon a member of their race as anything but a servant.

It just so happened that, at the very time that the Lindy Hop was first becoming popular in New York, I myself was in Jamaica, studying the dances there. When I returned to New York and saw the Lindy Hop for the first time, it was apparent to me that almost the entire pattern and certainly many of the specific movements were very similar to those urban Jamaican dances known as the *sha-sha*, or *mento*, which I had just been recording. This similarity was due, in part, no doubt, to the influence of the Jamaicans who had emigrated to America in increasing numbers. But it was due, also, I feel, to the fact that the patterns and the movements were fundamentally familiar, as part of a deep tradition of folk dancing, to American Negroes.[11]

The black people of the United States have come a long way since they glorified a white person by calling one of their dances after him — a long way in reclaiming their identity. Today, when they 'kill that roach', they know exactly whom they're stompin'; and when they do the Watusi, they are aware of whom they are praising. Moreover, today black people know that their dances constitute an art form, and that it is the most potent dancing in the world.

Hoodoo on the Bayous

Now, Chile, if you go wanderin' in the blue bayous
You'd better take a mojo-offering with you . . .

Hoodoo Slim

The Man without a Name

Hoodoo is the secret religion of the Afro-American. It is the result of a fusion of black and white, of the shotgun wedding of African and Christian religious beliefs. Under slavery the black psyche took refuge in its spiritual past. The gods of Africa were forced to go underground, where they are perhaps the most important for having done so. 'Undergrounding' was the religion's only chance for survival – indeed, the slave masters were loath for the Africans even to adopt Christianity, let alone keep up the religion of their homelands. But survive and thrive it did and anyone who believes that African religion has died in blacks in America simply does not know the black mind. 'It burns with all the intensity of a suppressed religion.'[1] In the face of repression blacks gave ample proof that Hoodoo 'works': they built and worshipped in an 'invisible' church.

And this was the case wherever they were enslaved: as we have seen, they wed their religion with Christianity and so escaped the scrutiny of their masters.

In 1526 a ship arrived off the coast of what has come to be known as South Carolina. In control of it were some five hundred Frenchmen and -women, come to try their hand at founding a new colony. Also on board were one hundred beings, black in colour, and so much resembling other members of the species *homo sapiens* that had it not been for the hue of their skin they would have passed for men. But the pink-skinned members of the vessel had declared these beings' humanity null and void, seeing as how they were lacking in those qualities which separate Man from beast. The so-called language of these creatures was a cacophony of growls and grunts; their religion was a mass of bewildering superstitions; culture? They had none. Running about the jungle all day hardly amounted to civilization. As an unmistakable sign that they were different, God had branded them with a hideous birthmark: they were *black*! Call them anything you like but, by God, don't call them men! Call them . . .

They were called everything except what they were. Never were they referred to or thought of as human beings. Never were they called, as a people or individually, by their true names. One summer's day, over 450 years ago, one hundred of these Men without Names were brought ashore in the United States. Their story is the story of the blues. The situation which gave rise to it is a unique one. While the whole of the New World was given over to slavery (including Mexico, a fact which historians have tried to deny, although the truth is that at one time there were as many as a quarter of a million black slaves there), the black slaves in the United States were dealt a particularly fiendish deal. Whereas they shared with other blacks the loss of freedom, they alone were deprived of their religion, that crucible in which blacks were able to keep African customs alive in Haiti, Cuba, Puerto Rica, Jamaica, Brazil, Guiana, Barbados and Trinidad.

> Probably never before in history has a people been so nearly completely stripped of its social heritage as the Negroes who were brought to America. Other conquered races have continued to worship their household gods within the intimate circle of their kinsmen. But American slavery destroyed household gods and dissolved the bonds of sympathy between men of the same blood and household. Old men and women might have brooded over memories of their African homeland, but they could not change the world about them. Through force of circumstances, they had to acquire a new language, adopt new habits of labour, and take over, however imperfectly, the folkways of the American environment. Their children, who knew only the American environment, soon forgot the few memories that had been passed on to them and developed motivations and modes of behaviour in harmony with the New World.[2]

Another commentator, Krapp, believes that the cultural disenfranchisement of black people was inevitable:

> The native African dialects have been completely lost. That this should have happened is not surprising, for it is a linguistic axiom that when two groups of people of different languages come into contact, the one on a

relatively high, the other on a relatively low cultural level, the latter adapts itself freely to the speech of the former, whereas the group on the higher cultural plane borrows little or nothing from that on the lower.[3]

What in the world is a 'linguistic axiom'? *Who* determines cultural 'levels'? And, above all, the blacks did not 'freely' adapt the English language which, even had it produced an infinite number of Shakespeares, they would have never heard about had they not been taken into captivity. Black people were plundered of their heritage and held down by main force, and had no recourse but to submit to a foreign culture. Thus arose the lie, still current, that the black man had no culture – a myth admirably suited to that cherished belief of whites that they were doing black people a favour by enslaving them: by a process of cultural osmosis blacks would become civilized. Today, this sham is at the root of white America's guilt. By advancing the phony theory of the biological inferiority of the black the whites seek to justify their crime.

> The South's dependence on the Negro is further obscured by the belief in the complete dependence of the black race upon the white race for moral as well as for economic support. The Negro is thought of as a child race, the ward of the civilized white man. We are told: 'The savage and uncivilized black man lacks the ability to organize his social life on the level of the white community. He is unrestrained and requires the constant control of white people to keep him in check. Without the presence of the white police force Negroes would turn upon themselves and destroy each other. The white man is the only authority he knows.'[4]

For 500 years white historians have been writing mythological histories about black people for white people, who have been content to accept them as fact – for to question them might lead to the revelation of some very painful home truths.

However, if black people did succumb to the yoke, they did so with very bad grace. If they did not succeed in regaining their freedom it was not for want of trying. In the very first colony in the United States to which Africans were brought, they revolted and gained their liberty. Much to their chagrin, whites discovered that if the people they had enslaved were without a culture, they were not without courage. Aptheker records that:

> the first settlement within the present borders of the United States to

contain Negro slaves was the victim of a slave revolt. A Spanish colonizer, Lucas Vasquez de Ayllon, in the summer of 1526, founded a town near the mouth of the Pedee river (South Carolina). Trouble soon beset the colony. Illness caused numerous deaths, carrying off Ayllon himself. The Indians grew more hostile and dangerous. Finally, in November, the slaves rebelled, killed several of their masters, and escaped to the Indians. This was a fatal blow and the remaining colonists – but one hundred and fifty souls – returned to Haiti in December, 1526.[5]

Far from seeing the whites as a 'civilizing' force, these Africans and Indians chased them back into the sea; after all, these were people who would scuttle their slave-bearing ships rather than let them fall into enemy hands (see p. 105). Aptheker catalogues six more rebellions which occurred between 1663 and 1700, at which time 'The constant fear of slave rebellion made life in the South a nightmare.'[6]

Like their brothers in the Caribbean the blacks in the United States frequently rebelled: the eighteenth century was riddled with revolts, with major outbreaks occurring in New York in 1712, and in South Carolina in 1720 and 1739. The successful overthrow of the French in Haiti filled the American slavers with dread.

Fresh in their memory were the horrors of the Negro revolution in Haiti. Toussaint L'Ouverture, who to Wendell Phillips was an apostle of liberty, was to them a demon of cruelty. How far the Negroes who surrounded them, who cooked their food and nursed their children, had been affected by civilization, and how far they retained their primitive savagery they were presumed to have brought from Africa, they did not learn until the Civil War.[7]

The truth is that black people never stopped rebelling, never ceased trying to gain control over their destiny. Apart from the better-known rebellions led by Gabriel (1800), Denmark Vesey (1822) and Nat Turner (1831), between 1700 and 1864 there were more than 150 insurrections by slaves. And, if that failed, they were not hesitant about taking the other way out: suicide. 'These savages, packed into the holds of vessels, were brought to the coasts of the United States. Many of them died on the way; many committed suicide – and that is a strange thing, as one finds the suicide rate among Negroes very low.'[8]

Black people undertook these revolts against overwhelming odds. They were vastly outnumbered by the whites, rarely numbering more than ten to a farm. Even as late as 1860 a quarter of all slaves were owned in groups of ten or less, and another quarter were held in groups of less than twenty. (Compare this with Haiti where it was usual for several hundred blacks to live on a plantation.)

Let no one attempt to belittle black people's courage in the struggle for freedom in the land of the free. Whenever they saw the opportunity to regain their liberty, they attempted it: by rebellion, or escaping to Canada, or – to use the words of that humane historian – 'strangely', by suicide.

The Man without a Name, that Man of Many Names – Nigger, Blackamoor, Coon, Tar Baby – the Man Declared to be without a Culture, the Man Said to be Biologically Inferior, the Erased Man, the Man Written Out of History, the Man Whose Colour was Declared to be a Curse: this *Man* (who was never allowed that august title) became, not in spite of, but *because of* the barbaric history of the country in which he was forced to live – the Unique Man, the Only Potential Man Realized, the Only New Man in the Whole of the New World.

What the Man without a Name Brought with Him

Having deprived blacks of all direct contact with Africa, whites sought to deprive them of every tangible connection with their roots, and to instil in their place the idea that Africa was a quagmire of barbarism – hence, blacks were better off where they were. Moreover, God had ordained it so, an irrefutable fact driven home by the Christian ministers who watched over their souls. Blacks ought to be thankful that the white man had come along and plucked them out of heathenism! What a blessing that the Christian Church had put them on the road to salvation! Though they were not 'men', they had the joy of saying 'Amen!' to the God of those who *were* 'men'. Wonderful as that was, it wasn't the only blessing America showered upon them: they also had the right (and duty) to serve those 'men', to slave for those 'men', to procreate for those 'men', to have their offspring sold up and down 'de ree-va' by those 'men' – hallelujah! Cee-vee-lie-say-shun at last!

Yet another gift bestowed upon blacks was the breaking-in or 'seasoning'[9] of their newly arrived colleagues from Africa. This important task was given to those who had proven themselves most competent in obeying their master. These 'drivers' were not only responsible for teaching the new arrivals their job but also English, perhaps the most important task in the whole of the seasoning process. That this system of setting slave to initiate slave proved successful is beyond dispute. But, alas, no system is perfect. What the whites didn't realize was that every new African brought to America was living proof to the slaves that Africa wasn't the woe-begone place they had been told it was. Here, before their very eyes, were blacks who spoke its languages and lived its customs. Africa's culture could not be gainsaid, for these people were living proof of its existence. And they, in their turn, seasoned the blacks in America, keeping alive the soul in man with their stories, religious instruction, music and dance.

> What magic formulae might not have been transmitted by these newly arrived Africans to a receptive ear? What discussions of world-view might not have taken place in the long hours when teacher and pupil were together, reversing their roles when matters only dimly sensed by the American-born slave were explained in terms of African conventions he had never analysed? Certainly during much of the slave period the masters did little to care for whatever needs the slaves might have had for instruction as to the nature of the world and the forces that activate it; the numerous complaints which the lack of adequate religious teaching for the slaves inspired in the earlier period of slavery, and the lax manner in which religion was later taught them, give ample justification for asking whether African belief and African methods of coping with the supernatural forces might not have been taught and thus perpetuated on this more humble level.[10]

Another source of the reinforcement of Africanisms was found in the slaves brought from the Antilles, who had kept their religion and culture very much intact. Louisiana, then under French rule, was the major point for these contacts. No sooner was the colony founded in 1718 than blacks were brought from Haiti, Martinique and Guadeloupe. These Africans brought with them not only their beliefs but their languages as well. Forced by their masters to embrace Catholicism, they utilized it as a veneer under which they practised their own religion: Voodoo. In 1782 Galvez, the Governor of the colony, complained about the blacks who had been brought from Martinique: 'These Negroes are too much given to Voodooism and make the lives of the citizens unsafe.'[11] In accord with this is Courlander's statement:

If one goes back just beyond the turn of the century, he finds that Negroes in Louisiana were familiar with the names of a number of West African deities, such as Limba, Agoussou, Dani (Dan), Liba (Legba or Limba) and others, all of whom had become syncretized (as in Haiti, Jamaica and Trinidad) with Christian saints . . . It is quite accurate to say that at the beginning of the nineteenth century Louisiana was part of a Caribbean culture.[12]

Dr Lorenzo Dow Turner, the greatest African linguist the United States has produced, found over 4,000 words of West African origin in the Gullah dialect of the blacks of the South Carolina and Georgia coasts. In the latter state he recorded songs in which 'whole African phrases . . . without change either of meaning or pronunciation', were found.

Unwittingly, the slavers had grasped a double-edged blade: seasoning cut both ways. By constantly bringing in new slaves they provided those blacks already on American soil with the means of reinforcing their ties with Africa. And they were blind to the fact that dances, songs and passwords could be used as keys to the spiritual world or to keep alive hopes. Seeing in everything black people did further proof of their backwardness, slavers gorged themselves on the illusion of their superiority, and became the victims of their own myths.

New Orleans was destined to be the setting for the three great cultural achievements the black American has given to the world: Hoodoo, the Blues and Jazz. A leading trading centre of the Caribbean, it has always been a cosmopolitan counting-house, where an astonishing variety of cultures collided and blended. It was also a curious scene where two races lived among one another without mixing, like an odd kind of club where the members saw each other but never met — at any rate, not in the open. Blacks and whites lived separate lives; except for purposes of work, whites had nothing to do with their slaves. Left to themselves in the hours of leisure, the blacks got on with their proper affairs, the main one of which was Voodoo, which in time came to be pronounced 'Hoodoo'. Likewise, the Obeah man became known as the Root Doctor. Hoodoo thrived because blacks had no faith in the whites' God, who existed only to condone whites' inhumane actions. Just as important was the fact that this God was wholly indifferent to the everyday happenings which constituted life; he descended from on high for a couple of hours on Sunday and then crept back to his retreat in heaven. But the black demanded a full-time God, one who would be there, around the clock, every day of the year. Their gods conditioned every aspect of their existence; their lives were a ceaseless task of interpreting the mysteries of Nature. Their metaphysics precluded all chance; everything is the result of the interplay between the human and the divine, and it is man's duty to seek the cause thereof. Herskovits has pointed this out.

In the region of Africa from which the slaves were principally drawn, the outstanding aspect of religion, noted by every writer who has dealt with these peoples, is its intimate relation to the daily round. The forces of the universe, whether they work good or evil, are ever at hand to be consulted in time of doubt, to be informed when crucial steps are to be taken, and to be asked for help when protection or aid is needed. Thus, while it is quite incorrect to describe the religion of the African as essentially based on fear, as has often been done, the very nearness of the spirits means that their requirements must be cared for as continuously and as conscientiously as the other practical needs of life.[13]

During the earlier period of American colonization the blacks contrived to keep their religion alive, for it was the only one capable of fulfilling their spiritual needs. As for Catholicism, they had incorporated it into their worship while still in Haiti: Jesus got high on palm wine and Mary and the saints boogied to the beat of the tom-toms. The blacks invoked their gods in secret ceremonies, dancing and singing in praise of the divine spirits. In her account of life in Louisiana, Mrs Channel makes the observation that,

On this plantation there were about one hundred and fifty slaves. Of this number, only about ten were Christians. We can easily account for this, for religious services among the slaves were strictly forbidden. But the slaves would steal away into the woods at night and hold services. They would form a circle on their knees around the speaker who would also be on his knees. He would bend forward and speak into or over a vessel of water to drown the sound. If anyone became animated and cried out, the others would quickly stop the noise by placing their hands over the offender's mouth.[14]

The practice of Hoodoo was also an act of political defiance, serving as a weapon against the teachings of the slavers and providing the blacks with a base of solidarity. Its secrecy was a means of operating 'behind enemy lines'. The codes invented by the blacks to hoodwink the whites were as innumerable as they were successful. Language (both African and English), signs, gestures, passwords, a wink — everything was employed, and though Big Brother was sometimes aware that something was going on behind the scene, all the eyes in the world didn't help: anything might mean anything.

By the end of the eighteenth century, Voodooism was firmly entrenched. This secret society extended through the entire slave population and among the free Negroes as well. A message could be conveyed from one end of the city to another in a single day without one white person's being aware of it. It is said that a Negro cook in a kitchen would sing some Creole song while she rattled her pots and pans, a song which sounded innocuous enough to any white listener, but at the end of the verse she would sing a few words intended as a message. Another Negro working nearby would listen intently and at the end of the second verse would hear the message repeated. This second servant would then go outside to attend to her duties. She would sing the same song and her voice would be heard by servants in the house next door. In this way, by means of a song, news of a meeting of a Voodoo society would be carried from one end of the city to another and upon the appointed night Negro men and women would slip from their beds before midnight and would assemble for their ceremonies. [15]

Another important factor in the rise of Hoodoo in this area was the bayous, those great, forbidding swamps wrapped in mystery. Impenetrable, a veritable spissitude of vegetation, reverberating with haunting sounds, they were the perfect place for the Voodoo ceremonials. In this uncharted no man's land the blacks felt safe from the slavers' prying eyes.

> A feast of moon and men and barking hounds,
> An orgy for some genius of the South
> With blood-hot eyes and cane-lipped scented mouth,
> Surprised in making folk songs from soul sounds.
>
> Meanwhile, the men, with vestiges of pomp,
> Race memories of king and caravan,
> High priests, an ostrich, and a juju-man,
> Going singing through the footpaths of the swamp. [16]

Cable, in his *Creoles and Cajuns*, describes the locations chosen for the sacred rites. 'It [the Voodoo ceremony] took place at a wild and lonely spot where the dismal cypress swamp behind New Orleans meets the waters of Lake Pontchartrain in a wilderness of cypress stumps and rushes. It would be hard to find in nature a more painfully desolate region.'[17]

Because of the sanctuary it offered them to practise their religion, the bayou became a part of the black people's heritage, representing a type of oasis in the midst of a land of persecution and trouble. There, on the ground where their people had come together to be reunited with the gods of Africa, their spirits were able to free themselves from the slavers' bondage and soar, and out of these stolen flights would come the music and words which became the blues, jazz, creole and cajun music.

The Voodoo Queen of New Orleans

From 1775 onwards there was growing concern on the part of the white authorities over Voodoo. Deprecating it as a 'dangerous and immoral' institution of 'Negro superstition', they did everything within their power to try and get the blacks to give it up. Pious-faced Catholic missionaries went the rounds of the plantations, white ladies formed committees and trooped through the streets of New Orleans, the police set up special night watches — but it was much too late even to hope to stem the tide. Voodoo was the characteristic trait of black life, and the more the whites tried to abolish it the stronger the blacks clung to it. It was the symbol of the blacks' refusal to accept their plight, the black torch which kept their hopes alive. There wasn't one black in a hundred who wasn't a Vodun; children were taught it at home, fed at the breast, as it were, its precepts. The lullabies sung to them, the bedside stories told to coerce them into sleeping, were but the stuff of Voodoo ideology. Every child of them anxiously awaited the day when they would be initiated into the mysteries of the cult, for that day when they, along with their fellow *hunos* (initiates) would pledge: '*Aizan of Africa, Aizan e: I will go, I will go to Africa!*' All blacks wore around their necks or carried in their pockets a mojo-bag, consecrated with the presence of a god and blessed by the Root Doctor. Not a night passed without one or more ceremonies being held at some secret spot on the bayous. New Orleans was in a Hoodoo ferment, and it was this which gave the blacks the strength to bear the incalculable pressures heaped upon them by the whites. Speaking in all seriousness, had it not been for the asylum their religion afforded them, it is arguable that there would be few sane black people in the United States today. Just as you cannot do to a people what Hitler did to the Jews and expect them not to react hysterically, you cannot deny a people their humanity for four hundred years and expect them to have maintained their pyschic equilibrium. Without a doubt, religion saved black people in the USA from a collective breakdown.

Some time around 1820 the leaders of the cult came together to elect a *mamaloi* and a *popaloi*, a queen and king, whose functions were to act as supernumeraries of the Grand Zombie (Great Snake). The position of the queen was the more important of the two, and the choice fell naturally on a young woman of striking appearance and unrivalled power named Marie Laveau. Even today an aura of respect and veneration surrounds her name, and no one has ever contested her place as the greatest of the Hoodoos.

Marie Laveau was born in the city over which she reigned, of free mulatto parents, on 2 February 1794. As a child she was noted for her piercing intelligence, the serenity of her bearing and the majesty of her demeanour. Initiated into the religion by her mother, she early showed signs of extraordinary insight, often experiencing trances from which she would emerge to make some pertinent pronouncement. Legend has it that while still a child a huge snake appeared in her bedroom one night and 'called' her to membership in the cult. From then on she undertook to fulfil her mission, and in time became a comforter to the worried, a curer of the sick and a provider for the poor and hungry. Even while she was in her teens word had spread throughout the various communities and plantations that she was a 'chosen'. By the time she was elected as the Voodoo Queen of New Orleans she was already a legend.

The accounts of her life are many and varied: worshipped by the blacks, she was detested by the whites. Saxon says of her that, 'We know nothing of her childhood, but as a very young woman we find her known to the police as a worker of black magic.'[18] Castellanos, in his *New Orleans as It was*, describes her thus:

> In her youth she was a woman of fine physique. Introducing herself into families as a hairdresser, she would assist in the clandestine correspondence of sweethearts, and aid youthful lovers. She was an essentially bad woman. Though Queen of the 'voudous', she exercised the ritual of the original creed so as to make it conform to the worship of the Virgin and of other saints. To idolatry she added blasphemy. She was the first to

popularize 'voudouism' in New Orleans, inviting members of the press, of the sporting fraternity, and others to the yearly festivals on St John's eve (24 June) at some spot not far from the bayou which bears that name. She also dealt in charms against malefices, and pretended to cure ailments produced by 'gris-gris' (little red bags containing powdered brick, yellow ochre and cayenne pepper, which were supposed to cause untold injury to the recipient) and other criminal devices.[19]

Another informant, George W. Cable, gave this account of her:

She (the Hoodoo Queen) reigns as long as she continues to live. She comes to power not by inheritance, but by election or its barbarous equivalent. Chosen for such qualities as would give her a natural supremacy, personal attractions among the rest, and ruling over superstitious fears and desires of every fierce and ignoble sort, she wields no trivial influence. I once saw, in her extreme old age, the famed Marie Laveau. Her dwelling was in the old quadroon quarter of New Orleans, but a step or two from Congo Square, a small adobe cabin just off the sidewalk, scarcely higher than its board fence. In the centre of a small room whose ancient cypress floor was worn with scrubbing and sprinkled with crumbs of soft brick – a Creole affectation of superior cleanliness – sat, quaking with feebleness in an ill-looking old rocking-chair, her body bowed and her wild, grey witch's tresses hanging about her shrivelled, yellow neck, the queen of the Voodoos. Three generations of her children were within the faint beckon of her helpless, waggling wrist and fingers. They said she was over a hundred years old, and there was nothing to cast doubt upon the statement. She had shrunken away from her skin; it was like a turtle's. Yet withal one could hardly help but see that the face, now so withered, had once been handsome and commanding. There was still a faint shadow of departed beauty on the forehead, the spark of an old fire in the sunken, glistening eyes, and a vestige of imperiousness in the fine, slightly aquiline nose, and even about her silent, woebegone mouth . . . One had but to look on [her daughter] to impute her brilliances – too untamable and severe to be called charms or graces – to her mother, and remember what New Orleans was long years ago, to understand how the name of Marie Laveau should have driven itself inextricably into the traditions of the town and the times. Had this visit been postponed a few months it would have been too late. Marie Laveau is dead; Malvina Latour is queen. As she appeared presiding over a Voodoo ceremony on the night of 23

June 1884, she is described as a bright mulatress of about forty-eight, of 'extremely handsome figure', dignified bearing, and a face indicative of a comparatively high order of intelligence.[20]

The following appeared in the *New Orleans Times-Picayune*:

It will not be amiss to relate the story of an octogenarian mammy, who says that Marie Laveau was not a wicked woman, but much maligned by her enemies, and that the powers she had were used for the good of others, as the following tale will prove. A certain wealthy young man in New Orleans, many years ago, had been arrested in connection with a crime, and though his companions were in reality the guilty ones, the blame was laid upon his shoulders. The grief-stricken father immediately sought Marie Laveau, explained to her the circumstances of the case, and offered her a handsome reward if she would obtain his son's release. When the day set for the trial came round, the wily 'voodoo', after placing three Guinea peppers in her mouth, entered the St Louis Cathedral, knelt at the altar rail, and was seen to remain in this position for some time. Leaving the church, she gained admittance to the Cabildo, where the trial was to be held, and depositing three of the peppers under the judge's bench, lingered to await developments. After a lengthy deliberation, though the evidence seemed unfavourable to the prisoner, the jury finally made its report, and the judge was heard to pronounce the words, 'Not guilty'.

The stories of her courage, her power and of her faith were legion. Even those who were ill-disposed to her – as most whites were – had to own that she was an extraordinary personality. One of these, G. William Nott, wrote about her in one of the local newspapers.

Again a narrative of Marie Laveau's strange career. In 1884 a violent hurricane passed over the city. She was then living in a shanty on Lake Pontchartrain. The force of the wind was so great that her cabin was wrenched from its foundations and hurled into the angry waters. Obliged to seek shelter on the roof, there she remained for several hours, discouraging the attempts of her would-be rescuers and telling them, '*Mo oule morri dan lac la*' (I want to die in this lake). However, she was finally prevailed upon to accept the assistance offered, and none too soon, for the cabin she was so loath to leave was completely shattered by the waves a few moments later. To this day, the superstitious darkies will tell you that not until Marie was safe ashore did the fury of the storm abate.

An old gentleman who remembers Marie Laveau from his childhood days will tell how she was held in dread by many of the residents below Canal Street, white as well as coloured. He describes her as having a 'Voltairean look', penetrating and taking in everything at a glance; an attribute quite disconcerting to the children of the neighbourhood, who would listen with terror when their black nurses threatened to 'give them to Marie' if they failed to obey.

Whether or not the famous Marie Laveau possessed supernatural powers has long been a subject of discussion among the ignorant. More enlightened people have dismissed her as a crass impostor, though not denying for an instant the prestige she held among her own race. However, with her death, 'voudouism' all but disappeared from New Orleans. The little that is practised today assumes a harmless form: a few chicken bones placed on a doorstep, a black cross mark on a front board, a bright-red powder sprinkled on the *banquette*; these are the last vestiges of the once dreaded 'gris-gris'.

The reverence with which the blacks looked up to their queen makes clear the high degree of esteem in which Voodo was held by blacks. As its chief representative Marie Laveau was looked up to as being favoured by the gods, and as proof that they had not abandoned their captive children. She became a symbol of their pride, a living proof of the glory of their culture. Her wishes were obeyed unhesitatingly, her pronouncements were unquestioningly believed, and no one ever dared to pit his or her will against hers. Wielding such power, she might have used it for her personal ends, but in fact the record shows that her actions were full of unselfishness and altruism:

Marie Laveau was the last great American witch . . . Her craft was jungle-born, African in origin, for she was Queen of the Voodoos, and by far the most important *voodooienne* ever to reign on this continent.

As such she was accused, by town gossip, of almost every crime of which humans are capable. She was never convicted of any, but it was whispered, especially during her later years, that she consorted with Satan . . . in a few instances wild stories about her also appeared in the newspapers of the day. For while she was still alive she became a legend. Yet there was another kind of legend, too. To many people she was known as a kind, charitable, almost saintly woman. She lived a very long time, and it is known that she tended the wounded brought back from the Battle of New Orleans in 1815, that she nursed numerous victims of the terrifying yellow fever epidemics, that she was considered a 'saint' by prisoners in the parish jail, among whom she visited for decades, bringing them food and clothing, as well as Voodoo charms. It is said that in times of financial depression she gave away all her money to the poor in her neighbourhood.

Voodoo is still a living religion, and right here in the United States. It may easily be that this is due almost entirely to the influence of Marie Laveau. Traces of it can be found all over the country. In her later years Marie trained a few people in its practice, and many others stole her secrets and carried them to New York, to Charleston, to Chicago, to the West Coast. Everywhere Voodoo practitioners know her name, recite it with awe, and tell tales of her, true, false and foolish.

It was Marie Laveau who popularized Voodoo. The meetings held at Bayou St John, just outside the city, were regularly attended by hordes of people.[21]

A man called Turner, a New Orleans Hoodoo doctor who had known Marie, told the black founder of the black American school of folklore, how he had seen the Great Snake in the Hoodoo queen's bedroom: 'He came to her room and spoke to her. He [coiled up] upon his altar and took nothing from the food set before him. One night he sang and Marie Laveau called me from my sleep to look at him and see. "Look well, Turner," she told me. "No one shall hear and see such as this for centuries." '[22]

This amazing woman, so intelligent, so physically attractive, embodied the religion of the black people. So proud and sure was she of it that she invited everyone to come and see its august ceremonies, to see for themselves the sincerity and beauty of its pageant. No wonder the whites hated her and did everything in their power to besmirch her memory! Yet, for all their animosity, no one dared to arrest her or to bring her to trial. Marie Laveau, Queen of the Voodoos, had her mojo workin'!

Marie Laveau (drawing by Willa Woolston)

Modest, portable house of images — note the pictures of the ancestors on the right and left (photo by Chris Parker)

Foday Musa Suso, a griot who
has followed the blues path
from Africa to Chicago
(drawing by Willa Woolston)

Suso with the author (photo by Maurice McElroy)

James Cotton (right) at the
Checkerboard blues club, 43rd St,
Chicago (photo by Bob Crawford)

Dennis Bovell (drawing by Willa Woolston)

Black church, South Side, Chicago (photo by Bob Crawford)

Pointing to the Promised Land (photo by Bob Crawford)

Singer conjuring her congregation (photo by Bob Crawford)

Acoustic bluesmen (drawings
by Willa Woolston)

Walter 'Shakey' Horton (photo by Bob Crawford)

Johnny Shines, who, like
Walter Horton, travelled with
Robert Johnson (photo by Bob
Crawford)

The bluesman (drawing by Willa Woolston)

Gaile Peters (photo by Chris Parker)

The Blue Princess (drawing
by Willa Woolston)

The Voodoo Ceremony

The importance of the Voodoo ceremonies celebrated during the era when black Americans practised their own religion (1790–1880) has been totally ignored by historians. From out of this 'golden age' of Hoodoo came the style of worship of the black Baptist Church, the black preacher, the 'conjure' songs in the blues, the blues singer's performance technique and the call-and-response reaction between him or her and the audience. As for the Afro-American dance, its debt to the Voodoo 'gathers' is obvious to the point that it precludes comment. The reasons for the vast influence these rites were to have lies in the basis on which they functioned.

The aim of the Voodoo ceremonial was possession. To the Vodun, to be possessed by the gods was the surest sign of having gained their favour. It meant that they considered the Vodun worthy of serving them, chosen as a vessel in which to deposit the divine spark. Liberating themselves from the inhibitions of their egos, the devotees cast off the shackles of the rational and made room for the deity who, upon entering their souls, took over and possessed them. Those thus favoured took on the attributes of the god whose servant they now were; by their actions their fellow worshippers knew exactly by which divinity they were possessed. The common idea of possession is that a person under such influence is totally out of control and runs amok. As concerns possession under Voodoo, nothing could be more false. On the contrary, the Vodun's actions under the power of a god are disciplined and controlled. The *houngan*, with deep knowledge of these occurrences, guides adepts step by step through the experience, avoiding its pitfalls and directing them to the fruits of its ecstasy. The attainment of this skill is the reward of a long and demanding apprenticeship, and it is for this reason that rites entailing possession are dangerous if undertaken without the proper guidance. Ignorant of the complexities involved in these rituals, the European declared them the product of heathenism. Which point brings us to the major divergence between African and Christian worship. African worship is communal, Christianity is personal; Africans attain the mystic heights of possession with the aid of their group, Christians (as in the case of Christ) privately; African worship utilizes music and dance, Christianity silence and stillness; at the highest level the African becomes, the Christian communes with, God. The use of music as a integral part of black worship has led to its being looked upon by blacks in a wholly different manner than that common among whites. To black people there is no such thing as 'art for art's sake'. Every poem blacks write, every wood carving they make, every tap on their drums has its 'instrumentality', is a medium, a means to an end. In the Voodoo ritual the purpose of the music, the invocations, the costumes, everything was to serve the gods, to invoke them so that they would enter into the participants.

The aim of African religion was lost on the whites, hence those accounts which have come down to us which show a total misunderstanding about the events they sought to describe: fine examples of people trying to interpret a language without knowing its alphabet.

Here in a fisherman's cabin sat the Voodoo worshippers cross-legged on the floor about an Indian basket of herbs and some beans, some bits of bones, some oddly wrought bunches of feathers, and some saucers of small cakes. The queen presided, sitting on the only chair in the room. There was no king, no snake – at least none visible to the onlookers. Two drummers beat with their thumbs on gourds covered with sheepskin, and a white-wooled old man scraped that hideous combination of banjo and violin, whose head is covered with rattlesnake skin, and of which the Chinese are the makers and masters. There was singing – '*M'alle couri dans deser*' (I am going to the wilderness), a chant and refrain not worth the room they would take – and there was frenzy and a circling march, wild shouts, delirious gesticulations and posturings, drinking, and among other frightful nonsense the old trick of making fire blaze from the mouth by spraying alcohol from it upon the flame of a candle.[23]

At some remote spot, usually near the borders of a dismal swamp, the members of the sect were wont to assemble, always in the dead of night, and after divesting themselves of their raiment, would gird their loins with a number of red handkerchiefs and encase their feet in sandals. These conclaves were shrouded in deepest secrecy. The manner of dress, however, varied at different times and places, with frequent modifications of the above-mentioned costume. The King and Queen, distinguished from the others by a blue cord fastened around the waist, would take their position at one end of the room, near an impromptu altar upon which rested the box containing the imprisoned serpent. After making sure that no intruders were within earshot, the adoration of the serpent would begin, the King and Queen exhorting their subjects to have entire confidence in their power, and to make known their individual desires. Thereupon, each according to his wants would step forward to implore the Voodoo God; one for the gift of domination over his master's mind, another for success in love, a third for a speedy cure and long life, a fourth for fortune, and so on. The King would then seize the precious box, lay it on the floor, and place the Queen upon the lid. No sooner had her feet touched the sacred receptacle, than she became possessed, and like a new Pythoness, her frame quivering, entire body convulsed, the oracle would pronounce its edicts through her inspired lips. On some she bestowed flattery and promises of success, while at others she thundered forth bitter invectives. As soon as the oracle had answered every question, a circle was formed, and the serpent replaced upon the unholy fane. Then each would present his offering, which the King and Queen would promptly assure them was acceptable to their Divine protector.

An oath was administered which bound the members not only to secrecy, but to assist in carrying on the work agreed upon as well. Then the famous Voodoo dance would begin. The initiation of a candidate usually inaugurated this ceremony. The King would trace with a piece of charcoal a large circle in the centre of the room, placing within it the sable neophyte. He would next thrust into the latter's hand a small package of herbs, horsehair, broken bits of horn, and other equally stupid fragments. Then striking him lightly on the head with a wooden paddle, the King would launch forth into a weird African chant. This chant, taken up by the chorus, would increase in volume, the gyrating dancer becoming convulsed. He would then drink some stimulating liquor, be led to the altar to take the oath, and finally lapse into a hysteric fit. Upon the termination of this ceremony, the King would place his hands on the box containing the snake, make a distorted movement of the body, communicate this impulsion to the Queen, who in turn would convey it to every one in the circle. All would now show signs of convulsions in the upper part of the body, the Queen being particularly affected, and going to the Voodoo serpent to gather a fresh supply of magnetic influence. Copious draughts of spiritous liquors are offered around, the hideous shouts grow louder, and general pandemonium is let loose. Fainting and choking spells succeeded one another, and a nervous tremor seemed to possess the entire audience. The dancers would spin round with incredible velocity, at times tearing their vestments and even lacerating their flesh.

The tumultuous orgy would continue, until the savage participants, entirely deprived of reason, fell to the ground from sheer lassitude, and were carried, panting and gyrating, to the open air . . .[24]

'Hysteric fit'; 'distorted movement of the body'; 'hideous shouts'; 'general pandemonium'; 'tumultuous orgy'; 'savage participants'; 'deprived of reason'; 'orgy . . . grown horrid'; 'hideous combination of banjo and violin'; 'a chant and refrain not worth the room it would take'; 'frightful nonsense': such are the epithets used by white observers to describe the blacks' religious worship – epithets which, far from describing it, serve only to highlight their authors' bigotry and ignorance. Even Dubois was, at the outset of his career, uninitiated into the true significance of the rites. In his *Souls of Black Folk* he takes up a middling stance:

The Negro has already been pointed out many times as a religious animal, – a being of that deep emotional nature which turns instinctively toward the supernatural. Endowed with a rich tropical imagination and a keen, delicate appreciation of Nature, the transplanted African lived in a world animated with gods and devils, elves and witches; full of strange influences – of God to be implored, of Evil to be propitiated . . . He called up all the resources of heathenism to his aid – exorcism and witchcraft, the mysterious Obi worship with its barbarous rites, spells and blood-sacrifice even, now and then, of human victims. Weird midnight orgies and mystic conjurations were invoked, the witch-woman and the Voodoo-priest became the centre of Negro group life, and that vein of vague superstition which characterizes the unlettered Negro even today was deepened and strengthened.[25]

After his trip to Africa Dubois began, slowly but surely, to recognize and to give credit to the profound significance of black worship. At the time he wrote *Souls* he was clearly labouring under the spell of his Western education – like so many others, he had not yet realized that for all their years in America black people still have their own way of thinking. Another point worth mentioning is the persistent harping by these authors upon 'orgies'. Whether or not these actually occurred is beyond historical validation; what does clearly emerge is the fact that since sex was a taboo in the Christian world, the surest way to decry black religion was to identify it with lewdness and to make out that it was a kind of pagan rite. Honest and objective observers have reported that the ceremonial of the Voodoos is anything but a fiesta, and anyone who comes along with the idea of 'having a good time' is soon put straight. Biased though these accounts are, what clearly emerges is the evidence of the importance the Hoodoo Mass had in so many facets of Afro-American culture.

High John the Conqueroo

Around the time of the death of Marie Laveau, black Americans suffered a prolonged and determined onslaught at the hands of Christianity, which went all-out to win them as converts. Newly 'enfranchised' by the sixteenth amendment, blacks made the mistake of believing they had become American citizens, in fact as well as in word. The result was a stampede to rid themselves of all reminders of their former state, and a blind rush to embrace the American way of life; the most obvious short cut to bring this about was to become Christian, black believers in the white faith. This they did with all the zeal with which they had formerly practised Voodoo. In this passionate bid to become Americans – i.e. to be made over in the white man's image – blacks castigated their negritude with contempt. 'Black' became shameful; running the entire gamut of Negroism, even the colours of their skins became to them matters for reproach. In doing so – let us not mince words – they dishonoured their race, ingloriously betraying the Nat Turners and Gabriels who had struggled so valiantly to restore to them their pride and freedom. Caught up in this grand illusion, like straw played with by a whirlwind, they sought to show the whites that they could be just as 'white' as Europeans! Piteous folly! The whites asked for nothing better, and as bait deeper to enmesh them in their toils, they held out to the blacks the chimera of Christianity, which promised all things in the next world and none in this. The surest proof that the white drive to convert the blacks to Christianity was but hocus-pocus – and the blacks should have seen this, for it was crystal-clear – is that even after they were joined in the same religion, the churches remained segregated. Even within the sanctity of the faith there could be no question of the joining of hands. Meanwhile, on the political side, all sorts of laws were passed to keep the blacks disenfranchised. With unparalleled hyprocrisy white 'senators' and 'representatives' passed laws which made the blacks slaves in everything but name. Men, whose names black students are taught to revere, either took part in or condoned these infamous bills which could never have been passed in a society worthy of being called humane. In short, in abandoning their own religion for Christianity black people made a miscalculation of dreadful proportions, the upshot of which was that they sold their culture for a lot less than twenty-six dollars and a handful of beads.

The only representative survivors of this whitewashing of black souls are the Root Doctors, the sole remnant of what had once been a thriving tradition. Their antecedents lay in the mists of the blacks' rise in Africa. They were revered not for themselves, but for the spirit which dwelt within them, and which manifested itself in their wisdom. The conjurors of mighty forces, they knew how to set them – both good and evil powers – into motion. By inexplicable ways Root Doctors know the inherent spirit of all things, know how to invoke and appease them. Nothing is beyond their power, there is no problem or illness for which they do not possess the remedy. They are either born with or acquire these powers – in any case, they are tellingly manifested.

> The first way [of becoming a Root Doctor] . . . is to be especially endowed with supernatural power. This most often takes the form of seizures similar to cataleptic ones. This, as it is explained, comes 'like a thunderbolt from a clear sky' . . . By whatever means the message comes it instantly makes the recipient qualified for the task, and he possesses all the techniques of the craft. These healers so strongly believe in their ability to perform cures that they not only become deeply insulted when one expresses disbelief in the method of diagnosis and treatment, but may say that this disbeliever can expect to be chastened by the supernatural power . . . Human selection by personal initiative is another means. In such cases a novitiate is apprenticed to a practitioner. An older doctor takes this novice under his care and gives him guidance, and in this way he learns by clinical contact with actual cases . . . Many practitioners state that in occasional crises they receive direct help from a voice which gives directions and tells of remedies that bring marvellous results which gain for the practitioner distinction and fame.[26]

The Root Doctors divine the future, concoct medicines, work spells, give advice and make charms to ward off evil and to bring good luck. They are influential and even feared personages. In Africa their profession was usually the monopoly of a certain family, handed down from mothers to fathers to their children. In America it was generally passed from teachers to pupils who, once their master felt they were qualified, set up on their own. Conjuring is a precarious art 'for spirits are a risky set to deal with'[27] – to be undertaken only by those with redoubtable courage and a true calling for it. Numerous are the misguided and over-enthusiastic souls living out their days in a world of wonder – the price of having toyed with the Root Doctor's craft.

In the United States the Root Doctor came to be called by various names: Wood Doctor, Fetisher, Vodun, Two-facer, Witchcraft Woman, Hootchie-cootchie, Wangateur, Priestess, Papa, Obi and Goofer-doctor.

The Root Doctors also fulfilled a social role in the black community. Under slavery, it was to them that their people turned for solace whatever the occasion or nature of the trouble. Divinely or humanly wrought, it was they who had the power to rectify it. Through their intercession the problem was either remedied or, at least, explained. They exonerated, rewarded or punished, according to the facts of the case. In a sense they came to represent to the blacks the fount of their own justice, for none whatsoever could be expected from the whites.

> It was a terrific social revolution, and yet some traces were retained of the former group life, and the chief remaining institution was the Priest or Medicine Man. He early appeared on the plantation and found his function as the healer of the sick, the interpreter of the Unknown, the comforter of the sorrowing, the supernatural avenger of wrong and the one who rudely but picturesquely expressed the longing, disappointment and resentment of a stolen and oppressed people. Thus, as bard, physician, judge and priest, within the narrow limits allowed by the slave system, rose the Negro preacher, and under him the first Afro-American institution, the Negro Church. This Church was not at first by any means Christian nor definitely organized; rather, it was an adaptation and mingling of heathen rites among the members of each plantation and roughly designated as Voodooism. Association with the masters, missionary effort and motives of expediency gave these rites an early veneer of Christianity, and after the lapse of many generations the Negro Church became Christian.[28]

As this statement shows, Root Doctors were godparents to the black ministers, in whose testifying and imprecations are to be found the smouldering embers of the African adepts, crying for their people to be set

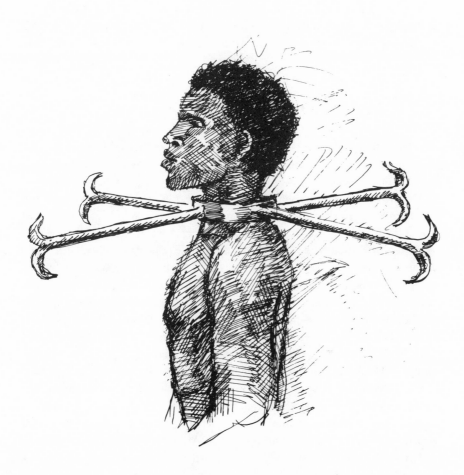

free. Ironically, it was the rise of these Christianized godchildren of theirs which was to relegate them to the obscure and undignified position they hold today. Jealous of their influence, black preachers used every weapon at their disposal – including the threat of eternal damnation – to break the Hoodoo doctors' power. From the pulpit they thundered out verbal brimstone at their competitors, identifying them with the devil and maligning their Africanness.

> Ole Satan am a liah an' a conjuror too:
> Ef you don't mind out he'll hoodoo you!

Shunted into the sidelines by the irresistible tide of black Christianity, the vocation of the Root Doctor is yet carried on, and they count among their clientele not a few of what might be termed the 'black sheep' of Christianity.

African magic as practised by the black people of the United States has ever lain under the opprobium of racist and cultural prejudice. That Moses parted the Red Sea, that Jesus walked on water, that Allah dictated the *Koran* to Mohammed, that Buddha achieved nirvana after being hit by a falling nut of the boa tree – these and a hundred other miracles are believed by the adherents of those respective faiths – at least they are taught with that aim in mind. But that a miracle should happen to blacks, that they should believe in miraculous charms, sends the world off into peals of laughter. When it comes to their magic then the world suspends belief in the supernatural and trots out arguments worthy to win prizes for pragmatism. As soon as some idea is advanced by black people credulity vanishes – in other words, racism comes to the fore. Why do people believe that Columbus discovered America? For the simple reason that he was white. In all sincerity, how can anyone credit him with such a feat when the American continents were replete with civilizations – the Incas, the Awaraks, the Mayas, the Aztecs and the numerous nations of the Northern continent? If the hype about Columbus is true then who was the first black man to discover Europe?

Racism apart, whites simply do not understand magic as it is interpreted by blacks. To cover this ignorance all sorts of spurious ideas are trotted out, such as Dollard's brainchild that magic as practised by Afro-Americans is:

> a means of accommodating to life when it is not arranged to one's wishes
> . . . Of course, one can think of the magical practices among the Negroes
> as lagging cultural patterns, which they are, but one can also think of
> them as forms of action in reference to current social life. Magic accepts

the status quo; it takes the place of political activity, agitation, organization, solidarity, or any real moves to change social status. It is interesting and harmless from the standpoint of the caste system and it probably has great private value to those who practise it . . . Magic, in brief, is a control gesture, a comfort to the individual, an accommodation attitude to helplessness. There is no doubt that magic is actively believed in and practised in Southern town and county today.[29]

If half of these allegations were true the world would be populated entirely by magicians, for when has life ever been 'arranged according to one's wishes'? As far as its 'taking the place of political activity' goes, that would make the US Senate, the British Parliament, the Japanese Diet, the General Assembly of the United Nations and quite a few other political bodies cabals of wizards and dervishes. The fact is that blacks were practising and believing in magic long before they had even heard of the place Columbus didn't discover; the fact is that far from being a substitute for it, magic was a *form of* blacks' political agitation; the fact is that the Afro-American has never accepted the status quo – which thought can only be wish-fulfilment on the part of the commentator.

Saxon, the self-constituted authority on black life in New Orleans, saw the subject in a more patronizing light: 'To understand properly the workings of this black magic, one must understand something of the Negro's characteristics. It must be remembered that he is intensely emotional, that he possesses a childlike credulity, that his imagination is easily inflamed, and that the powers of darkness are potent powers.'[30]

The surest way not to understand what magic means to its black believers is to use words to try and lasso and confine it. But the Western mind knows of no other way to express and explain itself . . . (To know when to *stop* thinking is a lost art, which some new Columbus ought to rediscover.) Why do black people believe in magic? Ask a fish why it stays in water. To the black mind, magic *is*. Anything more is tautology. Or, as the proverb says, 'White man's magic ain't black man's magic.'

Wangas and Mojos

In Hoodoo charms are the material manifestations of power. Believers in Hoodoo carry them to strengthen their will and to protect them from evil, though a charm can also be vocal — words which, when recited with faith, take on the attributes of the spirit they invoke. In the days of slavery, Hoodoo helped blacks to confound their enemies and sometimes to escape, if occasionally only through the doors of death. Through Hoodoo slaves' minds became supernaturally puissant, and they were able to call on powers of which the oppressor knew nothing. These 'invisibles' were represented by the Root Doctor's amulets: the *mojo*-hand, *wangas*, *tobys*, gris-gris, jacks, tricks, the black-cat bone, the High John the Conqueroo and others. They were composed of any number of objects: cats' claws, hair, teeth, roots, herbs, snakeskin, beads, bones, horns, bark, feathers, etc. Properly selected and proportioned, they were then sealed in a small bag or cloth, but as yet possessed no power. Only Root Doctors could give them that. They conjured the desired spirit to come and take its place in the charm. During this ceremony they may sit quietly and meditate or dance, chant and whirl about. When the spirit enters the bag then it becomes a 'charm', and the owner may call upon it in time of need. 'The Negroes,' wrote St Méry, 'believe in magic and that the power of their fetiches has followed them across the sea . . . Little rude figures of wood or stone, representing men or animals, are for them things of supernatural power, and they call them *garde-corps* (bodyguards).'[31]

Since the believer in Hoodoo sees the world as an interplay of multifarious forces, there are charms for every imaginable circumstance: love charms, bring-money charms, buried-treasure charms, keep-a-lover charms, get-rid-of-a-lover charms, wish charms, death charms. A black-cat bone possesses varied powers: love charm, money charm; and it gives its owner the power of invisibility. Voodoo or goofer dust must be procured from a coffin while the moon is on the wane; it is a mighty agent in the working of 'bad' Hoodoo. A *mojo* is a good-luck charm especially relished by gamblers and lovers; World Wonder Root is infallible in locating hidden treasure. The gris-gris — made from the crushed bones of the bird from which it takes its name — can revenge any wrong. High John the Conqueroo can break up a love affair, beat the law, ward off evil and make its possessor irresistible to whomever he or she fancies.

Working 'bad' Hoodoo is known as 'conjuring', which may be described as the left-hand branch of the Root Doctor's art. Conjuring is undertaken to 'put the whammy' on someone, to break up a happy home, to give a gift of seven years of bad luck, to drive people out of their wits, or to give a dose of the tombstone blues. In order to bring off this 'heavy' deal, the Root Doctor has recourse to special tricks: graveyard dust, a *mojo*-tooth, black-cat whiskers, the eyes from a blind frog or Marie Laveau's Special Calamity Powder. Once the trick has been prepared, Hoodoos put themselves into a deep meditation, in which they concentrate on the mental image of the intended victim. If the person is protected by a strong charm, Hoodoos will redouble the strength of their own until they can finally overcome the opposing force. Once this has been achieved the spirit is directed into the charm and it is given to the supplicant.

The next step is called 'Laying the Trick'. The owner of the charm waits for the new moon, so that the charm's power will increase along with the heavenly body. Then he or she puts it somewhere where the victim will come into contact with or step over it, which done, the victim will be 'whammied'. Another way of laying the trick is to sprinkle goofer dust around a person's bed or to put it into either their shoes or hat. The burning of goofer dust, shaped in the victims' image, will make them lose their personalities and go insane. Four nickels arranged in the shape of a cross with a lighted candle at the centre is held to be a sure way of bringing about death. Salt, sprinkled in a certain pattern outside doors, will bring bad luck on those who live there. Marie Laveau made gris-gris from saffron, salt, gunpowder and pulverized dried dog manure, all contained in a black bag. According to legend, it never failed to obtain her object. Puckett reports the case of 'a girl who set a hoodoo for a suitor who had stopped coming to see her. Within a short time this desultory suitor suddenly dropped dead while working in the field – the other Negroes knew he had been tricked.'[32] Bacon, in his essay 'Conjuring and Conjure-Doctors', was told,

When you are conjured you feel like you have never felt before in all your life. Uncouth thoughts take possession of your mind. If a rabbit had been used in working the hoodoo, you will become timid, and afraid of everyone, just as the rabbit is timid. If you are in doubt as to your condition you can verify your misgivings by telling your fortune with cards.[33]

Cable's statement about the blacks' belief in Hoodoo is categorical:

> But whatever may be the quantity of the Voodoo worship left in Louisiana, its superstitions are many and are everywhere. Its charms are resorted to by the malicious, the jealous, the revengeful or the avaricious, or held in terror, not by the timorous only, but by the strong, the courageous, the desperate. To find under his mattress an acorn hollowed out, stuffed with the hair of some dead person, pierced with four holes on four sides, and two small chicken feathers drawn through them so as to cross inside the acorn; or to discover on his doorsill at daybreak a little box containing a dough or waxen heart stuck full of pins; or to hear that his avowed foe or rival has been pouring cheap champagne in the four corners of Congo Square at midnight, will strike more abject fear into the heart of many a stalwart Negro or melancholy quadroon than to face a levelled revolver.[34]

That many black Americans still believe in Hoodoo is a fact. For them, it works. Its survival attests its success. 'This means,' says Herskovits about the Root Doctor, 'that the devices employed by these specialists have fulfilled their function to the satisfaction of their clients.'[35] Magic works by faith, and it would appear that, in the case of the conjure man, that faith has been justified.

Another account of the power of these charms, or 'Luck Balls', comes from Mary Alicia Owen, a Missouri Afro-Indian:

> How that ball (conjure bag) was made, what were its contents, Tow Head did not, at the time, know, though she gathered from the half-whispered gossip of the other aunties that it was the work of 'King' A-, a Voodoo doctor or conjuror of great power and influence.
>
> This A- was a curious half-barbarian, who never stayed long in a place, made his entrances secretly and mysteriously in the night, never confided in anyone, never spent money for anything but whiskey, and never lacked for the good things of the world. No cabin refused him shelter and the best bed and food it could afford. No one knew whence he came or whither he was going. When four taps were heard above the latch, someone flew to usher in the guest. 'A-'s dar', was the unspoken conviction. How he came was a matter of conjecture; it was generally conceded that he travelled at his ease on some strange steed of the devil's providing. In the course of the night came scores of darkies, some of them

from a distance of many miles, who eagerly purchased his remedies, charms, and 'tricks'.[36]

Some of the commoner prescriptions are worth quoting at some length.

To kill: get bad vinegar, beef gall, *filet* gumbo with red pepper, and put names written across each other in bottles. Shake the bottle for nine mornings and talk and tell it what you want it to do. To kill the victim, turn it upside down and bury it breast-deep, and he will die.

To make people love you: take nine lumps of starch, nine of sugar, nine teaspoons of steel dust. Wet it all with Jockey Club cologne. Take nine pieces of ribbon, blue, red or yellow. Take a dessert-spoonful and put it on a piece of ribbon and tie it in a bag. As each fold is gathered together call his name. As you wrap it with yellow thread call his name till you finish. Make nine bags and place them under a rug, behind an *armoire*, under a step or over a door. They will love you and give you everything they can get. Distance makes no difference. Your mind is talking to his mind and nothing beats that.

Black magic to free a criminal: secure a strand from the rope to be used to hang him and have 'Conjurer Doctor' say a prayer over it. Slip it to the condemned and he will go free.

A fetish to cause death: hair from a horse's tail, a snake's tooth, and gunpowder. Wrap in a rag and bury under your enemy's doorstep.

To drive a woman crazy: sprinkle nutmeg on her left shoe every night at midnight.

To get revenge on a woman: keep a bit of her hair and all her hair will fall out.

To make a woman drown herself: get a piece of her underwear, turn it inside out and bury it at midnight, and put a brick on the grave.

Black art used to influence people to win love: take some of the desired one's hair and sleep with it under the pillow. Rub love oil into the palm of your right hand. Carry a piece of weed called 'John the Conqueror' in your pocket.

To make a love powder: gut live hummingbirds. Dry the heart and powder it. Sprinkle the powder on the person you desire.

A love fetish: put a live frog in an ants' nest. When the bones are clean, you will find one flat, heart-shaped, and one with a hook. Secretly hook this into the garment of your beloved, and keep the heart-shaped one. If you should lose the heart-shaped bone, he will hate you as much as he loved you before.

To keep a lover faithful: write his name on a piece of paper and put it up the chimney. Pray to it three times a day.

To win back a husband: put a little rainwater in a clean glass. Drop in three lumps of sugar, saying, 'Father, Son, Holy Spirit.' Then three more lumps, saying, 'Jesus, Mary, Joseph.' Drop in three more lumps while making your request. Put the glass in a dark room (never before a mirror), and place a spoon on the top of the glass. Next morning stir the contents towards you, then, with back towards the street, throw the contents against the house or fence, saying, 'Father, Son, Holy Spirit, Jesus, Mary, Joseph, please grant my favour.' Water must not be spilled, for it must not be walked on.

To get rid of a man: Pick a rooster naked, give him a spoonful of whiskey, then put in his beak a piece of paper on which is written nine times the name of the person to be got rid of. The rooster is then turned loose in Saint Roch's cemetery. Within three day the man dies.

To get rid of people: in New Orleans it is said that a collector or salesman will never return if you sprinkle salt after him.

Dry three pepper pods in an open oven, then place them in a bottle, fill with water, and place under your doorstep for three days. Then sprinkle the water around your house, saying, *'Delonge toi de la'* (remove yourself from here), and the person will never return.

Aids to the lovelorn: love charms are particularly common and seem to be mainly small bits of conjuration practice which have come into popular use. Hair from your lover's head placed under the band of your hat, worn in your purse, or in your pocket nearest your heart, buried under your lover's doorstep, or nailed to a tree or post, will make that person love you; but, inserted in a green tree, it will run the owner crazy. The bow from your sweetheart's hat is equally effective in love affairs, worn in your shoe or in your stocking (if you lose it he will beat you to death), tied around your leg, or thrown into running water (if thrown into stagnant water he will go crazy). Else you may write a note and slip it in the hat band of the desired person, or pick up that person's track and lay it over the door. Others suggest the boy kissing his elbow in order to win a girl, or putting a letter from his lady love in a can and throwing it into running water. If a boy can contrive to have his eyes meet those of his girl and rub bluestone in his hands at the same time she is his for ever. If you pass between two persons of the opposite sex you will marry both of them.

To make someone move: take the hair off a dead black cat, fill its mouth with lemons that have been painted with melted red wax crayon. Wrap animal in silver paper, repeat your desire over it, and place it under the house of the person.[37]

Hoodoo in Black American Folklore

DE CUNJAH MAN

O Chillen, run, de Cunjah man,
Him mouf ez beeg ez fryin' pan,
Him yurs am small, him eyes am raid,
Him hab no toof een him ol' haid,
Him hab him roots, him wu'k him trick,
Him roll him eye, him mek you sick —
　　De Cunjah man, de Cunjah man,
　　O chillen, run, de Cunjah man!

Him hab ur ball ob raid, raid ha'r,
Him hide it un' de kitchen sta'r,
Mam Jude huh pars urlong dat way,
An' now huh hab ur snaik, de say.
Him wrop ur roun' huh buddy tight,
Huh eyes pop out, ur orful sight —
　　De Cunjah man, de Cunjah man,
　　O chillen, run, de Cunjah man!

Miss Jane, huh dribe him f'um huh do',
An' now huh hens woan' lay no mo';
De Jussey cow huh done fall sick,
Hit all done by de Cunjah trick.
Him put ur root un' 'Lijah's baid,
An' now de man he sho' am daid —
　　De Cunjah man, de Cunjah man,
　　O chillen, run, de Cunjah man!

Me see him stan' de yudder night
Right een de road een white moon-light;
Him toss him arms, him whirl him 'roun',
Him stomp him foot urpon de groun';
De snaiks come crawlin', one by one,
Me hyuh um hiss, me break an' run —
   De Cunjah man, de Cunjah man,
   O chillen, run, de Cunjah man!

James Edwin Campbell

Hoodoo is one of the main subjects of black American folklore, a spirit hovering about the life of the blacks irrespective of the particular aspect delineated. This omnipresence in the oral culture of the slaves and their descendants attests the near unanimous faith blacks once placed in it. Characteristic of these stories is the way in which Hoodoo Doctors are portrayed: they are mysterious and powerful figures who have the universal respect of the people. And they break the whites' law with impunity.

This wealth of homage proves that to their people Root Doctors were figures of pride and hope, and that their magic was a refuge to which blacks could always turn in time of need. Psychologically, they acted as counterbalances to the power of the whites: they were *blacks* endowed with vital cogency and, vicariously, the people shared in their glory.

These oral stories — a sort of spoken blues in which speech takes the place of music — are the first literature (in the European sense of the word) of the black people of the United States, and are the forerunners of the poetry and fiction of Dubois, McKay, Hughes, Cullen, Toomer, Wright, Brooks, Ellison, Himes, Joans, Baraka, Baldwin and of course, Hurston, who may be called the direct spiritual heir of Hoodoo in both the ethnology and fiction of the Afro-American. Her piece dealing with 'High John de Conquer' is worth quoting at length.

High John de Conquer came to be a man, and a mighty man at that. But he was not a natural man in the beginning. First off, he was a whisper, a will to hope, a wish to find something worthy of laughter and song. Then the whisper put on flesh. His footsteps sounded across the world in a low but musical rhythm as if the world he walked on was a singing-drum. The black folks had an irresistible impulse to laugh. High John de Conquer was a man in full, and had come to live and work on the plantations, and all the slave folks knew him in the flesh.

The sign of this man was a laugh, and his singing-symbol was a drum-beat. No parading drum-shout like soldiers out for show. It did not call to the feet of those who were fixed to hear it. It was an inside thing to live by. It was sure to be heard when and where the work was the hardest, and the lot the most cruel. It helped the slaves endure [. . .]

He had come from Africa. He came walking on the waves of sound. Then he took on flesh after he got there. The sea captains of ships knew that they brought slaves in their ships. They knew about those black bodies huddled down there in the middle passage, being hauled across the waters to helplessness. John de Conquer was walking the very winds that filled the sails of the ship. He followed over them like the albatross.

It is no accident that High John de Conquer has evaded the ears of white people. They were not supposed to know. You can't know what folks won't tell you. If they, the white people, heard some scraps, they could not understand because they had nothing to hear things like that with. They were not looking for any hope in those days, and it was not much of a strain for them to find something to laugh over. Old John would have been out of place for them [. . .]

There is no established picture of what sort of looking-man this John de Conquer was. To some, he was a big, physical-looking man like John Henry. To others, he was a little, hammered-down, low-built man like the Devil's doll-baby. Some said that they never heard what he looked like. Nobody told them, but he lived on the plantation where their old folks were slaves. He is not so well known to the present generation of coloured people in the same way that he was in slavery time. Like King Arthur of England, he has served his people, and gone back into mystery again. And, like King Arthur, he is not dead. He waits to return when his people shall call again. Symbolic of English power, Arthur came out of the water, and with Excalibur, went back into the water again. High John de Conquer went back to Africa, but he left his power here, and placed his American dwelling in the root of a certain plant. Only possess that root, and he can be summoned at any time [. . .]

So after a while, freedom came. Therefore High John de Conquer has not walked the winds of America for seventy-five years now. His people had their freedom, their laugh and their song. They have traded it to the other Americans for things they could use like education and property, and acceptance. High John knew that that was the way it would be, so he could retire with his secret smile into the soil of the South and wait.

The thousands upon thousands of humble people who still believe in him, that is, in the power of love and laughter to win by their subtle power, do John reverence by getting the root of the plant in which he has taken up his secret dwelling, and 'dressing' it with perfume, and keeping it on their person, or in their houses in a secret place. It is there to help them overcome things they feel that they could not beat otherwise, and to bring them the laugh of the day. John will never forsake the weak and the helpless. That is what they believe, and so they do not worry. They go on and laugh and sing. Things are bound to come out right tomorrow. That is the secret of Negro song and laughter.

So the brother in black offers to these United States the source of courage that endures, and laughter. High John de Conquer. If the news from overseas reads bad, and the nation inside seems like it is stuck in the Tar Baby, listen hard, and you will hear John de Conquer treading on his singing-drum. You will know then, that no matter how bad things look now, it will be worse for those who seek to oppress us. Even if your hair comes yellow, and your eyes are blue, John de Conquer will be working for you just the same. From his secret place, he is working for all America now. We are all his kinfolks. Just be sure our cause is right, and then you can lean back and say, 'John de Conquer would know what to do in a case like this, and then he would finish it off with a laugh.'

White America, take a laugh out of our black mouths, and win! We give you High John de Conquer.[38]

More circumstantial descriptions of Hoodoo practice and beliefs are related by former slaves:

A POCKET FULL OF CONJURE THINGS

Us children hang round close to the big house, and us have a old man that went round with us and look after us, white children and black children, and that old man was my great grand-daddy. Us sure have to mind him, 'cause iffen we didn't, us sure have back luck. He always have the pocket full of things to conjure with. That rabbit foot, he took it out, and he work that on you till you take the creeps and git shaking all over. Then there's a pocket full of fish scales, and he kind of squeak and rattle them in the hand, and right then you wish you was dead and promise to do anything. Another thing he always have in the pocket was a little old dry-up turtle, just a mud turtle 'bout the size of a man's thumb, the whole thing just dry up and dead. With that thing he say he could do 'most anything, but he never use it iffen he ain't have to. A few times I seed him git all tangle up and bothered, and he go off by hisself and sat down in a quiet place, take out this very turtle and put it in the palm of the hand and turn it round and round and say something all the time. After while he git everything untwisted, and he come back with a smile on he face and maybe whistling.[39]

OLD BAB, THE CONJURE MAN

Little pinch o' pepper,
Little bunch o' wool.

Mumbledy – mumbledy.

Two, three Pammy Christy beans,
Little piece o' rusty iron.

Mumbledy – mumbledy.

Wrap it in a rag and tie it with hair,
Two from a hoss and one from a mare.

Mumbledy, mumbledy, mumbledy.

Wet it in whiskey
Boughten with silver;
That make you wash so hard your sweat pop out,
And he come to pass, sure![40]

That's how the niggers say Old Bab Russ used to make the hoodoo hands he made for the young bucks and wenches, but I don't know, 'cause I was too trusting to look inside the one he make for me, and anyways I lose it, and it no good nohow!

Old Bab Russ live about two mile from me, and I went to him one night at midnight and ask him to make me the hand. I was a young strapper about sixteen years old, and thinking about wenches pretty hard and wanting something to help me out with the one I liked best.

Old Bab Russ charge me four bits for that hand, and I had to give four bits more for a pint of whiskey to wet it with, and it wasn't no good nohow!

Course that was five–six years after the war. I wasn't yet quite eleven when the war close. Most all the niggers was farming on the shares, and whole lots of them was still working for their old master yet. Old Bab come in there from deep South Carolina two–three years before, and live all by himself. The gal I was worrying about had come with her old pappy and mammy to pick cotton on the place, and they was staying in one of the cabins in the settlement, but they didn't live there all the time.

I don't know whether I believed in conjure much or not in them days, but anyways I tried it that once, and it stirred up such a rumpus everybody called me 'Hand' after that until after I was married and had a pack of children.

Old Bab Russ was coal-black, and he could talk African or some other unknown tongue, and all the young bucks and wenches was mortal 'fraid of him![41]

HOODOO

My wife was sick, down, couldn't do nothing. Someone got to telling her about Cain Robertson. Cain Robertson was a hoodoo doctor in Georgia. They said there wasn't nothing Cain couldn't do. She says, 'Go and see Cain and have him come up here.'

I says, 'There ain't no use to send for Cain. Cain ain't coming up here because they say he is a "two-head" nigger.' (They called all them hoodoo men 'two-head' niggers; I don't know why they called them two-head.) 'And you know he knows the white folks will put him in jail if he comes to town.'

But she says, 'You go and get him.'

So I went.

I left him at the house, and when I came back in, he said, 'I looked at your wife and she had one of them spells while I was there. I'm afraid to tackle this thing because she has been poisoned, and it's been going on a long time. And if she dies, they'll say I killed her, and they already don't like me and looking for an excuse to do something to me.'

My wife overheard him and says, 'You go on, you got to do something.'

So he made me go to town and get a pint of corn whiskey. When I brought it back he drunk a half of it at one gulp, and I started to knock him down. I'd thought he'd get drunk with my wife lying there sick.

Then he said, 'I'll have to see your wife's stomach.' Then he scratched it, and put three little horns on the place he scratched. Then he took another drink of whiskey and waited about ten minutes. When he took them off her stomach, they were full of blood. He put them in the basin in some water and sprinkled some powder on them, and in about ten minutes more he made me get them and they were full of clear water and there was a lot of little things that looked like wiggle tails swimming around in it.

He told me when my wife got well to walk in a certain direction a certain distance, and the woman that caused all the trouble would come to my house and start a fuss with me.

I said, 'Can't you put this same thing back on her?'

He said, 'Yes, but it would kill my hand.' He meant that he had a curing hand and that if he made anybody sick or killed them, all his power to cure would go from him.

I showed the stuff he took out of my wife's stomach to old Doc Matthews, and he said, 'You can get anything into a person by putting it in them.' He asked me how I found out about it, and how it was taken out, and who did it.

I told him all about it, and he said, 'I'm going to see that that nigger practises anywhere in this town he wants to and nobody bothers him.' And he did.[42]

The White Hoodoos

To the whites, Hoodoo was silly nigger superstition worthy of the primitive minds of the backward people who professed it. It was bad enough that they included Christian saints in their outlandish ceremonies, but actually to have credence in the mumbo-jumbo of those swindlers, the Hoodoo Doctors, to believe in their ghastly *mojos* and *wangas* – that alone was enough to prove their mental inferiority. Behind these charitable thoughts was the fact that under no circumstances would the whites admit the possibility of any religion which did not accord with Christianity having the merest tincture of truth. The religion of the blacks was a challenge which must be eradicated at any cost. Like lackeys running to the defence of their master, European and American men of science and history took up their cudgels and belaboured the blacks' beliefs with all the overwhelming power at their command. They inculcated in their readers' minds ideas about black people as derogatory as they were untrue. So successful were these fiendish efforts that even today the vast majority of whites believe themselves intrinsically superior to blacks. As for the blacks themselves, even they find it necessary to castigate the 'heathenism' of their past: 'I don't believe in none of that old Hoodoo!' No; now blacks too have become 'whitened', and believe in angels with wings, virgins giving birth to extremely human-like sons, and a place in the sky where the party never stops. 'I'm a Christian!' became the rallying cry of every black person who sought admission into the grace and favour of white people. Blacks hoped that by those magic words the doors of the kingdom would swing open and that they could charge the future with their 'merican 'xpress card. They quickly found out that they would forever have to leave home without it. In shunning Hoodoo blacks turned their backs on their negritude, thereby playing into their oppressors' hands. Hoodoo posed a threat to the whites' psychological domination over blacks, for which reason whites have never ceased to cast aspersions upon it.

> The dance and song entered the Negro worship. That worship was as dark and horrid as bestialized savagery could make the adoration of serpents. So revolting was it, and so morally hideous, that even in the West Indian French possessions a hundred years ago the orgies of the Voodoos were forbidden. Yet both there and in Louisiana they were practised.
>
> It is pleasant to say that this worship, in Louisiana, at least, and in comparison with what it once was, has grown to be a trivial affair.[43]

Notwithstanding the blatant racism of the above comment, Herskovits, one of the leading exponents of Afro-American history, paid its author, George Cable, this high tribute:

> One of the richest stores of data pertaining to Negro custom is the writing of George Cable, whose articles on New Orleans life . . . hold special significance for research into the ethnography of United States Negroes. Based on intimate knowledge of the locality and its history, it must be accepted as a valid document if only on the basis of its comparative

findings. It is thus a real contribution to our knowledge of life in this area during the time of slavery . . .[44]

Cable's own words convict him as a racist, and it was Herskovits's duty to call him one. History should be made of sterner stuff . . . and yet Herskovits says Cable's document is valid, and Herskovits is an honourable man . . .

There were other whites whose views on Hoodoo were diametrically opposed to Cable's, perhaps because they had intimate knowledge of black life which he, the self-proclaimed authority, lacked. Or perhaps they were just crazy? At any rate they shared in the life of the blacks, at least to the extent that they took part in Hoodoo ceremonies. Raised in the very midst of the black religion they could not but have become, to a greater or lesser extent, influenced by it. In this matter, it is impossible to overestimate the influence of the black 'mamas' on the white children they raised. They entertained and frightened them with the only stories they knew, and those tales were about Hoodoo. Even Cable goes as far as to admit this: 'And it is not only the coloured man that holds these practices and fears. Many a white Creole gives them full credence.'[45] Puckett expressed the same finding in 1926: 'Many people, both black and white, today, still believe in the power of the Voodoo Doctor.'[46]

The following accounts are by white authors. Apart from their interest from the racial viewpoint, they shed additional light on the subject of conjuring.

White men attended some of these meetings, as was the case with one held on St John's Eve between Spanish Fort and Milneburg, near New Orleans. Coffee and gumbo were served, and the men had to remove their coats so as not to break the charm. A small tablecloth in the centre of the room contained, in addition to cakes, beans, and corn, several bunches of feathers, candles, small piles of bones, and shallow Indian baskets filled with herbs. Dancing, gradually working into a frenzy, took place to the notes of a tomtom. Alcohol was spit upon the candles to make a flame and to fool the superstitious, but there were no snakes nor nakedness. In 1806 a Voodoo dance was held in Algiers on St John's Eve to invoke the powers to hold back a white girl's lover, preventing him from leaving for Baltimore as was his intention. The white girl's father discovered her, clad in her night clothes with bare feet and streaming hair, waving a wand while the Voodoos, all the while chanting in an unknown tongue, danced wildly about a cauldron containing serpents and frogs. One of the women was sprinkling a powder in the flames, which diffused a deathly sickening odour [. . .]

'In the centre of the room was a large vase containing a fetid mixture, and round about this, on three dishes of silver, many snakes calmly reared their heads. The scene was made brilliant by the light from hundreds of candles. In the four quarters of the hall stimulating perfumes burned on hearths.' Castellanos mentions a police raid of about 1860 or earlier where a group of women clad only in white camisoles were found dancing this Voodoo dance. Many white women of the highest walks of society were found among them. 'These facts are beyond controversy, and the scandal, attested by thousands, was made the subject of town gossip for many a year.'

One of the Voodoo songs stated that the queen, Marie Laveau, knew all kinds of *gri-gri* or charms; that she had gone to school with the crocodiles and alligators; that she had a speaking acquaintance with the Grand Zombi, and that when the sun went down every evening in a little corner of the wild woods he would come out of the bayou to teach Marie Laveau all Voodoo mysteries. Still another ran:

> '*L'Appe vini, li Grand Zombi,*
> '*L'Appe vini pour fe gri-gri!*

One of my informants, a white man of New Orleans, witnessed personally one of these Voodoo dances held between Spanish Fort and Milneburg, on St John's Eve in 1877 or 1878. An iron pot was swinging on a tripod with gumbo cooking in it. Claret mixed with cinnamon and aromatic herbs was warmed and served with the gumbo, but neither in the food nor in any attendant worship was any snake to be seen. All participants were naked and Marie Laveau beat time while the men − all of them white − and 'pretty yellow girls' danced around. Much immorality was in evidence around the deserted place. A later account tells of a meeting of mixed whites and coloured on the shores of Lake Pontchartrain for Voodoo purposes. Dr Alexander, a coloured Voodoo Doctor, the successor of Marie Laveau, presided, and here again a large number of white women of respectable middle-class families were found almost completely disrobed.

Another account testifies to the use of a 'strange mixture of Catholicism and Voodooism'.

In the first seánce [Mrs Helen Pitkin] tells of a white girl calling upon a Negro Voodoo-woman to obtain help in winning the man she loves. At the meeting, the girl is allowed to wear nothing black, and is forced to remove the hairpins from her hair, lest some of them be accidentally crossed, thus spoiling the charm. In the room were paintings of the various Catholic saints and an altar before which was a saucer containing white sand, quicksilver, and molasses, apexed with a blue candle burning for Saint Joseph (Veriquite). All the way through, there is this strange mixture of Catholicism and Voodooism. The 'Madam' kneels at the girl's feet and intones the Hail Mary of the Church, there is a song to Liba (Voodoo term for St Peter) and another to Blanc Dani (St Michael). The money collected for the seánce is put in front of the altar with the sign of the cross.

After the 'obi-woman' spewed wine upon all present, she sang and danced until the frenzy (spirit) came upon her. The white girl was asked to make her wish. She wished for the obstacles to her love to be removed. Gumbo and rice were served from the pot – which also contained snakes. Then the girl wrote her own name, her rival's name, and her lover's name on separate slips of paper. The slip containing her rival's name was put to soak in a dish of vinegar, salt and pepper, while her name and her lover's name were dropped into a dish of burning whiskey. A candle with seven notches in it was handed to the girl with the instruction to burn a notch each night for seven nights, repeating three Hail Marys each time. She was given a pinch of the *poiv' guine* from the saucer and told to put five grains in her mouth whenever her lover came near her, in order to soften him towards her. Also, when he first entered the house she was to make a glass of sugared water with *basilique* and throw it into the yard with her back towards the street. Again she was to put *poiv' guine* and clove in her mouth to get what she wanted from him; she must put a piece of his hair where the cistern water could splash on it; and she was to keep a piece of lodestone about her when he was near 'to ambition him'.[47]

By no means was Hoodoo confined to New Orleans and its environs. It was practised throughout the whole of the United States, in spite of the very hostile reaction it received from the whites. Root Doctors were jailed, fined and violently abused whenever they were caught practising their craft. The message was: if you're sick, go to a white doctor; if you need spiritual guidance, go to a Christian church. As they had done during the gory days when they had first arrived in America, the black medicine men and women once again had to go underground. 'So great was the number of Voodoo impostors,' wrote P.A. Bruce, 'practising their profession among the Negroes of New Orleans that in July, 1886, the Board of Health was compelled to interfere with a view to their suppression. Many are still there today, but they are less open in their methods.'[48] About the same time another observer stated that,

> it was estimated that in Atlanta, perhaps, a hundred old men and women practised Voodooism as a profession, telling fortunes, locating lost and stolen goods, furnishing love philtres, and casting spells upon people and cattle. Such incantatory beliefs are found in the Northern states as well, even in cities such as Philadelphia and Pittsburg. My own observations in Harlem lead to similar conclusions.

In his *Magic, Mentality and City Life*, Parks states, 'The Obeah men of the West Indies have many clients in the United States, and a recent issue of the *New York Age* announced that the Negro quarter around 135th Street, New York, was overrun with fortune tellers and witch doctors, many of them from the West Indies.' Another report, this one from Castellanos on the King of the Voodoos in New Orleans, compliments the police on a job well done.

> The prince of the occult science, styling himself 'Don Pedro', is now recognized head of the sect, and his adepts, as I am told, are legion. The police have, however, nearly broken up his business, having compelled him to go into hiding. The organization of the Voodoos, as an organization, has been suppressed in great measure by the efforts of our municipal authorities.[49]

These accounts are the same old, hackneyed refrain, one which has been droning in the lives of black people since they were forced to come to America.

> . . . references to the gods or religions of Africa were suppressed by the white masters as soon as they realized what they were — not only because they naturally thought of any African religious customs as 'barbarous' but because the whites soon learned that too constant evocation of the African gods could mean that those particular Africans were planning on leaving that plantation as soon as they could![50]

This comment, depicting the situation of black religion under slavery, could be used, without the slightest change, for describing the dilemma Hoodooists found themselves in. For a short time it looked as if the Man without A Name might achieve one. Having been freed, what was there to prevent him from living in his own way? Then, he would be able to proclaim – in a voice loud enough for the whole world to hear – his true message . . .

Like a great wave which surges only to expend itself before it reaches the beach, it rose in his throat and then died out before it could be pronounced.

Hoodoo Man Blues

We all believed in Hoodoo . . .

Muddy Waters

The blues repertoire is saturated with songs attesting the bluesman's credence in Hoodoo. To him, they conjure the supernatural forces he uses to overcome the obstacles in his path, for the bluesman who believes in Hoodoo thinks of himself as a privileged being in league with mighty spirits. Hoodoo songs, with their quasi-mystical themes, extol forces which are non-existent to the uninformed but very real to the initiated. By paying them homage the bluesman aligns them on his side; in some cases he may even be related to them. Through their intercession women can't help but love him; if he gambles he's bound to win; the law becomes something he sneers at. He carries charms which can upset the normal order of things: get in his way and he'll put the whammy on you! For these reasons the black Church singled out the lyrics of these songs as proof that the blues was 'the devil's music'. The concept of Hoodoo had to be done away with, all talk of 'conjures' and *mojos* had to be forever swept out of black people's minds, in order that the light of Christianity could shine through.

The faithful were warned not to listen to the blues and were sternly reprimanded if it came to be known that they did. Blues performers the righteous preacher indignantly castigated as tramps, drunkards and immoral vagabonds. Their songs were a sin in the eyes of the Lord and, as such, blacks must turn their backs on them. Hoodoo was a throwback to the jungle – to Africa – and heaven forbid that black Christians should have anything to do with the land of their origin. As one old song put it:

> Keep away from me 'hoodoo' an' witch,
> Lead mah path from the po' house gate;
> Ah pines for the gold'n harps an' sich,
> Oh, Lawd, Ah'll just set an' wait.

The black minister had his mission and carried it out; the bluesman, no less inspired, had his and fulfilled it. He put his argument to the people and let them decide. That he emerged victorious from the fray is to be seen in the fact that today no black preacher dare raise his voice against the blues. Black people have recognized the blues as their cultural heritage and have been outspoken in expressing their appreciation of the bluesman's work during the bleak period of black cultural and social unawareness. Even during the days when the black Church seemingly wielded supreme power over the black community they never wholly gave up their faith in the Hoodoo Doctor or their love of the blues, continuing to sneak out to the shack of the old man of many secrets and to gather around the blues singer whenever he or she appeared – and not only to listen, but also to participate, to tap the tambourine, to pluck the banjo or join in the singing. Music was their birthright, a communal possession to be shared by one and all. From the cradle blacks lived in a world of music. Someone was always singing – weeping and singing, working and singing, laughing and singing, dying and singing. Musically speaking, it was a rich and inspiring existence. In the same way, they lived in the mysterious sphere of Hoodoo – a world of invisible happenings, of magic charms and spells, presided over by the conjure men and *mambos*, who were in touch with the highest powers. Both were part of their inheritance, inalienable legacies bequeathed to them by their people. In 'Hoodoo blues' songs the two come together to function as a source of strength, to set off a reaction and bring about a desired effect. They act as magic – perhaps the first function music ever had. A few examples of the main types will illustrate these points.

Mojo songs are legion:

> Goin' to Louisiana to git myself a *mojo* hand
> 'Cause dese backbitin' womens tryin' fo' to steal my man.

> You may tip out sweet poppa, while tippin' is grand,
> But yo' tippin' will be over when Mamma gits her *mojo* hand.

In his 'Louisiana Blues' Muddy Waters tells of heading to the Hoodoo capital
to get his luck with the ladies fixed up:

> I'm goin' down to New Orleans
> Get me a *mojo* hand:
> I'm gonna show all you good-lookin' women
> Just how to treat yo' man.

On Fogyism:

> Why do some people believe in some old sign?
> You hear a hoot owl holler, someone is surely dyin'.

> Some will break a mirror and cry, 'Bad luck for seven years,'
> And if a black cat crosses them, they'll break right down in tears.

> To dream of muddy waters – trouble is knocking at your door,
> Your man is sure to leave you and never return no more!

Buster Benton's 'Spider in My Stew' describes an unlucky lover caught up in
the trick-bag of Obeahism:

> I been so unlucky, baby
> I found a spider in my stew
> Oh, I didn't know what happened, baby
> I got so much confidence in you.

> I wonder if somebody, people
> Been stirrin' somethin' up in my stew?
> Oh, I'm been gettin' awful sick lately, baby
> I just can't get along with you

> They got me scared to take a drink, people
> I'm even scared to take a bite
> Yes, I'm scared of all my women
> I just can't sleep at night!

On bad luck:

When de hog makes a bed, you know de storm is due.
When the screech-owl holler, means bad luck for you.

When a black cat crosses you, bad luck, I've heard it said.
One must have started 'cross me, got halfway and fell dead.

Screech-owl holler dis mawnin' right beside my front door.
I know when he hollered, trouble comin' back once more.

I heard a hound dog bayin', an' I felt so blue.
I dreamt he was in de graveyard, lookin' down at you.

On Gypsy women:

I went to see the Gypsy, she opened up my hand.
She said: 'My friend, you're worried, but I don't understand.'

Went to see de Gypsy to get my fortune tole
Gypsy done tole me: 'Darn yo' unhardlucky soul!'

You know, the Gypsy woman told me,
That you your mother's bad-luck chile
Well, you havin' a good time now:
But there'll be trouble after a while.

Muddy Waters

I been long gone
On Hoodoo charms and spells.
I get a thrill
When the devil rings my bell!
Gypsy women do with me what they will
Cuz I found and broke the Seventh Seal!

Hoodoo Slim

On the strength of Hoodoo:

She looked at the crazy man – he said, 'Now I'm not so dumb,'
I took her to a funeral – the dead jumped up and run.
She looked at a deaf and dumb boy – he said, 'Now I can speak,'

She stuck her finger in a blind man's face — watch the blind man now see!
                              Muddy Waters, 'She Moves Me'

Stop the things you're doin'
Dig-up: I ain't jivin!
I can't stand this foolin' around
I can't stand no puttin' me down!
I put a spell on you — because you're mine!
                    Screamin' Jay Hawkins, 'I Put a Spell on You'

I'm goin' back down to Kansas soon
Bring back my second cousin: Little John the Conqueroo.
                              Bo Diddley, 'I'm a Man'

I had this Gypsy boy, you see
He was always touchin' me
He warmed my body — cooled my mind
He had me thinkin' that I was divine.

He had me drinkin' Urban Voodoo Juice
I tried to get to California but he wouldn't cut me loose
He took my mind apart and put it together again
My baby's got me hooked on that ole Urban Voodoo Juice again!
                    Salome Arnold, 'Urban Voodoo Juice'

She took me away from ma baby
Yeah, she put the hurt on me!
She put ma mind in a rout
Oh, I couldn't hold out!

We lived in a shack on the bayou
Voodoo dust covered the floor!
I said: 'Baby, this can't last.'
She said: 'I print some mo' cash!'

I fell in love with
Sister Funky Divine!
                    Hoodoo Slim, 'Sister Funky Divine'

The best-known of all Hoodoo songs is Willie Dixon's 'Hootchie Cootchie Man' in which the Hoodoo man's fate and kit are described:

> The Gypsy woman told my mother
> Before I was born:
> 'You got a boy child comin'
> Gonna be a son-of-a-gun!'
>
> I got a black cat bone
> I got a *mojo* too
> I got the John the Conqueroo
> I'm gonna mess with you!
>
> On the seventh hour
> Of the seventh day
> Of the seventh month
> The seventh doctor say:
> 'He was born for good luck.'
> And that you see:
> I got seven hundred dollars
> Don't you mess with me!
>
> Because I'm here.
> Everybody knows I'm here!
> Well, I'm the Hootchie Cootchie Man.
> The whole world knows I'm here!

Hoodoo tells of supernatural agencies invading reality. To Hooduns they are a fact of life and they do everything they can to have them on their side – they get a *mojo*, keep on good terms with the Root Doctors, and wear their *wangas* around their necks. If they succeed in getting the powers behind them they become a force to be reckoned with. One of the Voodoo songs about Marie Laveau relates how she had gone to school with crocodiles and was in great favour with the Grand Serpent, who had taught her all there was to know about gris-gris. He told her that when her end came she would die but would return with him to Africa; and indeed, at her funeral her thousands of devotees piously waited for her to rise up and float back to her mother country on a rainbow cloud. Hoodoo is about faith, and Hoodoo songs are songs of power.

The Saints and the Hoodoos

Everybody . . . they . . . tell . . . me
That somebody done hoodooed the Hoodoo man!
                                    John Lee, 'Sonny Boy' Williamson

Hoodooing the Hoodoo Man

Hoodoo's greatest enemy was the many-headed hydra of American racism, a system of double standards as subtle as it was ignoble. On the one hand black people were slaves, mere chattels, treated with all the consideration due to pigs or a heap of lumber. This saved them from the dire fate that befell the Indians – whereas the only 'good Injun' was a dead one, blacks were *property*, too costly to be wasted. After all, economics was what slavery was all about.

Whereas education was not to be wasted on the slaves, the Churches of the land descended on them with all the zeal of neophyte missionaries sowing in virgin soil. (This is by no means a thing of the past, as witnessed by these words from Hugh Masekela: 'Central to the apartheid process is the Christianizing of the black man into an order-obeying, cheap servant. In that way we remain slaves – civilized slaves.') It was the 'benevolent' side of the familiar, accursed coin: sheer counterfeit for all its piety and cant. Church and State struck up a bargain worthy of the best high-street dime store in which it was found that slavery was compatible with the teachings of Christ. It was souls for sale!

To complete the confusion of this devil's work, slavery was illegal in some of the Northern states; surely this was the most confounded labyrinth in the history of any country in the world. In the same country people might either be free or slaves depending on which side of a line they stood! All whites were free; some blacks were, others were not; and those blacks who were not free might become so, and those who were free might become slaves! Whites joined with blacks to create the Underground Railroad to help enslaved Negroes escape north to freedom. Meanwhile, the Church played a game worthy of Jekyll and Hyde: it lent succour to the escapees in the North and countenanced slavery in Dixie. And all the while it preached its shameful brand of Christianity, condemning African beliefs and customs and 'whitewashing' the minds of the blacks. Its infernal pact with Caesar was to grant him the body so long as it got the soul. The usual outcome of this was what might be called a 'Christian Zombie' – a puppet under the spiritual control of hypocritical masters who had lost the keys to any mysteries they once might have professed. This Church – the American Church – was lacking both in compassion and courage, the two outstanding qualities of its founder.

As for the State, it has never stopped droning on to blacks that they are *American* and as such enjoy the rights of the Constitution . . . if only their colour would go away they could melt into the pot like everyone else . . .

Is it any wonder that black Americans strove – albeit with infinite reluctance – to discard their negritude? This attempt of theirs to Americanize, that is to *whiten* themselves, sad though it may be, is yet without blame: no contemporary mind, black or white, can possibly imagine to any realistic degree the hell that was slavery.

The Gods of Africa, the *loas*, did not achieve the resplendent reincarnations in the United States that had taken place in the West Indies and Latin America. Instead their forces were channelled into three different manifestations: Hoodoo or Root Doctors, the Christian Church, and the Blues.

We need not concern ourselves with the Christian Church here – we shall see it later on in our study of the Negro Spirituals. As for Hoodoo, we have seen its main features in the guises of Voodoo and Obeah. In the US it survived to become a far-flung but unorganized institution – too weak, in fact, to be called a Church thanks to the tireless efforts of the black Christian Church which, in its zeal to stamp out all throwbacks to African religion, left no trick untried. The State also did its share: Hoodooists were persecuted by law, and its adherents harassed, jailed and fined. The official (*sic*) black (*sic*) Church had sided with the whites, the powers in the land against superstition – that is, African beliefs.

Hoodoo took to the bayous. It survived, but only just; in place of the *grandes cérémonies* as practised in Haiti and Bahia it spread out over the Mississippi Delta – with its headquarters at New Orleans – in a freewheeling miasma of charms, spells and root cures. If it was rarely seen, it was always spoken of, whispered about. And this invisibility added greatly to its potency: it became legendary, wonderful and feared. Pregnant with mysteries, it gave birth to a rich folklore.

Black Americans knew Hoodoo existed but few of them had attended a *messe noire*. Besides, the fact that the Church was always warning them against it gave credence to its reality. But the pyschological need Hoodoo had fulfilled for the first slaves was now provided for in the sanctioned wailing of spirituals and the frenzied 'testifying' before the pulpits of the Baptists. Result: the Root Doctor had the blues.

The White Shepherd and the Black Sheep

I speak of the Christian religion, and no one need be astonished. The Church in the colonies is the white people's Church, the foreigner's Church. She does not call the native to God's ways but to the ways of the white man, of the master, of the oppressor. And as we know, in this matter many are called but few chosen.

Frantz Fanon

The history of the white Christian Church and its dealings with blacks is a tale worthy of the Bible, complete with a cast of millions, unholy temptations and an ever-hoped-for exodus. In this American version, however, it was not one man but a whole people who were crucified, and a whole nation which needs to be resurrected, for the land which ceaselessly boasts that it is the home of the free has yet to produce anyone inspired enough to tread unsinkingly upon the Mississippi. The spirituals of the peoples whose dark voices have rung up and down those great muddy waters for three centuries speak of this divine mariner's coming, a consummation devoutly to be wished in a land the religious history of which is a compendium of apostolic chicanery. The Christian Church's role in the enslavement represents the moral bankruptcy of its creed. When Nietzsche pronounced that God was dead he was merely proclaiming something more timid spirits knew but dared not express. The European god had, to all intents and purposes, been dead for centuries and was but a mummy exhibited upon suitable occasions for the benefit of tradition. Jesus, its protagonist, was a figure whose main teachings no one *really* believed in. He was merely employed by the ecclesiastical bigwigs to maintain the power of the rich and to cow the poor. Gabriel, blowing riffs worthy of Miles Davis, was put to work overtime to herald the revelation that Mr So-and-So was

king by *divine right*. This the Church announced after, no doubt, receiving a
message from its heavenly headquarters. The orders concerning blacks were
not so clear. The question of the age became, 'Can blacks be Christians?' and
it was attended by a whole host of related problems: did they have souls,
could they be admitted into heaven as angels, could the enslavement of
fellow believers be justified, etc. The crux of the problem was the whites'
concept of their religion. To them, Christianity was 'white': Moses,
Abraham, Jesus, Mary, Solomon, Herod — all were as white as if they had
been born in Finland or France. Forget the fact that they were all Jews, that
the Bible was the product of Hebrew culture! Far from admitting the
Jewishness of the hybrid faith, Europeans blamed the race of which Jesus was
a member for the death of the *Europeans'* saviour. By a paradox which can
only be described as pathological, Europeans have ever despised and hated
the Jews, whose religion forms the foundation of their Christian culture. But
in adapting it they sought to rid it of any overt Judaism — take a look at any
of the works of religious art in Christendom: the paintings of Michelangelo
in the Sistine Chapel, etc. Nowhere will you find evidence of the origin of
the race — not a trace of 'Jewishness', not a hint of the tinted skins of the
Middle East. These biblical representatives have Italian, German and Dutch
features. Leonardo's 'Last Supper' might have been posed for by a group of
Swiss villagers. The blond hair, blue eyes and pink skin of the figures
depicted in the religious tableaux of European painters are glaring reminders
that for the people of those periods Christianity was a club reserved for
whites.

Thus, there were no scruples to be overcome by the Church when it
acquiesced in, abetted and profited from slavery. As pagan idolaters Africans
were the Devil's disciples, excluded from the bosom of Christ — which alone
conferred the rights of humanity. They were non-persons, fit to labour for
the profit of the chosen. If they were thought to lack souls, blacks were
outside the bounds of ethics. Still, there remained a problem for the Church,
whose missionary zeal was not altogether quashed by the vast amounts of
lucre it gleaned from the colonies: the fact that the light of the holy
fisherman was not flooding into those dark minds, whether or not they had
souls, rankled in its conscience. At the same time, if blacks were granted
souls, how could the Church justify the bondage of a being imbued with
immortal essence? The contradiction would be glaring. Should all
Christians, regardless of colour, be free? Dare the spiritual fathers demand
that blacks be treated as fellow Christians? If such humane questions ever
arose in the cabals of the Church authorities they were hastily dismissed.

Only an inspired and revolutionary body could have undertaken such an epoch-making programme. Instead, these high-minded souls decided that it would be better (more profitable) to find a compromise which, while allowing them to fulfil their priestly mission to spread the gospel, would leave their, and the State's, revenues intact: the christianization of slaves need not affect their status as beasts of burden – their souls would be saved for the next world. 'They [the slaves] were handicapped in religious advancement because many owners believed that baptism made the slave free, which belief was prevalently held until 1729, when the Christian nations finally reached the decision that baptism did not mean manumission and that even a Christian could be a slave.'[1]

Even after the adoption of this vicious trick the blacks still had difficulty in fulfilling their spiritual needs. It was felt that, being inhuman, they had no right to bask in the divine grace. Slave owners were opposed to their chattels being converted to the white religion on the grounds that they would then possess a soul and their enslavement would, as a result, be unjustifiable. The Church got round this by pointing out to the owners that blacks' conversion would lead to their acceptance of their plight; it would inoculate them with the idea that their owners were placed over them by divine right. 'Religious instruction was initially used as a form of social control, as this early catechism shows: "Q: What did God make you for? A: To make a crop. Q: What is the meaning of 'Thou shalt not commit adultery?' A: To serve our heavenly Father, and our earthly master, obey our overseer and not steal anything." '[2]

Thus the Church joined in the slavers' rapacity. While willing that slaves' labour should go to their owners, the Church laid firm claim on their souls.

Father Raphael, the Capuchin, in a report dated 20 December 1724, deplored the fact that masters of slaves in Louisiana were solely bent on getting profit from the work of their slaves but cared not one whit about the salvation of their souls. Many, he stated, died without baptism, but those with whom the missioners came in contact were eager for instruction.[3]

In effect, the slaves' institutionalized religious activities lay entirely in the hands of their masters, most of whom were interested in slaves' conversion only if they thought Christian mores would reduce bondsmen's inclination for freedom. In her *Journal of a Residence on a Georgia Plantation*, Frances Kemble tells of seeing slaves living in the worst possible circumstances in

spite of their master's concern for their spiritual welfare. 'This man is known
to be a hard master; his Negro houses are sheds not fit to stable beasts in; his
slaves are ragged, half-naked, and miserable; yet he is urgent for their
religious comforts, and writes to Mr Butler about "their souls – their
precious souls".' And she goes on, about a white Baptist minister: '[he] is
very zealous in the cause of their spiritual wellbeing. He, like most Southern
men, clergy or others, jump the present life in their charities to the slaves,
and go on to furnish them with all the requisite conveniences for the next.'

And that was Christianity's promise to the slaves: do your work for the
white race and we'll guarantee you a place in the heavenly choir. In light of
this tailor-made fraud the white slavers encouraged the belief in the white
god, holding those blacks whom they found fitted their mode up as examples
of the enlightened pagan. Among these were the three famous black poets of
the colonial era, Jupiter Hammon, Phillis Wheatley and George Moses
Horton. Hammon (1715?–1802), says Marion Berghahn, 'conformed exactly
to "Sambo", the obedient type of slave, which was so dear to the hearts of
many slave masters'.[5] His 'The Kind Master and the Dutiful Servant'
certainly bears this out:

> Master
> Come, my servant, follow me,
> According to thy place;
> And surely God will be with thee
> And send thee heavenly grace.
> Servant
> Dear Master, that's my whole delight,
> Thy pleasure for to do;

In his 'An Address to the Negroes of the State of New York' (1787),
published at his ever generous master's expense, he says,

> Who of us dare dispute with God! He has commanded us to obey, and we
> ought to do it cheerfully and freely. This should be done by us, not only
> because God commands, but because our own peace and comfort depend
> on it. As we depend upon our masters for what we eat and drink and wear,
> and for all our comfortable things in this world, we cannot be happy
> unless we please them. This we cannot do without obeying them
> freely . . .

In his 'Address to Phillis Wheatley' he waxes fulsome, 'O come you pious youth! Adore the wisdom of thy God, in bringing thee from distant shore, to learn his holy word', and then goes on to remind her that she might have had the misfortune to have been left in the dark terrain of Africa and to have missed out on the riches of the Christian faith. As for Wheatley (1753–84), she couldn't have agreed more with him. Of Senegalese origin, she was stolen at the age of six and sold in Boston to a slaver whom Berghahn has the audacity to call 'a well-to-do and honest Methodist', and to state that his was a 'very religious house'. What kind of sense does that make? Can an adult who enslaves a child be 'religious'? Can a trader in human flesh and blood be 'honest'? Phillis the Senegalese was taken from the mother who gave birth to her, was deprived of her culture, that she might toil for a rich wretch who appeased his guilty conscience by instructing her in his religion, the brainwashing effects of which are clear from her poems:

> 'Twas mercy brought me from my pagan land,
> Taught my benighted soul to understand
> That there's a God, that there's a Saviour too;
> Once I redemption neither sought nor knew.

and

> I, young in my life, by seeming cruel fate
> Was snatched from Afric's fancy'd happy seat:
> What pangs excruciating must molest,
> What sorrows labour in my parent's breast?

Horton (1797–1883) presents a happy contrast to his poetical converts. An autodidact, his poems reflect his unwillingness to accept slavery as his fate.

> Alas! am I born for this,
>   To wear this slavish chain?
> Deprived of all created bliss,
>   Through hardship, toil and pain!
>
> How long have I in bondage lain,
>   And languished to be free!
> Alas! and I must still complain –
>   Deprived of liberty.

Horton hoped to buy his freedom and return to Africa, but his publisher stole his royalties, and he had to wait thirty years — until abolition — to gain his freedom.

In spite of what some authors — for instance, those who believe that a slaver can also be a moral person — would have us believe, most converted slaves never put their faith in Christianity, but used it as a ritual to mask their own beliefs. What happened throughout Latin America happened north of the border too: Christianity became a *black* way of worship, a means by which Afro-folk could testify to their beliefs without having the slaver on their backs. The whites, seeing the blacks talking about Jesus, believed that they were convinced by the rigmarole; little did they suspect — for it was common knowledge that blacks hadn't any intelligence — that the slaves' method of outsmarting their owners was to pretend to be as stupid as the whites thought they were. Not for a moment did the majority of black folk believe in the white minister who preached that they ought to be grateful for bondage; not for an instant did they put credence in a religion founded upon duplicity.

They say we are the Lawd's children, I don't say that ain't true,
But if we are the same like each other, ooh, well, well, why do they treat
　me like they do?

Dubois's summation of the history of the Christian Church and black people is as true today as it was throughout the whole of the period of slavery.

This paper is a frank attempt to express my belief that the Christian Church will do nothing conclusive or effective; that it will not settle these problems; that, on the contrary, it will as long as possible and wherever possible avoid them . . .

The proof of this to me lies chiefly in the history of the Christian Church and Negro slavery in America . . . we cannot forget that under the aegis and protection of the religion of the Prince of Peace — a religion which was meant for the lowly and unfortunate — there arose in America one of the most stupendous institutions of human slavery that the world has seen. The Christian Church sponsored and defended this institution, despite occasional protest and effort at amelioration here and there. The Catholic Church approved of and defended slavery; the Episcopal Church defended and protected slavery; the Puritans and Congregationalists recognized and upheld slavery; the Methodists and Baptists stood staunchly behind it; the Quakers gave their consent to it. Indeed, there was not a single branch of the Christian Church that did not in the end become part of an impregnable bulwark defending the trade in human beings and the holding of them as chattel slaves.[6]

With the passage of time the blacks remade the Christian Church in their own image, blending into it so much of their innate spirit that the whites complained that they were defiling it.

> In the *blacks'* quarter, the coloured people get together and sing for hours together, lengthened out with long repetition *choruses*. These are all sung in the merry chorus-manner of the Southern harvest field, or husking-frolic method, of the slave blacks; and also very greatly like the Indian dances . . . Who in the name of religion, can countenance or tolerate such gross perversions of true religion! But the evil is only occasionally condemned.[7]

These 'perversions' were the forerunners of the spiritual, that quintessentially black form of worship, in which Israel was used as a synonym for the black people's home and Egypt for idolatrous America. In the eyes of the slaves the Bible became a book of incidents paralleling their proper struggle; the lessons drawn from it acted as a crutch in putting up with the insupportable until the wrath of the Lord smote the infidels from the face of the earth. Of course, the Bible was but the hypocritical code of the oppressor.

> I realized that the Bible had been written by white men. I knew that, according to many Christians, I was a descendant of Ham, who had been cursed, and that I was therefore predestined to be a slave. This had nothing to do with anything I was, or contained, or could become; my fate had been sealed for ever, from the beginning of time.
>   . . . The Africans put it another way: when the white man came to Africa, the white man had the Bible and the African the land, but now it is the white man who is being, reluctantly and bloodily, separated from the land, and the African who is still attempting to digest or to vomit up the Bible.[8]

Or, as the black Americans say:

> White man use a whip
> White man use a trigger,
> But the Bible and Jesus
> Made a slave of the nigger.

The poisonous effect of the gospel of the White Shepherd permeates the whole of black American culture, which is, in the final analysis, a reaction to the white way of life. For to live a life of duplicity, blacks were at once proud of and ashamed of themselves, of the blues, of their colour, their hair, their features, their manners, even their way of thinking. The very gospels they read were illustrated with moving pageants of blond-haired, blue-eyed prophets and devils whose wicked features were encased in black. For four hundred years black people have been beguiled and betrayed by the Church of Christ: a pitiful record for a religion supposedly founded on faith, hope and charity. 'Come,' its new motto said, 'and I will make slaves of men.'

The White Shepherd, as seen by former slaves, is best illustrated by the following extracts.

I

We went to the white folks' church, so we sit in the back on the floor. They allowed us to join their church whenever one got ready to join or felt that the Lord had forgiven them of their sins. We told our determination; this is what we said: 'I feel that the Lord has forgiven me for my sins. I have prayed and I feel that I am a better girl. I belong to Master So and So and I am so old.' The white preacher would then ask our miss and master what they thought about it and if they could see any change. They would get up and say: 'I notice she don't steal and I notice she don't lie as much and I notice she works better.' Then they let us join. We served our mistress and master in slavery time and not God.

II

They had preaching one Sunday for white folks and one Sunday for black folks. They used the same preacher there, but some coloured preachers would come on the place at times and preach under the trees down at the quarters. They said the white peacher would say, 'You may get to the kitchen of heaven if you obey your master, if you don't steal, if you tell no stories,' etc.

III

The niggers didn't go to the church building; the preacher came and preached to them in their quarters. He'd just say, 'Serve your masters.

Don't steal your master's turkey. Don't steal your master's chickens. Don't steal your master's hogs. Don't steal your master's meat. Do whatsomever your master tells you to do.' Same old thing all the time.

IV

When Grandma was fourteen or fifteen years old, they locked her up in the seedhouse once or twice for not going to church. You see, they let the white folks go to the church in the morning and the coloured folks in the evening, and my grandma didn't always want to go. She would be locked up in the seed bin, and she would cuss the preacher out so he could hear her. She would say, 'Master, let us out.' And he would say, 'You want to go to church?' And she would say, 'No, I don't want to hear that same old sermon: Stay out of your missus' and master's henhouse. Don't steal your missus' and master's chickens. Stay out of your missus' and master's smokehouse. Don't steal your missus' and master's hams.' I don't steal nothing. Don't need to tell me not to.'

She was telling the truth, too. She didn't steal because she didn't have to. She had plenty without stealing. She got plenty to eat in the house. But the other slaves didn't git nothing but fat meat and corn bread and molasses. And they got tired of that same old thing. They wanted something else sometimes. They'd go to the henhouse and get chickens. They would go to the smokehouse and get hams and lard. And they would get flour and anything else they wanted, and they would eat something they wanted. There wasn't no way to keep them from it.

V

One time when an old white man came along who wanted to preach, the white people gave him a chance to preach to the niggers. The substance of his sermon was this: 'Now when you servants are working for your masters, you must be honest. When you go to the mill, don't carry along an extra sack and put some of the meal or the flour in for yourself. And when you women are cooking in the big house, don't make a big pocket under your dress and put a sack of coffee and a sack of sugar and other things you want in it.'

They took him out and hanged him for corrupting the morals of the slaves.[9]

GOD GOT A CLEAN KITCHEN TO PUT YOU IN

There wasn't no church on the plantation where I stay. Had preaching in Mr Ford's yard sometimes, and then another time the slaves went to white people's church at Bear Swamp. Boss tell slaves to go to meeting 'cause he say he pay the preacher. Dean Ears, white man, gave out speech to the slaves one day there to Nichols. Slaves sat in gallery when they go there. He tell them to obey they master and missus. Then he say, 'God got a clean kitchen to put you in. You think you gwine be free, but you ain't gwine be free long as there an ash in Ashpole Swamp.' White folks complain 'bout the slaves getting two sermons and they get one. After that, they tell old slaves not to come to church till after the white folks had left. That never happen till after the war was over.

TWO WAYS OF PREACHING THE GOSPEL

I been preaching the gospel and farming since slavery time. I jined the church 'most 83 years ago when I was Major Gaud's slave, and they baptizes me in the spring branch close to where I finds the Lord. When I starts preaching I couldn't read or write and had to preach what Master told me, and he say tell them niggers iffen they obeys the master they goes to Heaven; but I knowed there's something better for them, but daren't tell them 'cept on the sly. That I done lots. I tells 'em iffen they keeps praying, the Lord will set 'em free.[10]

The Rise of the Black Church

The steamroller of white racism made it inevitable, once the oppressors had deemed it worth their while to inoculate them with it, that blacks should adopt Christianity as their religion. Besides the fact that the masters prevented them from practising African creeds, black people, mentally brainwashed with the belief that 'white was right', came to adopt white attitudes to life, one of which was the turn-the-cheek syndrome as preached (but not practised) by their white brothers in Christendom. Blinded by the murky word of the minister they came to half-believe in the idea of biblical humility — that is, that it didn't matter how much they suffered on earth as long as they prepared their souls for the kingdom of heaven.

In spite, however, of such success as that of the fierce Maroons, the Danish blacks and others, the spirit of revolt gradually died away under the untiring energy and superior strength of the slave masters. By the middle of the eighteenth century the black slave had sunk, with hushed murmurs, to his place at the bottom of a new economic system, and was unconsciously ripe for a new philosophy of life. Nothing suited his condition then better than the doctrines of passive submission embodied in the newly learned Christianity. Slave masters early realized this, and cheerfully aided religious propaganda within certain bounds. The long system of repression and degradation of the Negro tended to emphasize the elements of his character which made him a valuable chattel: courtesy became humility, moral strength degenerated into submission, and the exquisite native appreciation of the beautiful became an infinite capacity for dumb suffering. The Negro, losing the joy of this world, eagerly seized upon the offered conceptions of the next; the avenging Spirit of the Lord enjoining patience in this world, under sorrow and tribulation until the Great Day when he should lead his dark children home – this became his comforting dream. His Preacher repeated the prophecy, and his bards sang:

> Children, we shall all be free
> When the Lord shall appear![11]

Once the whites' religion had been foisted on the slaves, the advent of 'black' Christianity was inevitable. First, because whites were in no manner prepared to worship alongside blacks; and, by and large, they still aren't. Second, the African concept of life made the blackening of Christianity a foregone conclusion due to the unique brand of religious fervour of black peoples with its source in the African psyche, the characteristics of which are abundantly manifested in the black style of worship. In short, the African psyche is *the spirit behind the people*. The oft-noted rhythm of black people is but the product of this spirit; and spirit, as we know, gives a subject its innate character. In this is to be found the inherent differences of different races and cultures, as well as the qualities of individuals. Clearly, then, black people were predestined to manifest any religion or way of life in a determinedly African fashion. Had they been transported to the moon and indoctrinated in its spiritual creed they would still have testified in their own way: the First Lunar Sanctified Church would have rocked in much the same way as do storefront tabernacles of Harlem. In the racial context, the concept of Fate has an unequivocal meaning: though it can be modified, the true nature (spirit) of a people can neither be created nor destroyed.

As far as institutionalized worship is concerned, blacks are no more 'religious' than whites – in the US both groups attend church in about equal proportions. Moreover, Sunday-go-to-meetings are largely social affairs from which no conclusions about faith or morals can be drawn. What differentiates blacks from whites is their belief in the existence of 'invisible forces' with whom they must come to terms. So individualistic is this belief that there are probably as many ways of handling the situation as there are Afro-Americans. The fact that white America has taught blacks to look upon these impulses as 'superstitions' has, while making them unwilling to verbalize these thoughts, not been able to remove them entirely. For, in truth, people of African descent are better identified by their mental make-up than by the colour of their skin. Herskovits broaches the subject this way:

> Underlying the life of the American Negro is a deep religious bent that is but the manifestation here of a similar drive that, everywhere in Negro societies, makes the supernatural a major focus of interest. The tenability of this position is apparent when it is considered how, in an age marked by scepticism, the Negro has held fast to belief.[12]

With their conversion to the teachings of Christ, blacks put all the fervour and faith they had once exhibited for Marie Laveau and the Voodoos into Christianity. Though he might be white, Jesus, according to the good book, was a most righteous man, who had gone out of his way to aid the needy and comfort the distressed. The Bible, with its archly painted goodies and baddies, could not but be conceived by the blacks as mirroring their life. Moral right was on their side, and it was a matter of time before an indignant God smote the Pharisees into the dust. Surely the zeal of the early black church meetings must have matched the most enthusiastic gatherings depicted in the Bible: apart from their religious 'bent', the blacks had no other way of socially expressing themselves, and so the church meeting became their theatre, their music hall, their costume ball, their opportunity for oratory and their social centre. Debarred from politics, the army, education, medicine and the arts, they naturally turned the only place in which they were allowed to congregate into a forum for all their suppressed talents. Many a would-be diplomat and frustrated general found a subsidiary outlet for talent in the pulpit; countless would-be actors have, in the guise of preachers, displayed their histrionic talents to pious but none the less noisy audiences. Protestations of faith worthy of being recorded in the annals of religion have been witnessed in these makeshift shrines. For these idolatrous wailings were the supplications of a downtrodden, brutalized, starving, afflicted, agonized – martyred and crucified – people. And, as far as they could tell, there was no end to the terror and work; the torment would end only with their death. On bended knees they asked, 'How long?' With shrieks of frenzy they pleaded for release from the labyrinth of horrors. Possessed by the holy spirit for a few moments, they experienced the forbidden joys of freedom, that sweet gift forever denied them. Together, a family bound tighter by suffering, they lifted their voices in a mighty chorus, beseeching God with songs of praise and hope, of redemption and deliverance.

> . . . relatively early, the Church, and particularly the independent Negro Church, furnished the one and only organized field in which the slave's suppressed emotions could be released, and the only opportunity for him to develop his own leadership. In almost every other area he was completely suppressed . . . Thus, through a slow and difficult process, often involving much suffering and persecution, the Negro, more than three quarters of a century prior to emancipation, through initiative, zeal and ability, began to achieve the right to be free in his Church. He demonstrated his ability to preach; and this demonstration convinced both Negroes and whites that he was possessed of the Spirit of God.[13]

As the spiritual head of this suffering community the black preacher assumed the role of chief. The servant of God and the interpreter of his word, he was revered as their counsellor and spokesman. In this, his personality played no small role: he had to inspire respect no less by his sensitivity than by his strength. He had to be able to instil the fear of the Lord into his flock, and to invest it with the holy spirit. He had to possess a good, strong voice and seemingly endless reserves of energy, to whip his flock into the ecstasy of worship. His sermons must ring true – to admonish sin and demand repentance.

To achieve his ends, the black preacher *performs* his sermons. Standing straight and stiff would never rouse his congregation; he shouts, whispers, threatens, pleads, jumps, dances, quakes, sings – in a word, he seeks to *conjure* his flock, to bring them to the state where they can be possessed by the Holy Ghost. '*Can you feel it?*' he screams. Next instant, he is in a trance, rapt in the divine spirit, on the brink of revelation. At a flick of his hand the music mounts, the voices of the choir lift on high, and the tranquil glory of salvation descends. No black preacher will last for long if he is not a good showman, if he is no good at transmitting his emotions to his assembly. It is no good feeling called to preach if you can't make your auditors *feel* your message. This transmission and the communal experience of God is the essence of African worship. Believers know that God exists because they literally feel the power of the supernatural passing through their own minds and bodies. The 'fits' black Baptists fall into are but the 'possession' of the Vodun by the *loas*. Only the names of the gods have been changed, in order to protect the innocent. Dunham notes this in her essay on black eurhythmics.

> In North America, however, there is less compromise and more real assimilation of African religious forms into European religious ideology. In 1938–39 I had occasion to direct a group in the Federal Writers' Project in an investigation of religious and magic cults in the city. Here, while the ideology was clearly and definitely Christian (with added flourishes), the entire pattern of religious behaviour associated with it was almost as purely African. The rhythmic percussion-type handclapping and foot-stomping, the jumping and leaping, the 'conversion' or 'confession' in unknown tongues which is a form of possession or ecstasy (induced, in some cases, by a circle of 'saints' or 'angels' closing in upon the person in rhythmic motion of a dance), the frequent self-hypnosis by motor-activity of the shoulders — all these African forms were present. This last type of movement, for example, is called *zepaules* in Haiti, and is formally recognized there as a basic dance movement of great ritualistic importance in Voodoo practice. In general form, even in function, the motor activity connected with the religious expression of storefront churches in this country is strikingly similar to that of the Haitian peasant.[14]

Dubois believed that this African form of possession was the most important factor in black American religion.

> [It] was the last essential of Negro religion and the one more devoutly believed in than all the rest. It varies in expression from the silent rapt countenance or the low murmur and groan to the mad abandon of physical fervour — the stamping, shrieking and shouting, the rushing to and fro and wild waving of arms, the weeping and laughing, the vision and trance.[15]

These indications of African hangovers in the worship of the former slaves would hardly surprise anyone familiar with the black Church. What is a matter for wonder, however, is the fact that the point had to be made at all – after which one can hardly fail to conclude that the warehouse containing the myths about black people is over-filled to bursting. Herskovits summed up the evidence of these African retentions as (1) spirit possession; (2) dancing with African steps and identical motor behaviour; (3) song that derives in manner, if not in actual form, directly from Africa; (4) references to crossing the River Jordan (from the African tradition of river-crossing); (5) wakes; (6) shallow burials; (7) passing of small children over coffins; (8) inclusion of food and money in coffins; (9) fear of cursing; and (10) improvisation of songs of ridicule.[16] Compared with all this, the Christian element of black worship is actually quite small. Instead of many, there is but one God; and the Bible replaces the legends of Damballah and Shangó. But, significantly, in the black Churches this solitary deity is conjured instead of being merely worshipped. Again, whereas in the white Church music is employed in an illustrative manner, in the black it is an indispensable part of the invocation, the bridge over which the God crosses to reach the devotee – note that the deity descends into the worshipper and not vice versa. Furthermore – and this is something whites have never grasped – though the images of Christ and the saints in Afro-American churches are of white folk, blacks always think of them as black – for in America there can be no question of God being void of a colour and race. Blacks see him in their image, and whites in theirs; the devil, naturally, being imagined as his opposite. Fear alone prevented the statues of the Christian saints from being smitten with a touch of the ole tar brush as, indeed, they were in the presbyteries of Bahia and Trinidad. Some black Americans do envision God as being 'colourless', which concept is but a manifestation of their wish that America should become a 'colourless' society. Experience, however, gives eyesight to all but the blindest of these unrealistic dreamers, who wake up from their illusions with a bang.

There was once a black man named Rufus, who read his Bible daily and went to church three or four times a week. Well, one day Rufus died and went up to heaven. He thought it a splendid-looking place and couldn't wait to get in and enjoy all those blessings his irreproachable conduct merited. He went up to the gate, where he was stopped by St Peter. 'Sorry,' said the saint, 'but no blacks allowed.' 'What?' cried Rufus, 'after all the penance I done done! Well, I'll tell you what, Mister St Peter – I'm going back to Earth to kick some ass!'[17]

Baldwin, the son of a preacher and who himself trained as one in Harlem, found himself confronted with this dilemma:

> And the blood of the Lamb had not cleansed me in any way whatever. I was just as black as I had been the day that I was born . . . It probably occurred to me around this time that the vision people hold of the world to come is but a reflection, with predictable wishful distortions, of the world in which they live.[18]

The black Christian Church was the only organization the whites permitted blacks to have – it, whites felt, as it had been conceived in a white image, must have a salutary brainwashing effect on the people they wished to subject to their will. The blacks, within the limits they were able to get away with, turned it into a Church of their own, making it the base of their social and cultural life.

> The Church as a social institution and as a system of belief did perhaps give the black community an overall universal context in which it could place itself, a structure which for some was a buffer against the grimmer aspects of reality, and a refuge and a source of strength for others. It could confer status upon its elders and leaders, and the emotionality and exuberance of its services and its music provided an outlet for repressed feelings, or for shared joys.[19]

Spirituals: The Sacred Metaphor

Under slavery, music was the only art form black people were able to practise, and that only in their spare time or during church services. The odd poet, such as Phillis Wheatley, hardly constitutes a movement; and those authors, painters and composers among the freemen in the North had no outlet for their talents. For under racism as practised in America the august role of 'artist' was looked upon as something beyond the scope of a person of colour. Just as judges, doctors, educators and other professionals were white, so it was believed that artistic creativity also was the exclusive preserve of the European. Here we have an unparalleled case of a whole people being denied the employment of its creative faculties. Blacks were thought to be unimaginative, dull, stupid, insensitive – in short, incapable of participating in 'higher' spheres of thought. To the whites, they existed as beasts of burden, on whom it would be useless to expend education. Lacking other outlets, they channelled their artistic talent into their music, which early separated into two distinct but interrelated branches: spirituals and blues. The former, which flourished in the black Church, are highly complex songs of deliverance – from the dual evils of bondage and the sins of the world. They plead for a 'better day' in both this world and the next. Employed as oral talismans, they call upon God to punish the white man for the wrongs he has perpetrated against black people, and summon those people to courage and perseverance. For a people deprived of other means, they become also a weapon against the bastion of racism, the 'sorrow songs' which summed up this long-suffering people's plight. Dubois calls them, 'the music of an unhappy people, of the children of disappointment; they tell of death and suffering and unvoiced longing toward a truer world, of misty wanderings and hidden ways'.[20] Songs of burden, of lament, of weariness; mystic songs describing the event of the second coming of the Lord and the establishment of justice on the earth. 'Through all of the sorrow of the Sorrow Songs there breathes a hope – a faith in the ultimate justice of things . . . Sometime, somewhere, men will judge men by their souls and not by their skins.'[21]

The spirituals served to lift black folk momentarily out of the drudgery of their everyday round, to remind them that within themselves there burnt a divine flame which no amount of servitude could extinguish. There *was* 'a balm in Gilead' – deliverance in this world (escaping to the North), and eternal life in the next.

Another valuable function of black church music was that it bound the community closer together, keeping them always mindful of the fact that they were a single family – hence the prevalent use of the words 'sister' and 'brother' between blacks. Just as a family shares a common fate, so did all blacks in America: all had come over 'in the same boat' and were caught in the same trap. Worshipping together, singing their communion in unison, a bond stronger even than blood was formed; a black definition of life came into being, a sense of identity so powerful that blacks all know their fellow blacks so well, comprehend so fully what they have been through without ever having met them.

This song invites the believer to move closer to the very sources of black

being, and to experience the black community's power to endure and the
will to survive. The mountains may be high and the valleys low, but 'my
Lord spoke' and 'out of his mouth came fire and smoke'. All the believer
has to do is to respond to the divine apocalyptic disclosure of God's
revelation and cry, 'Have Mercy, please.' This cry is not a cry of passivity,
but a faithful, free response to the movement of the Black Spirit. It is the
black community accepting themselves as the people of the Black Spirit
and knowing through his presence that no chains can hold the Spirit of
black community in bondage . . . Black music is unity music. It unites
the joy and the sorrow, the love and the hate, the hope and the despair of
black people; and it moves the people toward the direction of total
liberation. It shapes and defines black being and creates cultural
structures for black expression. Black music is unifying because it
confronts the individual with the truth of black existence and affirms that
black being is possible only in a communal context.[22]

The lyrics of the spiritual are religious metaphors for what the blacks
dared not tell the whites outright. 'I want my freedom!' they shout. 'Get off
my back!' they cry. 'Lord, deliver me from these devils!' they wail.

> See these poor souls from Africa
> transported to America;
> We were stolen, and sold down in Georgia.
>
> Working all day
> And part of the night
> and up before the morning light.
> When will Jehovah hear our cry
> and free the sons of Africa?

The legends and personalities of the Bible become symbols of the black
situation. Zion becomes the North, the harbour of freedom; Moses and Jesus
are the harbingers of the grapes of wrath; the Devil is the white man and Hell
is Dixie.

> Don't you see that ship a-sailin'
> bound for the promised land?

In his autobiography, *Up from Slavery*, Booker T. Washington tells what
spirituals meant to him and other slaves or ex-slaves:

Most of the verses of the plantation songs had some reference to freedom. True, they had sung those same verses before, but they had been careful to explain that 'freedom' in these songs referred to the next world, and had no connection with life in this world. Now they gradually threw off the mask; and were not afraid to let it be known that freedom in their songs meant freedom of the body in this world.[23]

The Afro-Americans' chanted biblical metaphors bear testimony to the fact that throughout their age-long trial of being first slaves and then victims in the United States, their spirit has never been defeated. Whatever it is — God, gods, justice, or their race — they *still have faith*. Not in the whites, to be sure; but in the hope that some day they will be able to walk the earth without the colour of their skin being held against them. God works in strange ways: did he not cleave a dry passage for Moses betwixt the waters of the Red Sea? Then why shouldn't the blacks win the same favour?

> Deep river, my home is over Jordan, deep river.
> Lord, I want to cross over into the campground!
> O, children! O don't you want to go to that gospel feast,
> Walk into heaven and take my seat!

and

> O freedom! O freedom!
> O freedom over me!
> An' befo' I'd be a slave
> I'll be buried in my grave,
> And go home to my Lord an' be free.
>
> My Lord delivered Daniel,
> Why can't he deliver me!
>
> When Israel was in Egypt's land,
> (Let my people go!)
> Oppressed so hard they could not stand,
> (Let my people go!)
> Go down, Moses, way down in Egypt's land
> Tell ole Pharaoh,
> Let my people go!

Cone is explicit about the undying faith blacks put into the words of these songs.

> There may have been many historical and sociological causes of the freedom of black slaves; but blacks viewed it as an act of God in history analogous to Israel's exodus from Egypt. Abraham Lincoln's decision to engage in war and issue the Emancipation Proclamation was seen as God's way of making justice a reality for black slaves on earth. This is why they lifted their voices to God in song:
>
> > Slavery chain done broke at last, broke at last, broke at last,
> > Slavery chain done broke at last,
> > Going to praise God till I die.
> >
> > I did tell him how I suffer,
> > In de dungeon and de chain,
> > And de days I went with head bowed down,
> > And my broken flesh and pain.
> >
> > I did know my Jesus heard me,
> > 'Cause de spirit spoke to me,
> > And said, 'Raise my child, your chillun,
> > And you shall be free.'

And he adds: 'The meaning of the song is not contained in the bare words but in the black history that created it . . . *Black history is a spiritual!*'[24]

Yes, it is a communal history, one that is still being written. Community songs are sung in church or out of church, and sometimes without the voice — then it is a silent and lonely dirge, but no less sanctified for that. At such moments the whole of black history becomes condensed, for a few indescribably beautiful and terrifying moments, in the person of the ex-slave's descendant, who experiences the meaning behind the spirituals, and solidarity with other black people. Spirituals and the history they relate are alive because that history is still being made; blacks are still suffering its effects. Or the individual experiences this history told in song while in communion with other blacks, where he or she actually sees this history evolving, sees it living in the faces and bodies of the worshippers, and hears its passionate strains reverberating to the high heavens. In the images of this holy pandemonium is witnessed, nay, experienced, four hundred-odd years of servitude and oppression and, just as importantly, the same amount of perseverance and struggle. Then they know that this strange belief called 'faith' has not been in vain! Pledging themselves to God, they renew their commitment to their race, its struggle, and the belief in its ultimate victory. A wave of unity sweeps through them all, the clan is reunited, the family has come together again. Every eye is joyful with recognition – Brother! Sister! The proud Spirit of Blackness reigns; the song, the singer, the story and the religion are one.

There is no music like that music, no drama like the drama of the saints rejoicing, the sinners moaning, the tambourines racing, and all those voices coming together and crying holy unto the Lord. There is still, for me, no pathos quite like the pathos of those multi-coloured, worn, somehow triumphant and transfigured faces, speaking from the depths of a visible, tangible, continuing despair of the goodness of the Lord. I have never seen anything to equal the fire and excitement that sometimes, without warning, fill a church, causing the church, as Leadbelly and so many others have testified, to 'rock'. Nothing that has happened to me since equals the power and the glory that I sometimes felt when, in the middle of a sermon, I knew that I was somehow, by some miracle, really carrying, as they said, 'the Word' – when the church and I were one. Their pain and their joy were mine, and mine were theirs – they surrendered their pain and joy to me, I surrendered mine to them – and their cries of 'Amen!' and 'Hallelujah!' and 'Yes, Lord!' and 'Praise his name!' and 'Preach it, brother!' sustained and whipped on my solos until we all became equal, wringing wet, singing and dancing, in anguish, and rejoicing, at the foot of the altar.[25]

In 1867 The Nation carried this description of a black church service:

The benches are pushed back to the wall when the formal meeting is over and old and young, men and women, sprucely dressed young men, grotesquely half-clad field hands – the women generally with gay handkerchiefs twisted about their heads and with short skirts – boys with tattered shirts and men's trousers, young girls bare-footed, all stand up in the middle of the floor, and when the 'sperichil' is struck up begin first walking and by and by shuffling around, one after the other, in a ring. The foot is hardly taken from the floor, and the progression is mainly due to a jerking, hitching motion which agitates the entire shouter and soon brings out streams of perspiration. Sometimes they dance silently, sometimes as they shuffle they sing the chorus of the spiritual, and sometimes the song itself is also sung by the dancers. But more frequently a band, composed of some of the best singers and of the tired shouters, stand at the side of the room to 'base' the others, singing the body of the song and clapping their hands together or on the knees. Song and dance are alike extremely energetic, and often, when the shout lasts into the middle of the night, the monotonous thud, thud of feet prevents sleep within half a mile of the praise house.

Amen to that. Black worship is an emotional event, the aim of which is to put the devotees in a state fit to receive the fruits of the blessings of the Lord. If you're sleepy, man, you'd best stay at home, because the spirit in the praise house is wide awake. Probably, the folks those folks prevented from sleeping had been asleep all their lives and needed awakening. Black believers utilize the spiritual and the dance – their voices and their bodies – as keys to the gates of the Kingdom, as interchangeable emotional states with freedom and deliverance. The strength of their faith demands that they testify, aloud and before witnesses, that they believe that

> When I get to heaven, gonna sing and shout
> There'll be nobody there to turn me out . . .

Another impetus to these communal sessions is the fact that the institution of the Church and its spirituals antedates the black family as a monogamous unit. Slaves were sold without the slightest consideration for their family ties – the fact that you had a mother or sister or brother or husband or wife today was anything but a guarantee that you'd have one tomorrow. The flash of a wad of greenbacks or the master's bad luck in a card game, and away went your nearest and dearest. The only real and lasting family was the race, every black person, anywhere and everywhere. Thus, coming together to sing the metaphorical jubilees became a reunion of the blood, a family symposium ostensibly held in order to praise the Lord. Under these circumstances, the church house becomes 'home', and the worshippers the clan, of which the preacher is the elder. The spirituals tell the story of this family, acting as a kind of history book in song. And that is why there have never been any 'professional' composers of these hymns or, rather, every member of the race is one. These dark cantatas rise up effortlessly from the depths of their beings, mournful echoes of their tragic past. Pervaded by the murmur of that sad melody which is the legacy of blacks' colour, they tell of the twilight of the olden days and the dawning of the new. The contents of these songs imply an effort towards the improvement of the black condition, the acceptance of the task and the determination to reach the goal. They prophesy the day when Sister Spiritual and Brother Metaphor will cross over the River Jordan.

Dealin' with the Devil

Concurrent with the rise of the spiritual, another kind of black music was being born, taking its shape from the same circumstances but interpreting them in an altogether different fashion. In lieu of placing its emphasis upon God, it dealt with the world as it is, in concrete and blatant terms. Still, as with the spirituals, its subject was the black experience, which is to say hardship and trouble. It focused on the realities of black life: racism, poverty, loneliness, suffering, work, love, human foibles and despair. In its own uncompromising way it too 'testified' to the black spirit, but in an earthy, all-too-human (for some) manner, its bold strokes faithfully mirroring the hardship which was the blacks' lot. In no uncertain terms it spoke of how the black people felt and, perhaps more importantly, who they were. Whereas the spirituals, by their Christian nature, linked blacks – however tenuously – with whites, the blues were totally black, a music which had come into being as a means of communication solely for that community. It spoke to them not about heaven, but about themselves; its 'revelation' was of their own weary lives.

Meanwhile, the black Church was doing all in its power to live up to the white concepts upon which it was founded. Hence, it was as natural as it was inevitable that it should see blues music as its enemy. For all its 'blackening' it was and has remained grounded in European traditions, a fact which put it in direct opposition to blues music which is, ideologically, rooted in African customs. The idea that blacks dislike blues because it reminds them of the 'bad old days' is a myth propagated by the black Church to cover its pro-white anti-black stance. For there can be no question of blacks not being reminded of those times – since they're still living them. Or are these supposed to be 'the good times'? If so, somebody had better announce it over

the radio, otherwise black people will never know. To those who believe that
these are the best of times I can only reply that in a free country you're free to
cling to any illusion you take a fancy to.

The truth is that the black Church didn't want to share its power over the
black community, for it early realized its position as the sole organized
institution among this otherwise wholly disenfranchised group. In 1900
there were over 24,000 black churches, or one for every sixty black families.
Their power was enormous, and Dubois says of them that, 'Such churches are
really governments . . .'[26] Just as their white counterparts had done in the
past, the black ministers went on a crusade to enforce the members of their
parishes to become, to act like, and to think like Christians. Anyone who
might see things differently was instantly branded as a friend of the Devil's.
The blues, in laying bare the facts of life – in speaking of sex, booze and good
times – was decried as being composed of songs inspired by the Wicked One,
bruited about the world in order to lead Jesus's lambs astray. In his history of
the blues, *The Devil's Music*, Giles Oakley sums up this fear on the part of the
Church of these unholy chants.

> There was however a parallel world to that of the Church, the world of
> secular amusement which lay alongside it, uneasily and with much
> tension; this was where the blues were sung. Their music considered
> 'sinful', or 'the Devil's music', blues singers were constantly being called
> to repentance, and children were always being warned away from the
> blues by their parents.[27]

This concept of the blues as singing praises to the Devil arose also because
of its Hoodoo elements. To the black Church these were no airy-fairy
musings but very real reminders of, throwbacks to African religion.
Hoodoo-Voodoo-Africa-Pantheism. Very un-Christian. The lyrics of the
blues make potent and overt reference to the faith they place in these
non-Western powers. Instead of appealing to Jesus, the blues singers say that
they're going to get themselves a *mojo*, that they're going to sprinkle goofer
dust around their babies' doors; instead of the Bible they consult with
Gypsies:

> I got a Gypsy woman giving me advice,
> I got a whole lot of tricks, keeping them on ice:
> I got my *mojo* working
> but it just won't work on you!

This was too black for the black Church. Hoodoo! Why, that would lead blacks right back to the jungle! The blues singer was the bane of the community.

The blues especially were the opposite side of sacred – blues singers went directly to hell, did not pass go, did not collect anything. You could sing gospel or the blues, but never both. The blues belonged to the Devil, with his high-rollin' ways and high-yellow women, and if you sang his music, the door to the Lord's house was shut to you . . . It was said from the pulpit that the Devil himself lived on Beale Street, and the blues was his music.[28]

Having committed itself to bringing its people into the mainstream of American life, the Church sought to get them to rid themselves of anything which might be a reminder of their origin. They were 'Americans', not Africans; and they were Christians and not Hoodooists. If they couldn't look white, at least they could act it. They must rid their very souls of their blackness, and refill them with the WASP ingredient.

The more conscientious Christian ministers among the slaves sought to get rid of 'all dem hedun ways', but it was difficult. For instance, the Christian Church saw dancing as an evil worldly excess, but dancing as an integral part of the African's life could not be displaced by the still white notes of the *Wesleyan Hymnal* . . . The Churches called sinful all the 'fiddle songs', 'devil songs', and 'jig tunes' – even the 'corn songs' were outlawed by some Church elders. Also, certain musical instruments, such as the violin and banjo, were said to be the devil's own.[29]

So white American culture was being bought at the price of the blacks' identity. In order to be American they must cut themselves off from their roots, and then, like actors in an old-time farce, don the masks of their oppressors. This show, played out daily on that stage which is the nation, would be a hilarious comedy if it were not such a sad tragedy. If all the dues black people have paid in America don't suffice to ensure their nationality, nothing ever will. The black Church's attempt to bring this about by influencing its congregation's soul has been a mistake of enormous proportions, from which only the direst consequences may be expected. Given the history of the country, it's hard to understand that blacks ever really believed that whites would accept blacks as 'equals'. Such a thought could have been inspired only in heaven, the laws of which place have no sway in the USA. All the black people's struggles were being sold down the river for a white song. And this was possible only because the self-constituted black leaders had embraced the whites' ways to the extent that they had lost their identity, as Leroi Jones points out: 'It was the growing black middle class who believed that the best way to survive in America would be to *disappear* completely, leaving no trace at all that there had ever been an African, or slavery, or even, finally, a black man. This was the only way, they thought, to be *citizens*.'[30] The adoption of this white spiritual persona meant that the blues would have to go. Singing and dancing must be performed only in church and in praise of the Lord. There must be no making of music which lauded pure, simple black life or black heroes. Love, when not conducted under the aegis of the minister, was a sin; sex out of wedlock was too damning even to be mentioned. Bluespeople sang of it because they were immoral, their fate already sealed. For in the matter of sex, blacks became just as frustrated as the whites.

What are we to make of such blatant descriptions of sexual love? Theologically, the blues reject the Greek distinction between the body and the soul, the physical and the spiritual. They tell us that there is no wholeness without sex, no authentic love without the feel and touch of the physical body. The blues affirm the authenticity of sex as the bodily expression of black soul.[31]

Yaller gal make a preacher lay his Bible down,
Good-lookin' high brown make him run from town to town.

The blues speaks about the facts of life, and if it doesn't it fails in its purpose. Now, sex may be immoral, but it's certainly going down. Blues singers leave the tales about virgin births to the preacher and tell their stories *'like it is'*. The day the blues begins to speak falsehoods or gloss over reality will mark its end as a living folk culture. Likewise, the day it rids itself of its Africanisms, it will become simply another 'American' form of entertainment, a thing to be listened to in between television commercials. The blues singers' function in the black community depends upon their depicting life in all its glory and deprivation. And the day they sing false their people will turn their backs on them, and seek truth elsewhere. So far, notwithstanding the Church's urgent warnings, the community has ever given blues performers credence, placing such a degree of faith in them that the blues has become known as a 'secular' religion – yet another reason it incurred the black minister's wrath. Why 'religion'? Because underlying the blues is the *faith* of the singer in black life; and the people's faith that he or she has faithfully described it.

> The blues are 'secular spirituals'. They are *secular* in the sense that they confine their attention solely to the immediate and affirm the bodily expression of the black soul, including its sex manifestations. They are *spirituals* because they are impelled by the same search for the truth of black experience.
>
> Like the spirituals, the blues affirm the somebodiness of black people, and they preserve the worth of black humanity through ritual and drama. The blues are a transformation of black life through the sheer power of song. They symbolize the solidarity, the attitudes and the identity of the black community and thus create the emotional forms of reference for endurance and aesthetic appreciation.[32]

The Church's 'devil' stance was taken over by the blues community and put to use to boost its aura. Singer Peetie Wheatstraw called himself the Devil's Son-in-law, and making a pact with the devil in order to become an outstanding musician became one of the accepted facts of blues lore. Bluespeople came to think of themselves as 'outsiders' to Christian religion, and in many cases even as damned souls, as Bessie Smith sings in her 'Blue Spirit Blues':

> Had a dream last night that I was dead
> Evil spirits all around my bed.
>
> The Devil came an' grabbed my hand
> Took me 'way down to that redhot land.

Peg Leg Howell complained that, 'I cannot shun the devil, he stays right by my side'; while Hoodoo Slim frankly admitted: 'Some folks believe in Jehu . . . ah, well, boys . . . Ah'm hooked on Hoodoo.'

But the dividing line between the blues and spirituals, and the role of the blues singer and the preacher has never been clearly defined: their roles overlap to the extent that they are often interchangeable. The blues crooner doesn't merely sing, he or she preaches in the same conjuring fashion as the man of God. Moreover, the symbolism employed is the same for, in the

black world, everybody needs salvation, and whether it's heavenly or earthly
is a moot point. Son House was one of the many bluespeople to 'find
religion', as he explains in his 'Preaching the Blues':

Oh I'm gon' get me religion, I'm gon' join the Baptist Church
I'm gonna be a Baptist preacher, and I sure won't have to work.

Oh I'm gonna preach these blues now, and I want everybody to shout,
Mmmmm, and I want everybody to shout,
I'm gon' do like a prisoner, I'm gonna roll my time out.

Oh in my room I bowed down to pray,
Say the blues come along, and they drove my spirit away.

Oh I had religion, Lord, this very day,
But the womens and whiskey, well, they would not let me pray.

Salome Arnold's 'Urban Voodoo Juice' is in a like vein, but unlike House she
is 'saved':

I took a peek into the dark
I took a trip to Babylon
I found and broke the Seventh Seal
And now the devil's after me, Lord help me if you will:

I was a bad mother-for-you, you can ask my friends
I was drinking Urban Voodoo Juice from beginning to end
I dropped my cross but I picked it up again
Oh Lord they got your blessed child hooked on Urban Voodoo Juice
    again.

Henry and Vernell Townsend, two dedicated Mississippi blues performers, told Giles Oakley in an interview in 1976 how they view 'the Devil's'
tag and the music itself:

HENRY: The Devil's music – don't think the Devil care for the truth, do
you? . . . So, the truth is, I guess I stick to my blues as the blues, and I'm
not afraid to play them because I'm gonna go to the burning place,
whatever it is. I'm not afraid of that!

VERNELL: I've heard old people say, down through the years, 'Oh, that's the Devil's music,' and then they give you a Bible quote, you know. They'll say, 'Because the Bible said "Make a joyful noise unto the Lord!" ' you know? They give you this reason. It *does* say that, but it doesn't say what *kind* of joyful noise to make to the Lord! The blues can be just as joyful as a spiritual.[33]

Taking its cue from Rome, the black Church sought to outlaw the blues and defame its practitioners, placing black secular music on a kind of moral Index of Forbidden Songs. Spirituals were the 'official' music of the Church, and the 'acceptable' songs of the community. The blues was taboo.

The Initiations

There are certain areas of black culture which are closed to the uninitiated.

Margo Crawford

Blue Hoodoo Man Blues

You'd better hear my warnin'
I'm gettin' madder every day
I don't want you to get so clean, baby
You just might wash your soul away!

Albert King

The Hoodoo Church was gone, sacrificed in the hope that if its followers shed their African identity they would become acceptable in the society in which they lived. Possibly it was one of the most expensive sell-outs in the history of the world, and, since the rulers of that society held all the trumps, it was a highly unlikely gamble. How this pitiably loaded game turned out is too well-known for details to be necessary. The blacks' bartering of their true Church for acceptance proved to be the height of folly. There is an African song which aptly describes the Afro-Americans' ordeal of their lost homeland:

> Marassaelo, I have no mother here who can speak for me;
> Marassaelo, I have left my mother in Africa

Luckily for them, blacks were still in possession of the 'invisible' side of their religion: folklore, slang, dances, cuisine and above all, music; in short, a *black* way of viewing and interpreting the world. But unlike their Haitian cousins they were no longer prepared from earliest youth to be receptive to things African; they were no longer sure if the tales of worship and power, of magic and healing, were true or false, miracles or superstitions. Were they to give credence to Hoodoo when they had never seen anyone possessed by a *loa*? Everything in their upbringing, their whole environment, denied its possibility; their Christian backgrounds told them that all those old stories were but stuff and nonsense, tricks used by the wily to overawe the gullible. But from whence, then, came those vague but all too real visions which assailed their minds during solitude? From whence those shrouded visitors who came in the night, who whispered things which, though half-understood, yet jolted them back to a sense of their true identity? These 'recognitions' – if they may be so called – were the core of Afro-Americans' personal *and* national dilemma: they *were* African too; or, to paint the problem in bolder colours, they were neither one nor the other – and they believed themselves to be both!

The Bluesman both personified and solved this bewildering situation. The epitome of the enigma, he was an American who believed in Hoodoo: he gave it free rein in his thoughts; it directed his seemingly directionless wanderings; it ensured his success in love and his luck in gambling. With its powers he could afford to be a rolling stone – sure to overcome any impasse the world threw in front of him.

Churchless, he praised God in his songs, and his listeners were reminded of the powers of the *loas*, of the forces the enemy could not understand, of their past glory and the history of their native land. These powers were their birthright; they symbolized and brought into focus those half-felt thoughts, those forms which unexpectedly dropped in during the night.

Music is one of the principal aspects of African religion – a manifestation of the gods themselves. It participates in the 'sacred' in the African mind, which – excuse the analogy – conceives of it as an indivisible trinity comprised of rhythm, dance and sound; that it should lack one of these is a concept alien to Africans' minds. To them music is *matter* and cannot exist without shape, form and mass. An African definition of music might be expressed as 'a movement born of sound'. This sound as traced by the human body is dance. Africans re-create the sound with their bodies and mimic it with their voices, the greatest of which is, for them, the drum. As the most consummate of manifestations, music is most worthy of being the vehicle of transport to the gods – it is the supreme offering, a synthesis of devotion, the ritual of power in motion. The body, the voice, become invocations to the Supreme. It is the means by which Africans overcome the opposition of the rational and break through to make contact with the spiritual: through music they come to the collective unconscious of the Ancestors. Freed from their everyday selves, they find their true selves, the essence of their beings, the Spirits of their blood. This magic called music is the key, the *open sesame* to the treasure house of the stored images of the primeval past. Having crossed the threshold they are in the presence of the gods, of the eternal messages of, specifically, their race, and universally, of Mankind.

In African religions the drums *speak* — they are the *guides* — and the worshippers' dance and voices complete the offering. The whole is the visible manifestation of the invisible messages being received. If participants achieve total contact with them they become 'possessed' — the god has taken over and controls them, their dance then becomes a hieroglyph of the god's personality.

Black Americans were divorced from all this — they had no natural organized Church of their own, no *houngan*, no rites, no prayers — in short, no ceremonial by which to give interpretation to their spiritual needs. The society they lived in had uprooted and destroyed all but the haziest remnants of their religion, which was now represented only by the rare Hoodoo Queen or Root Doctor. Besides, things were so contrived that they had to give nearly all their time to worrying about existence in a land of unrelenting hostility where their very colour was tantamount to a crime and relegated them to *official* poverty. Composed of violence and poverty, their life was a recipe for hopelessness.

On this bleak, troubled landscape there appeared a man . . . He was as poor and harassed as the rest of his brethren; as wretched and uneducated, as persecuted and disenfranchised as the rest. And yet, he was somehow different, possessing some kind of mysterious power, he posed an inexplicable threat to the order of things. He was a lone, restless, unstable figure; his shiftless, trouble-ridden life seemed the very synthesis of the black man's problem. As as such he posed a challenge to what the country stood for, and, more importantly, to his own people: if nothing else he was *free*. After all, there was a hint of defiance in his holding up his blue mirror in front of these people, singing of brown-skinned gals, jook dancing, and hootchie-cootchie. 'Look,' he seemed to say, 'and be proud of yourselves!' Of course he affected different people in different ways — some loved and others hated him. Some thought it best to forget the past; others to remember and cherish it. Those who saw 'black' as a stigma berated him for his 'nigger' ways, while others rejoiced that here was a man who had not lost his roots. The black Christian Churches, as we have seen, condemned him for playing 'the Devil's music'.

He was an unwelcome, incongruous figure, a would-be artist in a land which, having refused to acknowledge that blacks had ever had a culture, refused to credit him with the ability to participate in 'art' — *that* was the preserve of white people; artists came from Boston or New York and preferably from Europe. And since black people had long ago been relegated to their 'place', there was no need for them to have spokesmen.

Bluesman: the name itself sums up the black man's predicament. Maligned and misunderstood, he yet created the most important art form in American culture.

Far away, in the mysterious lands of Africa, when the griots (itinerant folksingers) pass, both men and women spit to show their contempt, for these singers are poets and sorcerers, and the people are afraid of what they do not understand . . . these singers have eyes full of nostalgia and their steps sink into dream's thickets. In dreams truer than reality the *loas* speak to them . . . reality was nought but the shade of a dream . . . [these men] form a world unto themselves . . .[1]

Can't You Hear Me when I Call?

Got one mind for the boss to see.
Got another mind for what I know is me.

The blues is a direct expression of the baneful dichotomy which characterizes being black in America, the phychological and moral scission of being an ex-slave now become free, and a national of a country where skin-colour determines destiny. In order to survive, black people had to develop a mental defence of double dealing, of making the whites believe that they accepted their lot. They had to pretend that they were 'good' slaves. They had to act as if they were stupid. And as if they were incapable of seeing the gross discrepancy between the whites' supposed belief in the words of Christ and their actions. In short, slaves had to deceive their owners in order to stay alive. 'Another ingredient of slave ethics was deception. To survive in an oppressive society, it is necessary to outsmart the oppressors and make them think that you are what you know you are not. It is to make them believe that you accept their definitions of black and white.'[2]

This duality permeated every aspect of black life: religion, conversation, social behaviour and more. And it does so today, for Afro-Americans have never felt *entirely* free in America. Indeed, I make so bold as to postulate the existence of two different kinds of freedom at large in the land, one white and the other black. What 'white' freedom is I am in no position to say – not having had the honour of being born in that condition. Black freedom is a very ambivalent thing: it is a very exciting, and sometimes even frightening, *condition*. For it arises from man-made circumstances, maintained and supported by white Americans. 'Such a double life,' noted Dubois, 'with double thoughts, double duties and double social classes, must give rise to double words and double ideals, and tempt the mind to pretence or to revolt, to hypocrisy or to radicalism.'[3]

The roots of the blues lie in a religion the blacks practised when whites weren't around – for like everything else from their homelands, African religion was proscribed. A knowledge of this 'invisible' religion is mandatory for a true comprehension of what the blues is about, for it employs words and metaphors which were originally meant for blacks only, and many, though in current usage, have become singularly distorted. A vast gulf separates the person who possesses the 'keys' to the blues and someone who doesn't. The former experiences the insights of the blues, the latter only the sound. Of course, music can be enjoyed solely for its melodies and poetry, but its magic comes alive if its 'message' can be understood. And the blues is a music which has a story to tell.

Blind to the richness of Afro-American folklore, and ignorant of the history which produced it, most people think of the blues as 'jive' or 'dance' music; they are guests at a feast who have lost their sense of taste.

There is a music in me, the music of a peasant people. I wander through the levee, picking my banjo and singing my songs of the cabin and the field. At the Last Chance Saloon I am as welcome as the violets of March; there is always food and drink for me there, and the dimes of those who love honest music. Behind the railroad tracks the little children clap their hands and love me as they love Kris Kringle. But I fear that I am a failure. Last night a woman called me a troubadour. What is a troubadour?[4]

The Bluesman as Artist

I'm walkin' by myself
— I hope you'll understand . . .

Jimmy Rogers

To practise any art demands a high level of seriousness, a willingness to face up to and surmount numerous hardships. In addition the bluesman has to pay a host of other 'dues' — his apprenticeship is followed by an unremittingly hard life on the road, the financial rewards of which are often meagre in the extreme. Why? The very simple answer to this isn't simple at all — indeed, it is fraught with social implications the nature of which lie beyond the scope of this book. It will, however, be sufficient for our purposes to state that the bluesman's plight has been and is due to the inbred anti-black stance in American culture: the fact that the blues was once known as 'the Devil's music' — by both blacks and whites, and more especially by the black Church — speaks for itself. The bluesman has always laboured under the scrutiny of suspicion; far from being given his due for the valuable contribution he makes to our culture, he is maligned, harassed and looked down upon. Cultural and racial put-down are the rewards reaped by the men and women who have created songs any musician in the world would be proud to have written. Instead of being celebrated they are *denigrated* — how sadly apt the term!

Hey, C.C. Ryder —
just look what you have done!

The bluesman is the undeciphered enigma on the American landscape, a lonely wanderer chanting a disturbing litany of past regrets and current complaints. He is a symbol of freedom, the outsider who says 'no' to the system. With only his voice and guitar he takes on the press, the television and, indeed, the powers that be.

My Black Name

My father's father used to tell me a lot about that. That's why this Boyd, that's just an identification for me like my social-security number. I don't respect that as nothing. 'Cause I'm no Boyd, man.

Eddie Boyd

Everything about the system of racism as practised in the United States was aimed at robbing the black of his or her identity. The first step was to proclaim him Man (or Woman) Without a Name. Blacks were deprived of their African appellations and forced to take European ones, thus signifying that they were chattels, belonging to Washington or Jefferson. This 'master's' misnomer carried all the weight and indignity of the branding iron, scorching a white label into the depths of the blacks' souls. But the affair was far more complex than that: it was also a ploy to dispossess them, once and for all of their Africanness, to destroy in them all thought of ever having had an African way of life. What did 'Van Buren' and 'Madison' have to do with Africa? The mere name told the world whose chattels blacks were; a European name carried with it the implication, 'He or she belongs to . . .' Even today, these pseudonyms tell to whom blacks used to belong. This fact, coupled with the metamorphosis of the colour of their skins into a stigma, effectively severed them from any claim to humanity, a domain whites declared as their private preserve.

Hamilton's nigger . . . Franklin's nigger . . . Calhoun's nigger-wench . . . *Nigger* . . .

The Man Without a Name was freely granted the use of that title, equivalent, in its contempt, with 'animal'. Like some accursed group of Atlases, blacks were forced to carry that ignominy throughout their lives as a punishment for not being white. And also . . . as a panacea to the whites' guilt, for yea, verily do I say unto thee, that much of the way racism evolved in the Land of the Free was due to the slavers' bad consciences. As Christians they had somehow to justify what they were doing to black people, who were living proof of the utter moral bankruptcy of their way of life.

The tragedy is all the more horrid because blacks came to believe what whites said about them. Their image of themselves was based on the oppressors' beliefs. They swallowed whites' lies that blacks were an inferior species originating in a barbaric land; they were mentally backward, lazy, savage and ugly. 'Black' became synonymous with evil, wickedness, crudity and stupidity; 'white' was good, honest, intelligent and desirable. In his study, *The Negro American*, Poussaint, the black psychologist, found that:

> From that point early in life when the Negro child learns self-hatred, it moulds and shapes his entire personality and interaction with his environment. In the earliest drawings, stories and dreams of Negro children there appear many wishes to be white as rejection of their own colour. They usually prefer white dolls and white friends, frequently identify themselves as white, and show a reluctance to admit that they are Negro. Studies have shown that Negro youngsters assign less desirable roles and human traits to Negro dolls. One study reported that Negro children in their drawings tend to show Negroes as small, incomplete people and whites as strong and powerful.[5]

Regarding the word 'black', Isaacs says that black Americans think of it as

> a key word of rejection, an insult, a fighting word. Prefixed to any name of obscenity, it multiplied the insult many times . . . Every time black was used or perceived in this way, the word African came after it, whether it was actually spoken or not, whether it was there or remained an echo in the mind. For the Africans were the blacks, the source of all blackness, the depths from which all had come and from which all wanted to rise.[6]

Blacks were ashamed of being black, and took no pride in their race: how could they when the whole culture in which they lived was structured to make them hate themselves? Black men and women hated each other, black lovers hated one another, black children hated their parents – all were mirrors reflecting the sin of having black skin instead of white. They had no need to wait to die in order to experience hell – they were born in it, encased in it, their souls housed in flames of ebony. And if, by some impossible mix-up, any of them got into heaven, let it be in white skin as well as robes! Otherwise, what would be the use of being a black angel – or were there ghettos in heaven too?

The colour of their skin barred blacks from ever entering into the American melting pot, that hodge-podge served up to the world (like cabbage in jars labelled 'caviar') under the brand name of the American Dream. Blacks were prohibited from being one of the fifty-seven varieties and, as we shall see, opted for being known as Brand X. But that would be much later, when that long-awaited thing known as 'black consciousness' developed. At the time of which we are speaking whatever consciousness they had was completely controlled by whites. Black ethnic identity was buried beneath a veritable Himalaya of falsehoods, misrepresentations, deceits, myths and fallacies. Of course, not all blacks bought this – Dubois' poem 'The Song of Smoke', written in 1899, proclaimed, 'I will be black as blackness can be' – but exceptions were few. They did, however, get the ball rolling.

Another of these avatars was a Tennessee-born blues singer and harmonica player named John Lee 'Sonny Boy' Williamson. He was the product of a musical tradition which had never lost contact with the life of black people. He saw life with an artist's eye: all the beauty and wonder of that suffering humanity was revealed to him. His sensitive mind plumbed the depths of its culture – the dialects, the family, the social customs, the dancing, the unstinting battle it waged to sustain its existence. He knew that they had nothing to be ashamed of, that the colour of their skin wasn't a badge of infamy but, on the contrary, because of what they had suffered, something they had a right to be proud of. He wanted to give them back their pride, to tell them that they could hold their heads up as high as the whites. Already one of the most popular black recording artists in Chicago, he knew that what he sang would be heard by his people all over the country. At his next recording session he was to record a song in which he not only boasted about the colour of his race, but which also reveals an important facet of the life of the bluesman. Standing tall and proud, his harmonica cupped in his hands like a conch sounding a triumph, he sang:

> I hear my black name a-ringin'
> All up and down the line . . .

Like a herald, come to deliver a timely message, he announced to black folk that they ought to be proud of their colour, their people and their origin. He also touched on one of the rites of initiation in the blues. In blues lore, this 'black' eponym denotes the *nom de guerre* he assumed when he became a bluesman. Significantly, he doesn't say 'blue' name; in using the word 'black' he is bragging about the colour of his skin. This black name is the antithesis, the refutation of his 'white' one, that ignoble hangover from slavery. The bluesman's black name is the one he chose when he realized that his mission was to be the interpreter and praiser of his people. In light of this, it would never do for him to appear in his new role under a misnomer bequeathed to him by the white slaver. When John Lee Williamson renamed himself 'Sonny Boy' he set the seal of his awareness on his 'new' self, and proclaimed to the world that he had renewed the bond between himself and his roots.

This courageous act had a long tradition behind it, for names have always played an important role in African life. They are magical entities which have a profound influence on the bearer's destiny, and as such are never lightly bestowed.

> Names are of great importance in West Africa. Names are given at stated periods in an individual's life and, as among all folk where magic is important, the identification of a 'real' name with the personality of its bearer is held to be so complete that this 'real' name, usually one given him at birth by a particular relative, must be kept secret . . .[7]

Even drums are given appellations in order to enhance their virtues: 'Some slit-drums are given proper names . . . The real purpose of the names is not to identify the instrument, but also to confer upon it the virtues they describe or to remind the musician and his neighbours of the truths and moral precepts on which everyday actions should be based.'[8]

This ritual denomination accords perfectly with naming as it functions in the blues. Once a bluesman takes on his black name he becomes a man with a mission. Henceforth, he is a member of that breed who have pledged themselves to the propagation of black American folklore. He is a guardian of his people's heritage, and his black name is the banner under which he will carry out his duties. As Edward Kamau Braithwaite explains in *The African Presence in Caribbean Literature*: 'The word (*nommo* or name) is held to contain secret power. People feel a name is so important that a change in his name could transform a person's life. That is why a Nigerian, for example, has so many names.'[9]

In the black world, to name is to conjure, to empower, to redefine and re-create. The bluesman's black name is the verbal symbol of his character and speaks volumes to his fellow musicians. Hence, the choice of this name is of the highest importance, for it will play a large part in the shaping of his destiny.* Names such as Muddy Waters, Koko Taylor, Lightnin' Hopkins, Ma Rainey, Big Walter Horton, Son House, Howlin' Wolf, Memphis Slim, Leadbelly, Big Bill Broonzy, Billy Boy Arnold, Mississippi John Hurt, and Sister Rosetta Tharp are pregnant with meaning.

Indicative of the new pride blacks experienced is Johnny Shines' comment concerning the word 'nigger':

> Anytime someone wants to call me 'nigger', I give him the privilege, because only a nigger could have subdued and gone through the things we, the black people, have gone through and survived. So, if you call me 'nigger', you only identify me as one of the strongest in the world. I feel like it's an honour, not a disgrace, to be called 'nigger'. To me it tells me I'm the strongest.[10]

. . . Memphis Minnie, Empress Betsy, Sunnyland Slim, B.B. King, Chicago Beau, Little Walter, Doctor Ross, Bo Diddley, Sugar Blue, Bobby Blue Bland, Little Esther, Johnny Guitar Watkins, Slim Harpo . . . Black names, bluespeople . . .

When Muddy Waters announced, 'They call me Muddy Waters: I'm the bluest man in Chicago-town!' he was proclaiming his identity. Snooky Pryor's words: 'You don't know my name and you don't know where I come from!' sum up the whole black–white relationship in America.

. . . Willie Dixon, Juke Boy Bonner, Screamin' Jay Hawkins, Son Seals, Big Voice Odom, Big Mama Thornton, Lazy Lester, Bukka White, the Aces, the Hoodoo Band, Eddie C. Campbell . . . Black names, blues heroes . . .

The day Sonny Boy glorified his black name he redefined both his role and his position *vis-à-vis* the white man. It was a momentous, defiant cry, meant as a challenge to everything the whites stood for. Years later the Black Muslims were to renew this challenge and fling off the slave masters' names and call themselves 'X'. After centuries of suffering the Man Without a Name had finally found one. Now, he could direct his energies to redeeming his past.

---

* So strong is this belief in the power of names that some bluesmen have changed their names for that of one of their deceased colleagues, a famous case being that of Rice Miller's assumption of John Lee Williamson's name 'Sonny Boy'.

. . . Taj Mahal, Magic Sam, Cleanhead Vinson, Maxwell Street Jimmy, Pinetop Perkins, Kokomo Arnold, Sister-So-Black . . . Blues names, black people.

The Road

I have been ramblin' and prowlin' since I was twelve years old
And I wouldn't stop ramblin' for all my weight in gold

Robert Nighthawk

The road is where the bluesman's faith is put to the test. Here, on the dusty, hostile line between two points – his place of departure and his destination – his knowledge and courage will be shown for what they are. This aspect of the bluesman's initiation is particularly intimidating because, fraught with unpredictability as it is, there is never an end to its trials and hardships. As long as he is 'on the road', he will be tested.

> The constant movement of blacks that Mark Twain noted in the 1880s could be paralleled in the lives of almost limitless numbers of blues musicians. Over and over again the theme of their songs was travel – 'I got to keep moving . . .', 'I got rambling, rambling all on my mind', 'I'm here today and tomorrow I may be gone'.
>
> To the white outsider the endless and seemingly pointless travel was hard to understand and something to be regretted. A liberal planter from Mississippi, lecturing in 1901, believed the blacks 'a restless people. Ever seeking change, they sometimes wander far afield . . . they move but in a narrow circle, yet always in the same vain, aimless quest . . .'[11]

The blueslife on the road is a lonely, weary and trying experience, and demands a constant rekindling of strength and faith.

> The first time I met the blues, mama, they came walking through the woods
> They stopped by my house, and done me all the harm they could.

Every day makes a new demand that he broaden his mental and spiritual horizons, until he comes to see the road, with its worries and disillusionments, and the blues as interchangeable entities: the blues road as a way of life, and that way of life as a song. The road brands him with its mark, his voice becomes burnished with its dusty winds, his lyrics paint its raw images, and his guitar quavers its candid meanings.

> Many days of sorrow, many nights of woe
> Bad luck and trouble, everywhere I go.

The road provides him, or in this case, her, with the material from which he fashions his song.

> I'm a young woman an' ain't done runnin' around
> Some people call me a hobo, some call me a bum,
> Nobody knows my name, nobody knows what I've done, [. . .]
> See that long lonesome road – don't you know it's gotta end,
> An' I'm a good woman an' I can get plenty of men.

For the bluesman the road is a living being, a redoubtable character capable of heavenly sweetness and incredible cruelty. He tells it his problems, admonishes it for its caprices, cajoles it to treat him right, and complains to it when things go wrong. It is both a seductress who lures him away from his loved ones and the fairy godmother who leads him back home.

> When I get back to Memphis, you can bet I'll stay,
> And I ain't gonna leave until the Judgement Day.

Only by passing through this unending fire of countless miles does the bluesman become wise and ripe – that is to say, *blue*. Only when he possesses the 'key to the highway', does he have the key to the soul of his people. The road symbolizes freedom and acceptance, and as such becomes a metaphor of black life.

> The blues don't ask you where you're going
> The blues don't care where you been . . .

To the bluesman the road may be likened to a song, the meaning of which becomes, spiritually speaking, the road within.

The Load

Every day, every day I have the blues . . .

Memphis Slim

The bluesman's load is a formidable one. The environment he practises in is hostile to his art: the whites hold it in contempt, and the blacks equate it with immorality and evil. To dedicate oneself to the blues is to take up a life-long crusade, not only for the music but also for the people it stems from. B.B. King says,

> Yes, I've been a crusader for it for twenty-one years. Without this, I don't think I could *live* very long — not that I think I'm going to live a long time anyway, but I don't think I could live even *that* long if I had to stop playing or if I couldn't be with the people I love so — the people that have *helped* me so much. I couldn't *live*! I try to give them a message. I try *hard* . . . I really began to fight for the blues . . . the things people used to say about those I thought of as the greats in the business, the blues singers, used to hurt me. They spoke of them as though they were all illiterate and dirty . . . To be honest, I believe they felt they were trying to lift the standards of the Negro, and that they just didn't want to be associated with the blues, because it was something still back *there* . . . The blues are almost sacred to some people, but others don't understand, and when I can't make them understand, it makes me feel bad, because they mean so much to me . . . I remember my childhood, the race problems, and how bad it was in the thirties. I remember how it hit us . . . maybe some people don't want to be reminded that it happened to them too.[12]

Undoubtedly, those who don't want to be reminded of the 'bad old days' dislike the blues because its message rings true. These people want to live television lives, want to bury their heads in the illusory sands of the so-aptly-named American Dream. There can be no place for wandering soothsayers in these would-be Peyton Places. By contrast, bluespeople are so wide awake to the realities of the society they live in that they seem to hit the mark even when they dream:

> If I had the power
> I'd make servants of kings and queens
> Now, please don't wake me, darlin'
> For once, let me finish my dreams!

In his ceaseless travels the bluesman criss-crosses the (so-called) most prosperous country in the world. His reality, however, is one long, unending reel of pitiful images, the actors in which are his people – labourers bent under the merciless sun; crowds of the unemployed; shacks stacked upon one another like mockeries of architecture; in every town an accumulation of hovels sporting the name of 'black belt' – and the larger the town the greater the squalor and hurt. The blues is still dogging his people:

> My burden's so heavy, I can't hardly see,
> Seems like everybody is down on me.

This hurt is one of the heirlooms he carries in his music, that old blues song first conceived by the first black people brought to these shores. This persistent suffering is the essence of his music, the blue soul pervading its spirit. Suffering is the determining gene of the bluesman's burden.

> I been scorned,
> Yea, I been talked about!
> I been abused
> And I been kicked out!

The bluesman sees his people caught up in a terrifying vortex, a nightmare reality the mechanism of which is arranged so that nothing in it can ever come out right for them – hell, man, he don't want to hear about the ten black pop stars who've 'made it' – the bluesman is concerned with twenty-five million crushed, exploited, troubled people! People whom history has branded, people whom those in power have condemned. He's using his song in multifarious ways: as a weapon against the oppressor; as a source of inspiration to his community; as a reminder of what was done to them *and* what they did to defend themselves – those glorious moments ignored by 'official' history as taught in the nation's schools. His songs are verbal books, musical portraits played in the key of *concern*. He preaches to the people lest they forget why 'black' has become equated with 'blue', the universal simile for sorrow.

> Why do they call me black when I'm so blue?

'The new priests,' says Cone, 'of the black community were the bluesmen and -women; and their songs were the blues. Like the preacher in the church, they proclaimed the Word of black existence, depicting its joy and sorrow, love and hate, and the awesome burden of being "free" in a racist society when one is black.'[13]

> I was born March the 15th – man, the year was 19 and 12
> Yes, you know, ever since that day poor Lightnin' ain't been doing
>   so well.

In that song, Lightnin' Hopkins speaks for his race.

Jookin' the Blues

> *I heard Papa tell Mama: 'Let that boy boogie-woogie: because it's in him and it's got to come out!'*
>
> *John Lee Hooker*

The jook joint is to the blues what the church is to the spiritual, and the bluesman, on stage, is in his pulpit. Contrary to the 'holy' atmosphere which reigns in the church, the jook joint is characterized by its rowdiness – the noise and smoke and drinking are necessities without which its character would be fatally altered, for that would alter the music, which is in no small way shaped by it. Together, the 'road' and the jook joint are the backbone of what – for lack of a better term – may be called the 'school' of the blues. Of course, black tradition admits of no such institution; one is simply born with the blues and dedicates oneself to it if one feels so inclined. No bluesperson has the time to sit down with a beginner, for so many hours a day, and teach him or her vocal phrasing, slide guitar techniques, syncopation, etc. Besides, these are merely technical matters which can be self-taught. The real essence of the blues is revealed in the bluesman's way of life. The beginner must first learn to *see*; then, over the years, he will become acquainted with the spirit of the blues, which is ineradicably rooted in the lives of black people and which, strange though it may seem, many black people are no longer in touch with. They are like sleepwalkers, blind to the treasures within and around them. But the bluesman cultivates this black spirit, and shines its light upon his people, for he knows that underneath the façade, they have got the blues. As Leroi Jones says, 'But again it was assumed that *anybody* could sing the blues. If someone had lived in this world into manhood, it was taken for granted that he had been given the content of his verses.'[14] No matter what its size, any group of black people represents a 'jook', or blues gathering, so long as they make music. If one sings, the others will respond, and the give-and-take exchange will envelop them in blues. It is easy to see, then, why the jook joint is the bluesman's natural element. He frequents the bars and honky tonks like one bewitched – in these smoke-filled dens of song and dance he recognizes the gatherings of his tribe. Here, the blue flame burns proudly and uninhibitedly: the congregation is free from the tribulations of the outside world.

The blues reflects the black world with an integrity which brooks no compromise. Black life is tough: it's tough to make a living, to raise children, to get an education, to stay out of trouble. Since money is the alpha and omega of life in America, it stands to reason that those with the least of it – the blacks – are going to be inextricably caught up in aggravation. The jooks are a microcosm of this world, which Oakley so eloquently described:

In the early 1900s the Monarch ('The Castle of Missing Men') had already established itself the favourite of the country people, with crap shooting, no closing time and barrels of whiskey on the counter. You could get any kind of moonshine, or dope, like reefers and cocaine. . . . There were regular killings and he [the bouncer] would just dump the bodies outside. The Monarch was one of a string of joints run by the 'Czar of the Memphis Underworld' Jim Kinnane – celebrated in one of Robert Wilkins' blues 'Jim Canan's'. He and his brother Thomas also had the Hole-in-the-Wall (a 'rough joint' according to pianist Sunnyland Slim), and the Red Light and the Blue Light. At one of Kinnane's places you could bump into Razor Cuttin' Fanny. 'Everytime you see her if you didn't give her that piece of bread and side of fish she cut your throat.' Or down at the Panama there was Mary the Wonder, a voodoo lady. At the Vintage there was prize fighting, at the Midway the sound of rolling blues piano. The favourite haunt of musicians was probably Pee Wee's, which like many of the Beale [Street] joints was run by an Italian. W.C. Handy used to hang out there in his Memphis days before the First World War and he knew plenty of blues musicians. The cloakroom was stacked with horns, guitars, violins, bull-fiddles and banjos, and anyone could just pick an instrument and play.[15]

This rough-and-tumble world — wherein the dictum, 'the life you save may be your own' was a truism — provided the bluesman with inspiration for his songs. The lyrics of 'Tin Pan Alley':

> They call it Tin Pan Alley
> Roughest place in town:
> They start cuttin' and shootin'
> Soon's the sun go down!

were born of scenes like this one, here described by a policeman. The scene is Beale Street in 1937:

This was the Hole-in-the-Wall, where they played craps all night and all day — but you never won anything on account of the fines — whatever you did, you were fined for it, spitting on the dice, or dropping them on the floor — and if you did win you never got away with the money. And this was the Monarch Club, poker mostly, where the boss once shot a nigger for knocking another one down — didn't allow no fighting in that club — but the nigger shot back when he was half dead, and they both died. And the bar was where Wild Bill shot it up and killed half a dozen. And Fatty was shot there too, and run out with five bullets in his back, and a nigger undertaker after him, and when he fell down that nigger sat right on his body till his own car came, so's not to lose the burying of him: a big funeral it was.

And here's where we got Koen for beating up a white woman at a party; she ran out on the street stark naked and him after her, and then he got into the basement here and we broke up the floor and threw tear-gas bombs down, and he got shot when he didn't surrender . . .[16]

The characters who peopled the blues world were often hardened bravos, whose colourful names boasted of their notoriety. 'Then there was Zack Slack,' recalled bluesman Tommy Pinkston, 'he played piano in a whorehouse; Ready Money, the oldest prostitute on Beale Street — we called her that 'cause she could always get ready money; Little Ona, the best pickpocket in the whole United States; Gorilla Jones, a prizefighter and a bootlegger who used to work with Machine Gun Kelly next to the Palace Theater.'[17] To the blues singer these larger-than-life characters epitomized certain characteristics of black life: its struggle, and its joys in spite of that struggle. The bluespeople knew that these hookers and gamblers were reacting to a situation imposed upon them by racism, as best they could. They knew that, given half a chance, many of these 'moral offenders' would lead completely different lives. These statements are no apologia for 'immorality' among blacks, but an attempt to put things in the correct perspective within the black experience in the US. The life of black people of, say, only thirty years ago, wasn't simply hard; in some cases it was unbearable. Slide-guitarist Hound Dog Taylor, who later made his name in Chicago's small clubs and taverns, recalls:

Back in the 1930s and 1940s it was rough. Nobody'd back you up. Everybody'd run like scared rabbits. At that time a white man would go into your house, grab your woman, even if she was sick, drag her out of bed and make her go out into the field, and you better not say anything to him.[18]

Knowing what they'd been through, there is no way the blues singer will deny any of his or her people — preacher or hustler, housewife or prostitute, sinner or saint — the songs are for them all, and *about* them all. Hence, when Koko Taylor pitched her 'Wang Dang Doodle', her invitation was:

> Tell Automatic Slim
> Tell Razor Totin' Jim
> Tell Butcher-Knife Totin' Annie
> Tell Fast-Talkin' Fannie
>
> We gon' pitch a ball
> Down to that Union hall
> We gonna romp and stomp 'til midnight
> We gonna fuss and fight 'til daylight

We gon' pitch a Wang Dang Doodle
All night long.

The jook scene was wild with excitement, as hustlers, steelmill hands,
loafers, field workers, drifters and gamblers ogled and danced with the babes
– young ones, old ones, tight ones, innocent ones, tough ones; with
man-eaters bedecked in sequins and holy-rollers in their Sunday-go-to-
meetin's. The whole place reeled to the beat – the rhythm of the music, of
money, of booze and sex. Bluesman Johnny Shines said of them:

> The joints, the places that we would play at, naturally they were in the
> coloured section of town, which was pretty big because there were quite a
> lot of coloured people living there [Helena, Miss.] then. Lots of music
> around too . . . The town was loaded with musicians. And lots of places
> to play there too. Jook joints, I'd guess you'd call them . . . Now, a jook
> joint is a place where people go to play cards, gamble, drink and so on. So
> far as serving drinks like you would in a bar or tavern no, it wasn't that.
> Beer was served in cups; whiskey you had to drink out of the bottle . . .
> See, they couldn't use mugs in there because the people would commit
> mayhem, tear people's head up with those mugs. Rough places they were.
> When you were playing in a place like that, you just sit there on the floor
> on a cane-bottomed chair, just rear back and cut loose. There were no
> microphones or PA set-ups there; you just sing out as loud as you can. [19]

The ambience of the jooks was akin to that of the Baptist church; both rose to
the pitch of hysteria. The difference, however, was that the worship in the
jooks was 'irreverent' – or, if you will, in honour of the good things of this
world. The dancers gesticulated in frenzied spasms, cutting loose the
floodtides – bloodties – and giving themselves up to the spirit of the blues.
Well might the preacher be envious of the zeal of this gutbucket worship. As
if attempting to redeem what had been denied them for so long, the jook
people danced with all the power of their souls, indulging to the hilt their
blackness. The spirits remembered! Teleguided by the drums, the winds of
that long-ago but never completely forgotten Yesterday, their way of life
Before Slavery, swept over them. They illustrated the music with their
bodies; the floor became a drum they played with their feet . . .

The rhythm is as old as Memphis Minnie's most remote ancestor . . .
Then through the smoke and racket of the noisy Chicago bar float,

Louisiana bayous, muddy old swamps, Mississippi dust and sun, cotton fields, lonesome roads, train whistles in the night, mosquitoes at dawn and the Rural Free Delivery that never brings the right letter. All these things cry through the strings on Memphis Minnie's electric guitar . . . Music with so much in it folks remember that sometimes it makes them holler out loud . . .[20]

The church and the jook are the hearts of Afro-American musical activity, and in the latter, it is the bluesman who ministers the beat.

How the Bluesman Casts His Spell

He warmed my body and cooled my mind –
He had me thinkin' that I was divine . . .

Salome Arnold

One of the most widespread misconceptions about the blues performer is that he or she is but a mere entertainer, and that the voice, guitar, piano, or whatever other instrument they play is their 'main' instrument. Of course entertainment is part of the offering, but performing the blues is of much greater significance than just this: the blues performance is a rite, in which the musician assumes the role of the 'elder' and the audience that of the 'initiate'. The purpose of this musical convocation is to invoke the spirit of the blues – i.e. of black people – and thereby unite its participants.

The blues are sung, not because one finds oneself in a particular mood, but because one wants to put oneself into a certain mood. The song is the Nommo which does not reflect but creates the mood. And this mood is melancholy only from the romantic point of view current since the time of the abolitionists . . . The blues do not arise from a mood but produce one. Like every art form in African culture song too is an attitude which effects something. The spiritual produces God, the secularized blues produce a mood.[21]

The performers' aim is to conjure – in the same sense as the preacher or Root Doctor conjures – their audience. They 'hoodoo' their listeners, by employing the call-and-response pattern traditional to African music. The 'Sing it brother!' and 'Tell it like it is, sister!' are identical to the 'Amens!' of the Church. And the 'true' instrument played in blues cult houses (jook joints) is the audience.

> A peculiarity of the African call-and-response pattern, found but infrequently elsewhere, is that the chorus phrase regularly commences while the soloist is still singing; the leader, on his part, begins his phrase before the chorus has finished. This phenomenon is quite simply explained in terms of the African musical tradition of the primacy of rhythm. Examples of call-and-response music in which the solo part, for one reason or another, drops out for a time, indicate clearly that the chorus part, rhythmical and repetitive, is the mainstay of the songs and the one really inexorable component of their rhythmic structure. The leader, receiving solid rhythmic support from the metrically accurate, rolling repetition of phrases by the chorus, is free to embroider as he will.[22]

The audience, as instrument, produces the spirit which shapes and develops the song. From belonging to the performer it becomes the property of the community; these individual statements are transformed into the testimony of the group – hence the bluesman's role as spokesman of the black people. 'For the blues singer does not in fact express his personal experiences and transfer them to his audience; on the contrary, it is the experiences of the community that he is expressing, making himself its spokesman.'[23]

The effectiveness of this depends upon how deeply he or she can tap the sleeping roots of the listeners' subconscious. A blues performer can only achieve this when his or her own 'soul' is intact. When these conditions are met, the effect on the audience can be overwhelming.

> His [Robert Johnson's] guitar seemed to talk – repeat and say words with him like no one else in the world could. I said he had a talking guitar and many a person agreed with me. This sound affected most women in a way that I could never understand. One time in St Louis we were playing one of the songs that Robert would like to play with someone once in a great while, 'Come on in My Kitchen'. He was playing very slow and passionately, and when we had quit, I noticed no one was saying

anything. Then I realized they were crying . . . both women and men.[24]

To achieve their ends performers use their voice, their body and their instrument.

> Elmore James will always remain the most exciting and dramatic blues singer and guitarist I've ever had the chance to see perform in the flesh . . . Wearing thick glasses, Elmore's face always had an expressive and dramatic look, especially when he was real gone on the slow blues. Singing with a strong and rough voice, he didn't really need a mike. On such slow tunes as 'I'm Worried', 'Make My Dreams Come True', 'It Hurts Me Too', his voice reached a climax and created a tension that was unmistakably the down-and-out blues. Notwithstanding that raw voice, Elmore sang his blues with a particular feeling, an emotion and depth that showed his country background. His singing was, I should say, fed, reinforced by his own guitar accompaniment which was as rough, violent and expressive as was his voice. Using the bottleneck technique most of the time, Elmore really let his guitar sound as I had never heard a guitar sound before . . . and when he gave free rein to his guitar, the people in the joint went crazy and some people ran to the bandstand throwing bills of one and five dollars at Elmore's feet.[25]

Above all, the performers conjure with their 'soul', the indefinable something which may be described as their connection with their past. If they can successfully invoke this they can move the most stolid and 'laid-back' audience to the pitch of hysteria. Then their spirit is liberated from the straightjacket of Western mores and reverts to its 'old' and 'true' self. It dances, shouts, jumps, laughs and weeps. It is this 'African' style of emotionalism which accounts for the fact that the atmosphere of the jook joint and the black church are the same. Thus it is that the Gods of the Black Past visit their Lost Children in Texas or Chicago, in Baton Rouge or Harlem. A good blues performer must needs be something of a sorcerer, and a great blues band is comprised not only of superb musicians but also master conjurers. For the blues is the culmination of a tradition of which conjuring is an indivisible part.

Robert Johnson at the Crossroads

I stand at the crossroads, baby,
Now there's no turnin' back:
I'm here to make a deal
Let the Devil deal the pack!

Blue Bob Crawford

Robert Johnson's life presents one of the most fascinating stories in the whole of blues history. His biographers are divided into two camps: the bluesmen who knew him and believe that he made a pact with the Devil at the crossroads; and the folklorists, who don't. The former are black, the latter white; and this division has no small weight in determining the manner in which his story has come down to us. In confronting his history the folklorists find themselves up against an enigma they are at a loss to explain, and so they resort to hazy images which portray him as a mystery, cipher, puzzle, etc. He is a 'man of mystery'; a 'problematic figure'; even 'the personification of the existential blues singer' – whatever *that* is. To these commentators, the story of his having made a pact with the Devil has made him a legendary figure – not, they would have us believe, because there can be any foundation to it, but because it cloaks him in an aura of occult mystique. In the main they present his life as the saga of a romantic troubadour, who revelled in sex and booze and indulged his sense of wanderlust by roaming happy-go-luckily along the sunny trails of America. The deal at the crossroads adds to the charm of this blueslife – and, it sells records: so better leave it in. Finally, there comes the perfect ending: the hero dies young. 'Like Housmans's athlete, like Orpheus, Keats and James Dean, he was kissed by the flame of youth and never lived to see the effects of the infatuation wear off.' This comment, by one of the most prolific writers on the blues, is a blatant 'whitening' of black culture. What, in the name of the Devil, has Robert Johnson got to do with Keats, James Dean *et al*? Surely the likes of Magic Sam, Jimi Hendrix, Minni Ripperton and Bob Marley are more apt comparisons. Lacking the keys to the inner meanings of the blues, these authors distort his story so that it reads as some *Hamlet*-like drama. The true clue to it lies in a proper understanding of the lore of the crossroads.

There was nothing whatever 'romantic' about being black in Mississippi in 1911, the year in which Johnson was born. Nor was there any particular luck in being born into a family of cotton-pickers. And it was decidedly a misfortune to have had the previous father of that family run out of town by a white lynch mob, on account of having dared to talk back to some rednecks, who followed up this good deed by getting the wife and children evicted from their land. While separated from her man, this woebegone woman met a labourer named Noah Johnson, and it was from this union that the bluesman was born. They bequeathed to him all they had: chronic poverty. But he also inherited the black South – its frightened souls, folk tales, ecstatic religion, Hoodoo, and music. Over all this – as a bonus for being black – racism held sway over the land. Like a plague, it decimated the black populace, consuming its energies and murdering its hopes. The Godson of Defeat, it had never forgiven them for having gained their freedom. Its mandate was to keep them down; its method was terror. The Ku Klux Klan, the police, the state laws – spectres created to ensure the dominion of the whites over the blacks. No, there were no blacks striking up James Dean poses in Mississippi in Robert Johnson's day; but there were plenty of scared, hungry, helpless black folk just trying to stay alive. Bluesman Eddie Boyd remembers those days:

> And I was nothing but a seventeen-year-old boy . . . So that's how I got back to Memphis without getting killed. And this bad chief of police from West Memphis, Ark., called Cuff, he was such a cruel white man. Man, he'd have kicked babes out of pregnant women's stomachs right there in West Memphis, Ark. He came that night, him and four other men, looking for me at my mother's and her husband's shack where they were living there on a sawmill job. He ripped my mother's mattress up looking for me, in that one-room shack. I was such a small boy he thought I could have been hiding in there.[26]

Young Robert observed and listened, trying to piece together into some kind of coherency the evil contradictions of life. His stepfather had had to escape dressed in the disguise of a woman; his mother had lost her land; his sisters and brothers were living with relatives in four or five different places. And he – he was surrounded by his skin, the colour of which the whites had declared war on!

The only haven open to him was the blues. Somehow, the people who played it appeared to have risen above circumstances. They talked of faraway places, cities like New Orleans, Memphis and Chicago; they spoke of notorious good-time women and big-shot gamblers; they told about *wangas* and charms which gave a person supernatural powers. He longed for their freewheeling way of life and, above all, for their power to confabulate that life into song. To be a bluesman would give him the right to partake of that wandering, devil-may-care existence, and the means of telling his people what was on his mind. For wondrous things were happening to him. Looking out over the fields, he had visions of a world bathed in the light of peace. Or he saw his life transformed by love and happiness, a life in which he need not be ashamed of his colour or features. At night, sweet voices came to whisper to him secret messages – things he dared not tell to anyone. He had dreams of a world in which there were no white people – no one to tell him that he was 'wrong' for being black. Other times, his mind was invaded by nightmares, of scenes in which the whites threw off their masks and forced his people back into slavery. And, trying to escape through the swamps, he would hear the bay of the dreaded hounds on his trail; then, the fearful chain could clink around his neck, and before him there would stand the devil, dragging him down into hell . . .

During the time he lived with his stepfather (he who had escaped) in Memphis – between the ages of three and nine – his brother Charles had given him lessons on the guitar, which instrument he had laid aside for the harmonica. Now, in his late teens, he resumed it, passing his apprenticeship in the company of the awesomely gifted Son House, and his accompanist, Willie Brown. According to their statements, his playing left a whole lot to be desired. As Son House recalled in *Living Blues*:

We'd all play for the Saturday-night balls, and there'd be this little boy standing around. That was Robert Johnson. He was just a little boy then. He blew the harmonica and he was pretty good with that, but he wanted to play the guitar. When we'd leave at night to go play for the balls, he'd slip off and come over to where we were . . . He'd get where Willie and I were and sit right down on the floor and watch from one to the other. And when we'd get a break and want to rest some, we'd set the guitars up in a corner and go out in the cool. Robert would watch and see which way we'd gone, and he would pick one of them up. And such another racket you never heard! It'd make the people mad, you know. They'd come out and say, 'Why don't y'all go in and get that guitar away from that boy!

He's running people crazy with it!' I'd come back in, and I'd scold him about it. 'Don't do that, Robert. You drive the people nuts. You can't play nothing. Why don't you blow the harmonica for 'em.' But he didn't want to blow that. Still, he didn't care how I'd get after him about it. He'd do it anyway.

About this time he suffered a personal tragedy: his fifteen-year-old wife died in childbirth. Though there is no record of how he took this blow – for he never spoke about either his family or personal life – it is clear by his actions that he must have suffered a kind of breakdown, which his creativity turned into a spiritual asset. Confronted with yet another crisis, this young man sought a means of transforming his life, by transforming life itself into a work of art. Disillusioned with the 'reality' the white world imposed upon him, he turned to the world of magic, to the supernatural powers promised by Hoodoo, which was nothing less than the complete antithesis of the white man's power. Having realized that music was a kind of magic, he sought out magic to gain control over it. His quest led him into the bayous and, when he returned two years later, he was a changed man and the best guitar player anybody had ever heard. His mentors were forced to eat their words:

> Willie and I were playing again out at a little place east of Robinsonville called Banks, Miss. We were playing there one Saturday night, and all of a sudden somebody came in through the door. Who but him! He had a guitar swinging on his back. I said, 'Bill!' He said, 'Huh?' I said, 'Look who's coming in the door.' He looked and said, 'Yeah. Little Robert.' I said, 'And he's got a guitar.' And Willie and I laughed about it. Robert finally wiggled through the crowd and got to where we were. He spoke, and I said, 'Well, boy, you still got a guitar, huh? What do you do with that thing? You can't do nothing with it.' He said, 'Well, I'll tell you what.' I said, 'What?' He said, 'Let me have your seat for a minute.' So I said, 'All right, and you better do something with it, too,' and I winked my eye at Willie. So he sat down there and finally got started. And man! He was so good! When he finished, all our mouths were standing open. I said, 'Well, ain't that fast! He's gone now!'[27]

The stories about his phenomenal technique are legion. Every musician who heard him talks of his playing in wondrous terms, and many fell under the spell of both the music and the man, following him like disciples trailing after a guru. Now began those travels which seem the very diathesis of the blueslife – Memphis, St Louis, Texas, Chicago, New York, California – and everywhere he went he left unforgettable impressions of himself. The man who emerged from the swamps was no ordinary hoboing minstrel, but a *bluesman* in the profoundest sense of the word. In two short years he had become a man with an aura. Johnny Shines, who was his foremost disciple, said of him,

> Robert was one of those fellows who was warm in every respect – in *every* respect. Even, you know, it's natural for men not to like a musician too much. But Robert was a fellow very well liked by women and men, even though a lot of men resented his power or his influence over women – people. They resented that very much, but, as a human being, they still liked him because they couldn't help but like him, for Robert just had that power to draw.[28]

In 1936 he made his first recordings, travelling with a white record agent named Ernie Ortle to San Antonio, Texas. Though one of them sold over 5,000 copies, Shines says that 'about 75 or 100 dollars was all the money he ever got'. Two years later he was again in the studio, this time in Dallas, where he laid down the last eleven songs he would ever record. Their lyrics spoke of the composer as a doomed man. And he was. Fourteen months later he would be dead, poisoned by a jealous husband at a party he was playing at, a few miles out of Greenwood Mississippi.

The question of whether or not Johnson made a pact with the Devil at the crossroads hinges upon two considerations: first, is such a thing possible?; second, do the facts of his life tally with the assertion?

The answer to the first question must be sought in the cultural and social background in which he grew up. Johnson was a product of the Mississippi Delta, a kind of muddy jungle ever at the mercy of the great stream to which it owes its existence. If many of its wonders are known, many more remain unknown – dark, forbidding, uninhabited bayous which the neighbouring inhabitants contemplate with awe and foreboding. It takes no great feat of the imagination to conceive of them as the abode of malignant spirits. Shrouded in darkness, they are a network of stagnant pools and impenetrable foliage – in short, the stuff no man's land is made of. In them, one is seized by a feeling of helplessness, by a kind of mental vertigo, born of the consciousness of one's weakness in relation to the power of Nature.

Inexplicably, at the same time, the visitor to these outlandish outbacks also experiences a kind of union, a communion with the savage scene. If one remains among these bayous for a length of time, it is possible to give oneself up to them and begin to feel at one with their solemn and spooky trappings. The environment of the bayous is too resilient not to affect those who live in them.

Johnson chose to go into those wild backlands. And certainly not simply to 'get away from it all'. If that had been his aim he had only to hop any of the dozens of freight trains which passed through the area, bound for distant points in every direction. No, he went into the delta swamps in search of that music which would clear up his frustrations and unlock his talent. He went to deal with the Root Doctor, who finds in the swamps a fit sanctuary for his practice and worship. Here, in this terrain not unlike that in which his predecessors first discovered the secrets of Nature, he is free to invoke the spirits – and free from molestation by the whites. He and the environment are as one, complementing and completing one another: it sustains him and he worships it. The Hoodoo is Lord of the bayous.

The tradition of making a pact at the crossroads in order to attain supernatural prowess is neither a creation of the Afro-American nor an invention of blues lore, but originated in Africa and is a ritual of Voodoo worship. It is doubtful whether Johnson could have written the lyrics of his songs without having been initiated into the cult for, as I shall proceed to show, the symbolism involved in them is highly complex and of a nature which makes it highly improbable that they were simply things he 'picked up'. This knowledge is only to be had from one deeply versed in Hoodoo lore – from the Root Doctor – who, in turn, would reveal it only to one who had given proof of his seriousness to the cult. Johnson had to convince the Hoodoo Doctor that he was in earnest about pledging himself – hence the two years in which he disappeared into the bayous, the two years of which the only information he would give was that he had sold himself to the Devil.

Legba: Master of the Crossroads

In Voodoo the god of the crossroads is Legba, one of the most powerful in the whole of the pantheon. 'No consideration of the roles played by African deities in New World religions should omit mention of Legba.'[29] Legba is a capricious and often malicious character, who delights in double-crossing those who put their faith in him. Courlander describes him as:

> One of the most important of Haitian *loa*, frequently the first invoked in any service. He is the guardian of the gateway, the crossroads and the highway. He is a divine trickster who is both feared and loved, a force that is capriciously malevolent or benevolent. Legba's mischief and tricks are directed against the other deities and human beings. He is the intervener between mankind and the deities. It is in this sense that he 'opens the gate', providing a channel of communication between man and *loa*. In Dahomean lore, Legba's mischief is often in the realm of sex . . . The Dahomean Legba is remembered elsewhere in the New World, notably in Dutch Guiana, Brazil and Cuba. Until relatively recent times he was known among the Negroes of Louisiana by the name of Papa Lebat.

Haitian Vodun spoke of Legba in these terms: 'The *Mait Carrefour* (Master of the Crossroads) is like the president. Legba is like a minister. God sent *Mait Carrefour*. He commands Baron Samedi. Before going to the cemetery to perform black magic you must pass the crossroads, and therefore he is able to restrain you if he is not properly worshipped.'[30]

In Haiti, certain charms, called *garde carrefours*, are made with earth taken from the crossroads. One of the songs sung to invoke Legba runs:

> Attibon Legba, open the gate for me
> You see, Attibon Legba, open the gate for me, open the gate.
>
> I will enter when I return.
> I salute the *loa*!

The literal meaning of the invocation is, 'Open the gate, and I shall return to pay (salute the *loa*) what is due.' Métraux explains how these pacts are made: 'The Voodooist seeking co-operation of a god in order to achieve some ambition or simply wishing to put himself under the god's special protection, can make the god a formal proposal of marriage. Henceforth, they will have a common destiny.'[31] 'A common destiny' . . . and we have seen how Legba is a nefarious trickster whose pleasure is to hoodoo those who call upon him. Also, it should not be forgotten that, in black religions, to invoke the gods is to offer oneself for possession by them. If Johnson made a pact at the crossroads with Legba, in essence, this is what he was doing – a claim which he was by no means alone in making. Ledell Johnson, brother of guitarist Tommy Johnson, explained in *Living Blues* how his brother had struck his deal at the crossroads:

Now, if Tom was living, he'd tell you. He said the reason he knowed so much, said he sold hisself to the devil. I asked him how. He said, 'If you want to learn how to play anything you want to play and learn how to make songs yourself, you take your guitar and you go to where the road crosses that way, where a crossroad is. Get there, be sure to get there just a little 'fore 12:00 that night so you know you'll be there. You have your guitar and be playing a piece there by yourself . . . A big black man will walk up there and take your guitar, and he'll tune it. And then he'll play a piece and hand it back to you. That's the way I learned to play anything I want.

The evidence here presented proves that, first, the lore of making a pact with the Devil at the crossroads had come to the Delta area as part of the Hoodoo religion; second, that musicians of Johnson's era believed that the forging of such a deal was possible; and third, that they believed music to be connected with magic, and that this magic could be obtained by invoking the spirits.

Magic, Music and Possession

Johnson's songs present the visions of a haunted mind, obsessed with the idea that it will have to pay the Devil his due. In other words, he was possessed by the idea of death – that is, of getting out of this life and into the next as quickly as he could. His songs are the laments of a soul too sensitive to face up to the brutal realities of its existence. For Johnson was a creative genius in every sense of the word, by which I mean that he came to embody the art he practised. He 'created' his – for lack of a better term – 'neurosis' the same as he created his songs; his genius gave birth to those very hellhounds he thought were following him when, in fact, they were inside him. That he made a pact at the crossroads, I don't doubt for a moment; but it was he who supplied the demon of the lore, the 'big black man', Papa Legba with his guitar, with the power to overwhelm him. In order to turn his neurosis into art he promised his soul for, aware that the hounds could not be kept at bay for long, he wisely chose the road to power rather than end up in some house for the mentally ill. His was the Nat Turner style of creativity, which either begets great artists or social revolutionaries. Turner saw blood in the sky, Johnson 'blues falling like hail'. He needed the curse of the crossroads in order to justify the existence of such visions; having made his pact he felt that it was all right to see things in a way no one had ever seen them before. The Devil became his excuse for being a genius – a word, by the way, none of his white biographers has yet used to describe him. Just as he turned to music because of its magical qualities, so he turned to magic in order to strengthen his music. This was only natural, for talent of his calibre is a kind of magic, and magic has ever been a quality of music to the black mind. Johnson's genius lay in his realizing that music could be used as an antidote to the suffering in his life, as a defence against the evils perpetrated by the whites. Even so, he knew that his powers – human and otherwise – were too tenuous to hold out. But, having made his pact, things became 'clear' – in his 'Stones in My Passway' he says:

> I got stones in my passway
> And my road seems dark as night
> I have pains in my heart
> They have taken my appetite
>
> My enemies have betrayed me
> Have overtaken poor Bob at last
> And there's one thing for certain
> They have stones all in my path.

In Hoodoo lore certain stones have great powers, and can be used to work both good and evil. Speaking of the Candomblés of Brazil, Pierson says, 'In Africa, certain stones appertain to specific deities . . . it is believed, however, that the stones should not be touched, since the *encantado* (sanctified spirit) will possess anyone who does touch them.'[32] In Haiti, these stones are called 'thunder stones', and belong to Damballah, who sometimes incarnates himself as one. 'Stones in my path' tells us that Johnson felt that his 'enemies' were closing in on him, and was calling on the master of the road for help — *Attibon Legba, open the gate for me* . . .

He became immersed in his magic-music, in his special relationship with
the Devil. When he sang his songs he was addressing what was to him a very
real presence:

> Early this morning
> When you knocked upon my door
> And I said: 'Hello, Satan —
> I believe it's time to go.'

The Evil One had kept his side of the bargain, and soon it would be time for
'poor' Bob to keep his.

> I got to keep moving
> Blues falling down like hail
> Ummmmmm
> Blues falling down like hail
> And the days keep on worrying me
> There's a hellhound on my trail

He became infatuated with his dark secret, or rather, he so identified it with
his life he felt his actions might betray him. Researcher Mack McCormick
says people told him of Johnson secretly playing his guitar and, when he
found out they were listening, he would stop. Another of his habits was to
turn away from people when he played, so that they couldn't see his
technique. Then again, he was the classic loner, wrapt up in his inner
thoughts even when he was with a friend. For no friend could understand
what he was going through, the horrendously rich nightmare he was living.
'Things like this often happened,' said Shines, 'and I think Robert would cry
just as hard as anyone. It was things like this, it seems to me, that made
Robert want to be by himself, and he would soon be by himself. The thing
that was different, I think, was that Robert would do his crying on the
inside. Yes, he was crying on the inside.'[33]

Then, at the age of twenty-six, having already sung his way into blues
history, Legba deceived him. 'I'm sick,' he told the divine prankster, 'but
I'm still playing.' Honeyboy Edwards, who was performing with him on that
tragic occasion, has given this account in *Living Blues* of what happened:

A fellow give a dance, he lived in the country, but he come to the little city and picked the boys up out of the little city and carry them back in the country and play on a Saturday and Friday night. And when we get through, they'd bring us back in our old cars, back to town where we lived at.

How I got it, this fellow said Robert was messing around with his wife or something like that. So Robert came back to Greenwood and went back the next Saturday night out there. So he gave some of his friends some whiskey to give Robert a drink — I was lucky I didn't drink none of the whiskey, but I don't guess they was trying to give it to me. His friend give it to Robert — you see, he give it to him to drink because he had it in for Robert and his wife. But still he kept him to play for him! I think this fellow was named Robert.

About 1:00 Robert was taken sick when he was playing. All the people just came out the city and said they wanted him to play, 'cause they was drinking and all them having a good time, and they was begging him to play, and he played sick. And they said he told the public, he said, 'Well, I'm sick, y'all see, but I'm still playing, but I'm still sick. I'm not able to play.' About 2:00 he got so sick they had to bring him back to town . . .

In acute suffering, he survived for two days, after which he finally expired.

Did Robert Johnson seek out or meet a Hoodoo Doctor during his wanderings in the bayous who initiated him into the cult, thus providing him with the knowledge to invoke Legba, the master of the crossroads? Did he make a pact with this 'Devil' in order to play 'the Devil's music'? We'll never know. What is certain is that in the span of a couple of years he went from playing the guitar so badly that it hurt people's ears, to being a performer in a class by himself. At the same time, from being a 'boy' he became a man with extraordinary charisma, capable of moving a crowd to tears and attracting many men, destined to become famous in their own right, as his disciples. We also know that he was secretive to a fault about his technique. Most importantly, he himself told his friends that he had made a deal with the Devil, and that he would have to pay for it. His fellow musicians believed him, seeing nothing implausible in the undertaking. Not only his playing, but his 'new' personality lent credence to the assertion. He had gone seeking strength and had come back a man of power — not just a bluesman, but a *Hoodoo* bluesman. The way the postulated thesis of his going to the crossroads fits into the Hoodoo tradition is almost uncanny. Compare, for instance, his story with that of the Dahomean tale 'Man Against the Creator':

> Awe reached the sky. Mawu (Legba's mother) said to him: 'What are you looking for?' Awe said to Mawu, 'My knowledge is great. I now seek to measure my knowledge with you.'
>
> He made a statue of a man. But it could not breathe, nor talk, nor move.
>
> Mawu said to him, 'Your knowledge is not enough.'
>
> Mawu left Awe, and Awe went back to earth. But Mawu sent death to follow him.
>
> However, Awe mastered Legba's knowledge and became a practitioner of magic. Awe and Death are the two friends of the world.
>
> Legba (the seventh son of Mawu) led this man down the road to the market, and told him all that had to be done to make magic charms.

Moreover, music as a magic medium is an accepted idea in black culture. Bebey, speaking of the *griots* of West Africa, says,

> A *griot* is not merely an African witch doctor or sorcerer, although some *griots* do dabble in witchcraft. They usually specialize in the art of invoking supernatural beings of all kinds and sing their praises in order to ensure pardon, protection or goodwill. However, the role of the *griot* in West African society extends far beyond the realm of magic. The fact that music is at the heart of all the *griot*'s activities is yet further proof of the vital part he plays in African life.[34]

Johnny Shines voices the idea of music and magic in the comment he made about the first time he saw Howling Wolf perform: 'I thought he was a magic man. They had an old saying about people who sold their soul to the Devil to be able to play better than anyone else. I thought Wolf was one of these.'[35]

People think wrongly about magic: magic looks exactly like reality – only its effect is different.

In spite of the evidence, Johnson's biographers are either sceptical or deny outright his having made a pact. It is significant that none of them brings Hoodoo into the picture. But, then, how could they have, when none of them knew about Legba, or the *loa* stones, or of the African concept of the partnership between music and magic? This is pardonable, but their arrogance is not. They deal, not with what Johnson believed, but with what *they* themselves believe. They don't believe in Hoodoo, so . . . But, *whose* story is this? The only thing which matters is what Johnson believed. Possession? Why not? To hoodooists, the thing is not only possible, but desirable, a sign of high favour. Perhaps it was Johnson's misfortune not to have been born in Brazil or Haiti – for, a few hundred miles from the clinical climes of the Great Union, possession takes place daily, and no one finds it 'impossible'. When I read the whitewashed accounts which have so far appeared of Robert Johnson, I experience a kind of vertigo, so similar in attitude are they to the earlier accounts by whites of African culture and music. The old taboos, rehashed and updated, lurk beneath the 'objective' interest. While extolling Johnson's music – the Devil's music – they erase the obvious role Hoodoo played in it. The fact that Mister Bluesman Son House, Mister Bluesman Johnny Shines and Mister Bluesman Robert Jr Lockwood believed in his 'pact' goes for nothing. So be it. But stop obscuring the history of the blues with your ideas, stop 'interpreting' for the world how black people think – because you don't know! Robert either made or believed he made a deal with the Devil, and whichever way he did it – physically, symbolically, or imaginatively – he did it out of desperation. However it was, he certainly contracted a mystic obligation with the spiritual world. Those stones in his path, the midnight vigil at the crossroads, the flight from Satan's hounds – all became so inextricably bound up with his vision of the world that they became the signposts of his destiny. The ever-mounting consciousness that he himself was a 'crossroad' all but unhinged him, and left him tottering in a nightmare world on the borders of which were insanity. Oakley put his finger on it when he says, 'At times he seems scarcely able to control the extremities of feeling which press on him or the tensions and neuroses which drive, harry and confuse him. As if on the edge of an abyss of complete psychic disintegration his voice changes from high frenzy to little-boy vulnerability.'[36]

By some kind of genial mysticism he transformed the chaos of his life into art, forging a new path for the blues to follow and giving a new interpretation to Hoodoo, breathing new life into the most awesome of the initiations, the Crossroads.

Revelations pass unseen to the uninitiated. Johnson was 'called' to Hoodoo the same as he was 'called' to the blues: to bear witness. With his 'Hell Hound on My Trail' he gave utterance to the well-nigh hopeless condition of his people. In this sense, his art is the logical outcome of events, while his life is the blues revealed, a towering monument to the music he played. His story encapsulates the whole of its history and his songs are the archetypal expression of its true meaning. There were stones in his pathway; he left gems in ours.

Transculturation: Black and White Blues

Thus the blues – the Black Slave lament – was offered up for the admiration of the oppressors.

Frantz Fanon

Ever since black people were forced to come to the Americas historians and sociologists have been writing about their 'acculturation', a word which implies that the exchange was one-sided, that blacks have contributed nothing to the cultures which have risen in the New World. This theory of acculturation has been bandied about by generations of American academics – even those 'liberals' who supposedly champion the black cause. This word, 'acculturation', contains within it the very germ of the Great Lie whites have wanted to believe about blacks and want blacks to believe about themselves. Why is it still in use today when the Cuban ethnologist, Fernando Ortiz, introduced the word 'transculturation' into academic grammar more than forty years ago? Transculturation is the exchange which takes place when peoples of different cultures meet. Why the perseverance in the use of that obviously one-sided, nay racist term 'acculturation'?

The truth of the story of America is that black people brought a great deal with them, and have had just as much influence upon whites as whites have had on them. Nothing in these Original Thirteen Colonies plus Thirty-seven has escaped black influence, be it the Christian Church, the English language, poetry, art, folklore, cuisine or Bo Derek's hairstyle. It is an inescapable fact that American culture is a mulatto. Even the special brand of racism in this continent was conceived and dedicated to the proposition that it be a 'reaction' to black people. So, in the name of the Father, the Son and the Holy Ghetto, let us do away with, for once and all, all talk of blacks being 'acculturated' and speak about what really happened.

The aspect of the transculturation this book deals with is not blacks' adoption of the English language, European instruments or cultural influences made by the Indians on blacks, etc; but with the recent appreciation and performance of the blues by whites. Whites have heard the blues ever since they enslaved the black people: they were there at its origin, acting as catalysts. Blind, deaf and dumb to any culture but their own, they heard but never listened to the music of their slaves – for in truth, what could those barbarians know about singing and instruments and the other refinements which go to make art? Thus the racist musicologist, H.E. Krehbiel, wrote in 1914: 'Why savages who have never developed a musical or other art should be supposed to have more refined aesthetic sensibilities than peoples who have cultivated music for centuries, passes my poor powers of understanding . . .'[37] Krehbiel's powers of mind were not as 'poor' as he pretended, for whites everywhere agreed with him. American 'culture' was lily-white, and heaven forbid that it should ever be besmirched with the taint of the ole tarbrush. And yet, by 1800, both Church and vauDeville – the sacred and secular forms of American entertainment – had been strongly influenced by the slave. The theatres put on parodies of black life, known as 'minstrel' shows, with white actors, singers and dancers made up with black faces. The object of this hideous entertainment was to show how funny it was to be a slave and black. Not content with having stolen their freedom, these 'artistes' were filching their music and dance. Meanwhile, the churches throughout the land were being lit up by the blacks' fiery form of worship: 'The Great Revival, as it came to be known, was sweeping the country into a religious fervour and, incidentally, spreading revivalist songs into every corner. For the first time white Americans found a way and a place to let go, to "act like a nigger" with impunity.'[38]

Dubois' analysis of the black Church reveals one of the key features of this transculturation:

> Moreover, the religious growth of millions of men, even though they be slaves, cannot be without potent influence upon their contemporaries. The Methodists and Baptists of America owe much of their condition to the silent but potent influence of their millions of Negro converts. Especially is this noticeable in the South, where theology and religious philosophy are on this account a full half-century behind the North, and where the religion of the poor white is a plain copy of Negro thought and methods. The mass of 'Gospel' hymns which has swept through American churches and well-nigh ruined our sense of song, consists largely of debased imitation of Negro melodies made by ears that caught the jingle

but not the music, the body but not the soul, of the Jubilee songs. It is thus clear that the study of Negro religion is not only a vital part of the history of the Negro in America, but no uninteresting part of American history.[39]

Secular music, as made by the two races, had an almost identical development. Even in the compartmentalized structure of the scene, black music was heard, played and danced to by whites – though most of them either didn't realize it or pretended not to. It was admitted that 'they' had rhythm, but black music was as segregated from whites as the people who created it. It was known as 'race' music – that is, music for black ears only.

Whites did appreciate black music, on condition that it was performed by members of their own race. Whenever blacks were permitted to perform in front of whites they did it not in the role of artists, but as servants, the object being to keep them in their 'place'. (While singing in New York with Artie Shaw's white band, Billie Holiday was asked to use the service elevator, the hotel's white patrons having complained of a black using the same one as they. The Lady refused, and left the band.) And rare was the white performer or critic who spoke out in defence of the black musician. There was plenty of jibber in the defence of the music, but precious little about the people who played it. Apart from the very odd exception, these so-called friends of black music were nothing but time-servers, hypocrites who prided themselves on doing the music a favour when what they were actually doing was making a living. Not one of these glorified Judases ever lost *his* job or walked out of *his* gig because of undignified treatment meted out to black artists. Straddling their positions of go-betweens with the consummate skill of tightrope virtuosos, these 'cool' folks had the best of two worlds. As whites, their meagre talents lifted them to heights the most talented of blacks could never aspire to, let alone achieve. Thus, Paul Whiteman was the King of Jazz, Benny Goodman the King of Swing, Fred Astaire became known as a great 'jazz' dancer, June Christy a renowned 'jazz' singer; while John Hammond was credited with being a veritable Columbus, having 'discovered' a number of blues artists who were never 'lost'.

The change on the American scene which was to bring about a metamorphosis as far as the blues was concerned was the era of the beatnik. Characterized by their non-conformity to traditional American values, they sought a new kind of pioneer freedom akin to that preached by Thoreau and

Emerson, the upshot of which was a species of philosophical and cultural rebellion. They laid themselves open to everything, with the proviso, however, that it go against the American grain: Buddhism, Latin American poetry, Surrealism, American Indian folklore, Zen meditation, jazz and blues. In this all-embracing programme there was no room for racism – blacks and Indians were *people*, and they possessed a *culture*. In their quest for a more natural way of life, the beatniks could not but realize that black musicians represented a redeeming force on the arid landscape of American art, that their sufferings had given them a different perspective from whites', and that their music was one of the portals to a more humane future. As for the blues, they knew that it was the most viable folk tradition in the land, and that its lyrics contained truths which applied to everyone, regardless of race. The reason the beatniks were able to understand and in some measure even to identify with blacks is that they too were 'outsiders' – people who didn't fit comfortably in the American pie. They were jailed by redneck cops who didn't like their looks; they were harassed by stalwart citizens who didn't cotton on to their way of life; in short, the news was delivered to them in bold print that the Land of the Free was anything but what the slogan claimed.

By the time the beatnik had been transformed into the hippy society was staggering under its contradictions. The hippies – because of their greater numbers – were much more confident than their predecessors. They took direct action and protested vehemently against the war in Vietnam and crusaded with black people for civil rights. For the first time in American history white Americans were trying to look their situation straight in the face and, though they often blinded, were calling a honky a honky. They were also – a thing which never crossed the beatniks' minds – calling themselves bluespeople, for by now, whites not only listened to the blues, they also played it, and in some cases even lived its lifestyle. White youth was leaving home, leaving university, leaving security, and taking to the open road to find out what life in America was all about. The Alabama bus rides, the Kent State massacre, the Chicago police riots and a host of other delights served up courtesy of the Establishment left nothing to be desired for young America's inquisitiveness. And, after all this, who could say that they didn't have the right to sing the blues? They had been treated like white niggers! Young whites latched on to the blues like white on rice; black bluespeople were yet again 'discovered' and pop journalists wrote reams of interviews in which the blueslife was served up with soulful panache. After which it was as logical as it was inevitable that whites should appear on stage with blacks, that whites and blacks should form bands together, and that all-white blues bands should come into being. The blues had become a mulatto. Apart from English, blacks and whites now had another language in common. And the phenomenon wasn't confined to the United States. In the late fifties, Great Britain also experienced a blues wave. Led by Alexis Korner and Cyril Davis, it proved to be the chrysalis from which nearly every major British pop figure or group was to emerge: John Mayall, Eric Clapton, the Rolling Stones, the Beatles, Jack Bruce, Eric Burdon and a score of others. These musicians learned their craft from listening to and playing the songs of Willie Dixon, Howling Wolf, Bo Diddley, Muddy Waters, Billy Boy Arnold, Eddie Boyd, Jimmy Rogers, Sonny Boy Williamson, Junior Wells, James Cotton, Jimmy Reed . . . all of them black bluesmen. Battered by broadsides from both sides of the Atlantic, the floodgates, which had so long held black music back, crumbled.

Understandably, whites were at first nervous about playing the blues, a music so long identified with blacks that the mere mention of it brought them to mind. The first white blues performers were proud to play with the masters of the art, and blacks were just as proud to have them at their side. It was a double-barrelled vindication: black culture was being accepted by whites and whites were being allowed to participate in it. Then, almost inevitably, things went wrong. The ravings of a racist press, combined with the hysterical adulation by whites of certain of the performers of their own race, began to erode and destroy the crucial relationships – based on mutual respect – which had been built up between black and white performers and their audience. To begin with, the press and the record companies got up to their old tricks, one of which was the attempt to redefine the blues in order to take it out of black culture and appropriate it for white music. To this end the blues was called 'a universal music', and 'the blues aren't black or white, but human . . .'[40] The argument – waged exclusively by white journalists – reached such a pitch that it became a question of whether the blacks had anything to do with the blues at all: 'The central question changed from "Can a white man sing the blues?" to "Can a *black* man sing the blues?" because after the Cream the whites had the terminology all sewed up. With the skill of a surgeon, popular culture removed "black" from "blues", leaving the term free to become almost synonymous with British groups . . .'[41]

'True to form' – as the saying goes – the whites were taking over the blues. Having 'accepted' it, they were going to make it theirs. The blues was going to become universal, which meant white. An outstanding example of this whitewashing was the Seegal-Schwob Blues Band's 'Concerto for Bluesband and Symphony Orchestra' – as alien to black culture as it is futile. Once again, blacks were being written out of history; the whites were yet again making history all by themselves and writing themselves into the leading role. In their omnipotence, the whites failed to take into account the reaction of the blacks, as all along they had failed to understand what the blues meant to them. 'OK,' the blacks said, 'you shuffle, I'll deal.'

The game was played in December 1968, in Memphis, at the Stax Records Review. The performers were Wilson Pickett, James Brown, Isaac Hayes, Arthur Conley, Eddie Floyd, Rufus and Carla Thomas, Sam and Dave . . . and Janis Joplin *and* the Audience. Michael Bane, who witnessed the scene, gives this account:

> Janis Joplin . . . had, in essence, picked up the torch from the white blues kids, the bluesman's burden. She was, as she told everybody within earshot, a blues singer. Not a *white* blues singer, not a white girl singing the blues, but the next step on the evolutionary ladder; from spirituals to gospel to blues to rhythm and blues to rock to her. The beat had been passed on to the next generation, and Janis Joplin was holding the torch.
>
> . . . She became increasingly obsessed with the idea of the blues, though, and the melancholy that went with that music. People had to understand, she told a newspaper interviewer in San Francisco in the late 1960s, that it was the white kids now who were carrying the torch. The blacks used to have it, she said, and now it was hers.
>
> She went to the microphone, took a hit off the bottle, and said 'Hi-ya'. There was a smattering of applause, a few knowing glances exchanged. Then she launched into 'Ball and Chain', and it was clear what Janis Joplin was attempting to do. The acknowledged queen of white blues singers had come to Memphis to remove the adjective colour from her title. She had come to Memphis defiantly, to throw her colour in the face of this exhausted crowd who'd done everything short of crawling on their knees for Carla Thomas, the woman *they* called the Queen of Soul. Think white people can't sing the blues, she told this black audience. Well, listen to this, Memphis!
>
> Wrong crowd, wrong night, wrong town. The crowd wasn't having any honky bullshit. There were rumbles that were clearly not applause. Janis was singing wonderfully, but she was simply no match for the intensity of what had passed before her. The call-and-response electricity

simply wasn't there. She had nothing to tell this particular crowd about the blues, because they had lived and eaten and slept with the blues; they knew the way the blues tasted, felt and smelled. The electricity passing through the audience was all wrong, exactly the opposite of the blues feeling. The singer seemed to be communicating that she had a *right* to sing the blues. The audience became overtly hostile — *When you say you got a right to sing the blues, then you and me ain't talking about the same blues.*

She finished her first number, and there was a smattering of applause. Most of the audience had already headed for the exits. She did one more number, then stopped abruptly. 'If you don't want to listen,' she said, 'then I'm going to leave.' And she walked off stage in a blind fury, still the best white blues singer there was . . . The next morning the local newspaper mentioned that Miss Joplin was upset by the audience's lack of response.[42]

The audacity of this would-be High Priestess of the Blues is matched only by her insensitivity. Unfortunately, her case is all too common in the relations between whites and blacks. Suffering under the delusion that whatever a white person does is superior, and that whites have only to say something for it to be true, Joplin believed that blacks were going to hail her as the Great Blues Hope! The victim of her own illusions, she envisioned herself sitting on the throne once occupied by Ma Rainey and Bessie Smith; by Victoria Spivey, Billie Holiday and Dinah Washington! She, the descendant of slavemasters, thought that she could conjure the souls of black folk! They knew that she had never had the black blues; that she had experienced a different kind of blues.

The oft-posed question, 'Can whites play the blues?' ought to be retired. Undoubtedly, they can — since they do it. Paul Butterfield, Elvin Bishop, Alexis Korner, Mike Bloomfield, Tony McPhee, the J. Geils Band, the Allman Brothers, Charlie Musselwhite, John Hammond Jr and Johnny Winter have played the blues with a dedication and expertise which entitles them to the right to be proud of their achievement. However — and as far as I know they have never claimed to be — they can never be *bluespeople*. Why not? Because the blues is not something they *live* but something they *do* — which makes all the difference in the world. What distinguishes the bluesperson from the blues performer is cultural-racial make-up, which can only be inherited by a descendant of an ex-American slave. Africans, for all their 'soul' and the blackness of their skin, are not bluespeople. They play the blues but do not claim that title. The suffering they underwent during colonization was a different experience – just as inhuman, but different from slavery as it was institutionalized in the United States. Fine African blues performers like Manu Dibango, Francis Bebey, Sam Kelly and Rachid Bahri have never called themselves 'bluesmen'. They know that the blues is the result of a 'peculiar' experience. So what right have whites – who even lack the merit of having the same colour of skin as bluespeople – what justification have they, I say, to call themselves bluesmen and -women? Their white skin bars them from ever living the blueslife, for in America skin colour is EVERYTHING, the alpha and omega of a person's destiny. There can be no question of white people suffering in the same manner as people with black skin – in America, they couldn't even if they wanted to. Their suffering is *different*.

The blues is part of the white American's heritage, but it is different from the other arts: it is the product of a special kind of inhumanity one people suffered at the hands of another. The outcome has been an art form so deeply imbued with the stamp of that experience that it is inseparable from the people from whom it springs. The blues is the cultural memorial of slavery, a musical memoir commemorating the history of blacks in the United States. Unlike other arts, its intrinsic spirit can only be transmitted by blood or, if you like, psychically. No amount of enthusiasm, no amount of time spent living with black people, will ever endow a non-Afro-American with it. 'Only people who have been down the line,' says James Baldwin, 'know what this music is about.'[43]

Anyone – French, Ethiopian, Mongolian – can play a 'blues'. But only a black American can *be* a bluesperson. He alone was the Man Without a Name, the Nigger, the Sambo. He alone *lives* the blues.

The Blue Princess

There She is, with her blue smile:
My glory is to sing the praises of the Ethiopian.

L.S. Senghor

If there is any treasure hidden in these vast walls, I'm sure that it has a sheen that outshines gold – a tiny, pear-shaped tear that formed on the

cheek of some black woman torn away from her children . . . a shy tear
. . . on that black cheek, unredeemed, unappeased — a tear that was
hastily brushed off when her arm was grabbed and she was led toward
those narrow, dank steps that guided her to the tunnel that directed her
feet to the waiting ship that would bear her across the heaving,
mist-shrouded Atlantic . . .

Richard Wright

All the wealth of the future cannot make up for what you have suffered.
Instead, it is you who enrich us, you with your blue voice — Empress Bessie
. . . Ma Rainey . . . Clara Smith . . . Mary Dixon . .

The blues woman is the priestess or prophet of the people. She verbalizes
the emotion for herself and the audience, articulating the stresses and
strains of human relationships.

James H. Cone

Across the fields there comes the heady sound of your blue sonority, from
out of the shacks, rising above the ghetto, wafting across the swamps — sing
for us, O Most Nobly Born, for you are our beloved — Mamie Desdoumes
. . . Ethel Waters . . . Lil Hardin . . . Ruby Walker . . .

> Her skin is like the dusk on the eastern horizon,
> O can't you see it, O can't you see it,
> Her skin is like the dusk on the eastern horizon
> . . . When the sun goes down.

Jean Toomer

Blue Horizon-Blue Mother; Blue Flame-Blue Lover; Blue Star-Blue Child
— O, Our Lady of the Blues — sing! — Bertha 'Chippie' Hill . . . Sippie
Wallace . . . Lucille Hegamin . . .

'Play music!' shouted the Blues Singer. 'Play music!' she shouted. Echo of
the slamming door. 'Play music! Play music!' cried the crowd. Louder and
louder the Blues Singer shouted, against the booming bass, 'Music!
Music!' Around her, the frantic faces, the yelling feet, the sweating
laughter. 'Music! Music!' cried the Blues Singer, rising to her feet.
'Music! Music!' cried the crowd. The music shouted on.

William Gardner Smith

Now, more than ever, we need your song to give us strength: Sister of All the Blues, keep the Sound for us — Alberta Hunter . . . Ida Cox . . . Big Mama Thornton . . . Katie Webster . . . Mamie Smith . . .

> I cannot praise, for you have passed from praise,
> I have no tinted thoughts to paint you true;
> But I can feel and I can write the word;
> The best of me is but the least of you.
>
> Claude McKay

Without your voice, this song is robbed of its essence. If there were no 'You', the blues just wouldn't be blue — Billie Holiday, Dinah Washington, Koko Taylor, Aretha Franklin, Gaile Peters . . .

The Bluesman's Greatest Song

> *Subdued and time-lost*
> *Are the drums — and yet*
> *Through some vast mist of race*
> *There comes this song.*
>
> *Langston Hughes*

The reality is American; the dream is Black.
The language is American; the voice is Black.
The instruments are American; the sound is Black.
The marrow is American; the spirit is Black.

Black and Blue — an Afro-American in the truest sense of the word — the bluesman shoulders his load, content in the knowledge that his greatest song is his way of life.

Glossary

Agayú the *orisha* of those who are weighed down by burdens, interchangeable with St Christopher

Aleyo (in Santeria) non believer

Assotor largest and most important drum in Vodun rites

Bongoism (also known as the Convince Cult) beliefs of the Jamaican Maroons. Adherents are called bongo men and women.

Botao (from the Spanish to recoil) act of the female turning away from (resisting) her partner during the *yuka* dance

Brujeria (Cuba) witchcraft, black magic

Budu Voodoo

Calenda West Indian dance of African origin, well known in New Orleans, where it became a hybrid through mixture with European tradition

Candomblé Yoruba rites in Brazil

Chica Afro-Cuban dance which the Spanish renamed and modified as the fandango

Cumina Jamaican cult which worships the dead

Damballah Wedo one of the greatest of the Haitian *loa*, god of fertility and rainfall, personified as the snake and the rainbow

Encantados Venus of the Vodun pantheon, the symbol of purity, often identified with the Christian Virgin Mary

Garde-corps protective charm worn to ward off evil

Gèdés in Voodoo, deities of the graveyard, led by Gèdé Nimbo

Goofer dust dirt taken from a grave and used in the confection of *wangas*

Griot West African poet-musician-historian, guardian of the people's folklore and history. 'The death of a griot is like the burning of a library'

Gris-gris bird whose bones are used for making charms

Hoodoo (US) Voodoo

Hounfor (also *humfo, huno*) Vodun temple

Houngan Vodun priest

John the Conqueroo perhaps the most powerful charm in black American folk belief

Lambis conch trumpet used in Vodun ceremonies in Haiti

Legba guardian of the gateway, the highway and the crossroads. The messenger of (and to) the gods, Legba is also the divine trickster. Every Vodun ceremony begins with a sacrifice to him

Loa (*loaloachi*) spirit(s) which possesses people during Vodun religious rites

Macandal *wanga* taking its name from the great Haitian freedom fighter

Macumba Afro-Brazilian religious beliefs, derived from the Yorubas of Nigeria

Mambo Vodun priestess

Maroons runaway slaves

Maroon dance religious dance of the Jamaican Maroons. A part of Cumina (the worship of Shangó), the Maroon dance is performed to a special rhythm provided by bongos

Mojo (US) Hoodoo love charm

Naniguismo Afro-Cuban brotherhood based on the Efik secret society of southern Nigeria. Their rites honour Baron Samedi and the gèdés

Nyannego member of the secret brotherhood of the Naniguismo

Obeah Homeopathy and magic by conjuration practised in Jamaica

Ogun Feraille Vodun god of war, patron of blacksmiths and hunters

Orisha Yoruba god or goddess

Poro West African secret society

Samedi, Baron guardian of the graveyard who delights in wreaking havoc during the Vodun ceremony

Santeria practice of magic in Cuba (where it is also known as *lucumí*), Puerto Rico, Trinidad and Brazil (see *macumba*), derived from the Yorubas of southern Nigeria

Santero/a practitioner of Santeria

Shangó god of fire, thunder and lightning in the Yoruban pantheon, one of the greatest deities in Cuban Santeria and Brazilian *macumba*

Toby (US) Hoodoo charm

Vodun/Vodoun rites and belief of the Avada 'nation' in Haiti; a *loa*

Wanga Vodun charm employed for malevolent or selfish ends

Yuka Afro-Cuban dance performed in 2/4 or 6/8 time, forerunner of the rumba

Notes

Origins: *What is the Blues?* (pp. 3–6)

1. Raboteau, Albert J., *Slave Religion: The 'Invisible Institution' in the Antebellum South* (Oxford University Press, 1979)
2. Johnston, Sir Harry, *The Negro in the New World* (EP, 1970)

Haiti: *The Invisible Religion* (pp. 7–37)

1. Roscoe, John, *The Baganda: An Account of Their Native Customs and Beliefs* (F. Cass, 1965)
2. Hambly, W.D., *Serpent Worship in Africa* (Field Museum of Natural History, Chicago, 1931)
3. Levy-Bruhl, Lucien, *The Soul of the Primitive* (Allen and Unwin, 1928)
4. Leonard, Arthur Glyn, *The Lower Niger and Its Tribes* (F. Cass, 1968)
5. Wake, C. Staniland, *Serpent Worship and Other Essays* (G. Redway, 1888)
6. Labat, Père, *Nouveau Voyage aux Isles de l'Amérique* (1698)
7. Dalzel, Archibald, *History of Dahomey. Inland Kingdom of Africa* (F. Cass, 1967)
8. Nassau, Robert Hammill, *Fetichism in West Africa* (Duckworth, 1904)
9. Price-Mars, Dr, *Ainsi Parla l'Oncle* (La Habana, Casa de la Americas, 1968)
10. Ellis, Alfred Burdon, *The Land of Fetish* (Chapman & Hall, 1883)
11. Burton, Sir Richard, *A Mission to Gedele, King of Dahome* (Routledge Kegan Paul, 1966)
12. Bennett, Lerone, *Before the Mayflower. A History of Negroes in America* (Johnson Publishing Co, Chicago, 1964)
13. St John, Sir Spenser, *Hayti, or the Black Republic* (F. Cass, 1972)
14. Laws of Jamaica (Code Noir)
15. Bonsal, Stephen, *The American Mediterranean* (Hurst & Blackett, 1913)

16. Huxley, Francis, *The Invisibles* (Hart-Davis, 1966)
17. Fermor, Patrick Leigh, *The Traveller's Tree* (J. Murrary, 1950)
18. Métraux, Alfred, *Voodoo in Haiti* (André Deutsch, 1959)
19. Fouchard, Jean, *The Haitian Maroons: Liberty or Death* (Edward W. Blyden Press, New York, 1981)
20. Ibid
21. Ibid
22. Ibid
23. Métraux, op cit
24. Seabrook, William Buehler, *The Magic Island* (Harrap, 1929)
25. Métraux, op cit
26. Alexis, Jacques Stephen, *Les Arbres Musiciens* (Gallimard, Paris, 1957)
27. Prichard, Hesketh, *Where Black Rules White: Journey Across and About Haiti* (Irish University Press, 1972)
28. Bonsal, op cit
29. Métraux, op cit
30. Ibid
31. Much of this material on Macandal is from Fouchard, op cit
32. Carpentier, Alejo, *The Kingdom of this World* (Penguin, 1975)
33. Fouchard, op cit
34. Ibid
35. Sannon, Pauléus, *Histoire de Toussaint L'Ouverture* (Paris, 1898)
36. Malenfant, Colonel, *Des Colonies, et Particulièrement de Celle de Saint Domingue* (Paris, 1814)
37. Fouchard, op cit
38. Jahn, Janheinz, *Muntu* (Faber & Faber, 1961)

Jamaica: *My Name is Obeah* (pp. 39–56)

1. Reports of the Council, *Treatment of the Slaves in West Indies* (1789)
2. Burdett, William, *Life and Exploits of Mansong, Commonly Called Three-Finger Jack, the Terror of Jamaica* (1800)
3. Beckwith, Martha Warren, *Black Roadways, a Study of Jamaican Folk Life* (Chapel Hill, 1929)
4. See Anon, *Hamel, the Obeah Man* (London, 1827) and Khan, Ismith, *The Obeah Man* (Hutchinson, 1964)
5. Garvey, Amy Jacques, *Philosophy and Opinions of Marcus Garvey* (Universal Publishing House, New York, 1926)
6. Cronon, E. David (ed), *Marcus Garvey* (Prentice Hall, 1973)

7. Cronon, E. David, *Black Moses* (University of Wisconsin Press, 1955)
8. Ibid
9. Marable, Manning, *Blackwater* (Black Praxis Press, 1981)
10. Ibid
11. Cronon, *Black Moses*, op cit
12. Clarke, Sebastian, *Jah Music* (Heineman, 1981)
13. Simpson, George Eaton, *Religious Cults of the Caribbean* (Institute of Caribbean Studies, University of Puerto Rico, 1980)
14. Ibid
15. Clarke, op cit
16. Ibid
17. Johnson, Linton Kwesi, *Dread Beat and Blood* (Bogle L'Overture Publishers, 1975)
18. Garvey, Amy Jacques, op cit

Cuba: *The House of Images* (pp. 57–69)

1. Montejo, Esteban, *Autobiography of a Runaway Slave* (Bodley Head, 1968)
2. Jahn, Janheinz, *Muntu* (Faber & Faber, 1961)
3. Ibid
4. Montejo, op cit
5. Ibid
6. Ibid
7. Ibid
8. Ibid
9. Jahn, op cit
10. Ibid
11. Ortiz, Fernando, *Los Bailes y el Teatro de los Negros en el Folklore de Cuba* (Havana, 1951)
12. Montejo, op cit
13. Marinello, Juan, *Poetica, encayos en entusiasmo* (Madrid, 1933)

Brazil: *Obatala in the Backlands* (pp. 71–9)

1. Pierson, Donald, *Negroes in Brazil: a Study of Race Contact at Bahia* (University of Chicago Press, 1942)

The Drum (pp. 81–7)

1. Bebey, Francis, *African Music: a People's Art* (Lawrence Hill, New York, 1975)
2. Courlander, Harold, *The Drum and the Hoe* (University of California Press, 1960)
3. St Méry, Moreau de, *Description Topographique, Physique, Civile, Politique et Historique de la Partie Française de l'Isle de St Domingue* (Philadelphia, 1797-8)
4. Hurston, Zora Neale, *Jonah's Gourd Vine* (Duckworth, 1934)

The Dance (pp. 89–97)

1. St Méry, Moreau de, *Description . . . St Domingue* (Philadelphia, 1797-8)
2. Labat, Père, *Nouveau Voyage aux Isles de l'Amérique* (Paris, 1722)
3. Ortiz, Fernando, *Los Bailes . . . Cuba* (Havana, 1951)
4. St Méry, op cit
5. Jahn, Janheinz, *Muntu* (Faber & Faber, 1961)
6. Ortiz, op cit
7. Ibid
8. Ashbury, Herbert, *The French Quarter* (Jarrolds, 1937)
9. Cable, George Washington, *Creoles and Cajuns* (Doubleday, New York, 1959)
10. Herskovits, Melville, *The Myth of the Negro Past* (Harper & Bros, New York, 1941)
11. Dunham, Katherine, 'The Negro Dance' (*Proceedings of the 29th Congress of Americanists, 1949,* University of Chicago Press)

Hoodoo on the Bayous (pp. 99–150)

1. Hurston, Zora Neale, *Mules and Men* (Indiana University Press, 1978)
2. Frazier, Edward Franklin, *The Negro Family in the United States* (University of Chicago Press, 1966)
3. Krapp, 'The English of the Negro' (*American Mercury* 2, pp.190-5, 1924)

4. Herskovits, Melville, *The Myth of the Negro Past* (Harper & Bros, New York, 1941)

5. Aptheker, Herbert, 'The Negro Slave Revolts' (*Science and Society* I, pp.512-38, 1937)

6. Ibid

7. Ibid

8. Saxon, Lyle, *Fabulous New Orleans* (Century, 1928)

9. See Crawford, Margo, *The Seasoning of the Negro under Slavery* (Doctorate Thesis, University of Chicago, 1978)

10. Ibid

11. Courlander, Harold, *Negro Folk Music* (Columbia University Press, New York, 1963)

12. Ibid

13. Herskovits, op cit

14. Channel, quoted in Puckett, Newbell Miles, *Folk Beliefs of the Southern Negro* (Dover, 1970)

15. Saxon, op cit

16. Toomer, Jean, *Cane* (Harper & Row, 1969)

17. Cable, George Washington, *Creoles and Cajuns* (Doubleday, New York, 1959)

18. Saxon, op cit

19. Castellanos, *New Orleans as it was* (New Orleans, 1895)

20. Cable, op cit

21. Tallant, Robert, *The Voodoo Queen* (Robert Hale, 1957)

22. Quoted in Hurston, op cit

23. Cable, op cit

24. St Méry, Moreau de, *Description . . . St Domingue* (Philadelphia, 1797-8)

25. Dubois, William E.B., *The Souls of Black Folk* (Constable, 1905)

26. Herskovits, op cit

27. Ibid

28. Dubois, op cit

29. Dollard, J., *Caste and Class in a Southern Town* (New Haven, 1937)

30. Saxon, op cit

31. St Méry, op cit

32. Puckett, op cit

33. Bacon, 'Conjuring and Conjure-Doctors' (*Southern Workman*, 24, 1895)

34. Cable, op cit

35. Herskovits, op cit

36. Owen, Mary A., *Voodoo Tales as Told among the Negroes of the South West*

(Putnam, New York, 1893)
37. Hurston, Zora Neale, op cit.
38. Ibid
39. Botkin, Benjamin A., *Lay My Burden Down: A Folk History of Slavery* (Phoenix Books, Chicago, 1945)
40. Ibid
41. Ibid
42. Ibid
43. Cable, op cit
44. Herskovits, op cit
45. Cable, op cit
46. Puckett, op cit
47. Pitkin, Helen, *Angel by Brevet* (Philadelphia, 1904)
48. Bruce, P.A., *The Plantation Negro as a Freedman* (New York, 1889)
49. Castellanos, op cit
50. Jones, Leroi, *Blues People* (William Morrow, New York, 1963)

The Saints and the Hoodoos (pp. 151–83)

1. Wilson, G.R., Religion of the American Negro Slave (*Journal of Negro History* VIII, 1923)
2. Oakley, Giles, *The Devil's Music: History of the Blues* (BBC, 1976)
3. Gillard, John T., *The Catholic Church and the Negro* (Johnson Reprints, 1969)
4. Kemble, Frances, *Journal of a Residence on a Georgia Plantation in 1838-9* (Cape, 1961)
5. Berghahn, Marion, *Images of the African in Afro-American Literature* (Basic Afro-American Reprint Library)
6. Dubois, William E.B., *The Souls of Black Folk* (Constable, 1905)
7. William Howard Russel, quoted in McPherson, J.M., *The Negro's Civil War* (Vintage Books, 1973)
8. Baldwin, James, *The Fire Next Time* (Penguin, 1970)
9. Botkin, Benjamin A., *Lay My Burden Down: A Folk History of Slavery* (Phoenix Books, Chicago, 1945)
10. Ibid
11. Dubois, op cit
12. Herskovits, Melville, *The Myth of the Negro Past* (Harper & Bros, New York, 1941)
13. Dubois, op cit

14. Dunham, Katherine, 'The Negro Dance' (*Proceedings of the 29th Congress of Americanists, 1949*, University of Chicago Press)
15. Dubois, op cit
16. Herskovits, op cit
17. Beauchamp, L.T., *The Black Pages of Wisdom* (Epoch Press, St Louis, 1977)
18. Baldwin, op cit
19. Oakley, op cit
20. Dubois, op cit
21. Ibid
22. Cone, James H., *Spirituals and the Blues* (Greenwood, 1980)
23. Washington, Booker T., *Up from Slavery* (Oxford University Press, 1945)
24. Cone, op cit
25. Baldwin, op cit
26. Dubois, op cit
27. Oakley, op cit
28. Bane, Michael, *White Boy Singing the Blues* (Penguin, 1982)
29. Jones, Leroi, *Blues People* (William Morrow, New York, 1963)
30. Ibid
31. Cone, op cit
32. Ibid
33. Oakley, op cit

The Initiations (pp. 185–232)

1. Burr-Reynaud, Frédéric, *Anathèmes* (La Presse, Port-au-Prince, 1930)
2. Jones, Leroi, *Blues People* (William Morrow, New York, 1963)
3. Dubois, William E.B., *The Souls of Black Folk* (Constable, 1905)
4. Johnson, Fenton, 'The Banjo Player' from *Visions of the Dusk* (Chicago, 1944)
5. Poussaint, Alvin, 'A Negro Psychiatrist Explains the Negro Psyche', *New York Times* Magazine, 20 August, 1967
6. Isaacs, quoted in Berghahn, Marion, *Images of the African in Afro-American Literature* (Basic Afro-American Reprint Library)
7. Braithwaite, Edward Kamau, *The African Presence in Caribbean Literature* (Benin)
8. Bebey, Francis, *African Music: a People's Art* (Lawrence Hill, New York, 1975)

9. Braithwaite, op cit
10. Shines, Johnny, quoted in *Living Blues* 22, July/August 1975
11. Bane, Michael, *White Boy Singing the Blues* (Penguin, 1982)
12. Oakley, Giles, *The Devil's Music: History of the Blues* (BBC, 1976)
13. Cone, James H., *Spirituals and the Blues* (Greenwood, 1980)
14. Jones, op cit
15. Oakley, op cit
16. Ibid
17. Ibid
18. *Blues Unlimited* 95, October 1972
19. Shines, op cit
20. Hughes, Langston, 'Here to Yonder' (*Chicago Defender*, January 1943)
21. Jahn, Janheinz, *Muntu* (Faber & Faber, 1961)
22. Waterman, Richard, 'African Influence on the Music of the Americas' (*Proceedings of the 29th Congress of Americanists, 1949*, University of Chicago Press)
23. Jahn, op cit
24. Shines, op cit
25. Adins, Georges, *The Legend of Elmore James* (UAS 29109)
26. *Living Blues* 35, November-December 1977
27. *Sing Out!* XV
28. Shines, op cit
29. Simpson, George Eaton, *Religious Cults in the Caribbean* (Institute of Caribbean Studies, University of Puerto Rico, 1980)
30. Courlander, Harold, *The Drum and the Hoe* (University of California Press, 1940)
31. Métraux, Alfred, *Voodoo in Haiti* (Andre Deutsch, 1959)
32. Pierson, Donald, *Negroes in Brazil* (University of Chicago Press, 1942)
33. Shines, op cit
34. Bebey, op cit
35. Shines, op cit
36. Oakley, op cit
37. Krehbiel, H.E., *Afro-American Folksongs* (Schirmer, New York, 1914)
38. Bane, op cit
39. Dubois, op cit
40. From an advert for Joe Cocker in *Rolling Stone*, 1969
41. Bane, op cit
42. Ibid
43. Baldwin, James *The Fire Next Time* (Penguin, 1970)

Index